THE ART OF THE CHORAL CONDUCTOR

pg. 3 87

The Art of the Choral Conductor

Volume One

CHORAL TECHNIQUE

William J. Finn

Price $3.75 $4.00

C. C. BIRCHARD AND COMPANY, BOSTON

3-46

This book is dedicated to all the Paulist Choristers,
past and present.

PREFACE

The history of music in the United States during the Twentieth Century, when written, will contain an important chapter on the renaissance of choral art. This country has fostered the oratorio since the early years of the Nineteenth Century. Large mixed choruses have been established in many of the great cities and in some of the smaller ones, without, it must be confessed, paralleling those qualities of precision and refinement that distinguish our important symphonic ensembles, which began a few decades later.

Not until the first decade of the Twentieth Century did the chorus begin to revive, in this country, those splendors that are its ancient heritage. In church and in concert hall, in the public schools of some communities, and even in the colleges and universities where the living arts long had languished, music lovers encountered, most of them for the first time, those expressions of beauty which it is the prerogative of the finely wrought vocal ensemble to initiate. There followed a growth, especially of unaccompanied choral art, that is the most important musical phenomenon of the age. Colleges, especially the smaller sectarian groups, made the chorus an agent of cultural publicity second only to the football squad, and actually more important than the track team.

Since the greatest choral music, ancient or modern, is ecclesiastical, it was inevitable that leadership in the movement should have developed in the Church, mother of the arts and preserver of all learning in ages more barbarous but not more ruthlessly materialistic than the present. That leadership, assumed by right of talent and achievement, devolved upon The Reverend William J. Finn, C.S.P., who founded the Paulist Choristers of Chicago in 1904 and speedily made this group the foremost of its kind, not only in this country, but actually in Europe as well by the unanswerable test of competition with the great choirs abroad.

Removing to New York, Father Finn repeated in that center the great service he had rendered in Chicago, carrying his evangel of pure choral art to the radio as well as to the concert hall. His activities were not limited to the choir of men and boys. Great mixed choruses engaged him with profit so that his experience as choral conductor presently embraced the whole field.

Every great conductor is a great teacher. From the training of choristers to training of conductors is a short step and one taken early in his career. The fruits of this vast practical and pedagogic experience were recorded in the two volumes of "The Art of the Choral Conductor," a work of authority and importance because it solves the problems, not only of ancient ecclesiastical music, but of all the interesting and exciting modern schools.

These books should be in the library of every choirmaster, whether his medium is the choir of men and boys, or the mixed ensemble; for the churches of all denominations lag woefully in the important department of musical culture. Music has achieved expressions of the devotional spirit that are suggested but not realized by the drama of ritual or the word of Holy Writ.

To ignore this great music is to worship God in the ugliness of illiteracy (of a kind). There is nothing, in all the world of tone, that defines with similar completeness those mysteries of faith, which forever escape verbal statement but which Palestrina, Byrd, Lasso, Dowland, Lotti, Ingegneri, and other polyphonic masters have stated in tone. Wrought of intermingled melodies this music rises like sounding incense before the high altar bearing the spirit of man to that other world which he seeks. Or, if this idiom omits certain accents of modern feeling, there is the vital new school of Russia, poignant and dramatic, or the interesting American school just coming into life and discovering its own kind of beauty. Sooner or later this music must replace the Mendelssohnian school of our grandfathers, at least to the abandonment of much that is sterile and platitudinous.

Whether he is bound by the conservatism of his congregation, or by pecuniary limitations, the choirmaster still must perform his functions to the best of his ability. In "The Art of the Choral Conductor" he will find all his problems stated and solved and at the same time will be stimulated to a realization of the dignity of his art and the wealth of its literature.

GLENN DILLARD GUNN

Washington, D. C.
April 25, 1939.

CONTENTS

Volume I

CHORAL TECHNIQUE

CHAPTER I

Choral Musicianship

"There is not any musicke of instruments, whatsoever, comparable to that which is made by the voyces of men, when the voyces are good, and the same well-sorted and ordered."

WILLIAM BYRD (1542–1623)

It is the purpose of the writer of this treatise to set forth the principles and practices of choral technique by which a high degree of ensemble artistry may be achieved and maintained. These elements and agencies will be presented as systematically and comprehensively as possible in the two major aspects of the choral art. One aspect concerns the vocal development of the choral unit, the other concerns primarily the conductor in his role of interpreter. Mastery of the very considerable subject matter comprised in these two distinct but inseparable phases of choral direction is essential to the conductor, if he would escape mediocrity. His chorus must be free from the inartistic blemishes of poor vocalism, unsuitable timbres, inadequate blending and imperfect balance. His readings of the compositions must be guided by the interpretative needs of many and diverse schools of music.

His first task is, obviously, to build his chorus into a singing instrument of musical quality, for if the director fail to produce an aesthetically convincing choral tone, the cultivation of merely technical excellences, and facility in interpreting many styles of music correctly, will be necessarily futile.

The primary requisite for choral effectiveness is beauty of tone. Any degree of ugliness in any of the single lines of a chorus will prevent the ensemble from being an artistic musical agency. Beauty, in one or other of its many forms, is the only medium through which music can successfully address the aesthetic instincts of listeners. Beauty is of the essence of music; without it, one can produce only a counterfeit of the art; according to the structure and mood of a composition it must manifest itself in elegance, grace, charm, sympathy, elegy, brilliancy, radiance or sublimity.

3

The ultimate basis of choral artistry is sheer loveliness of tone. Except in bravura, grotesque and violent episodes, where simulation of emotional reactions is indicated, this must be its pre-eminent virtue.

Just as no degree of finger-technique and interpretative virtuosity can make Chopin sound well on a piano out of tune, so no measure of skill in interpreting Gregorian Chant, 16th century Polyphony, Bach or modern music can compensate for the unmusical sounds which are the handicap of the average poorly trained modern chorus.

Therefore, the choral director must be a master of vocalism and ensemble singing. He must know how, scientifically, to train the voices of the single parts of his unit and how to merge all the parts in a homogeneous blend. Also, he must understand the relationship of instrumental accompaniment to choral singing; this means that he must know organ registration and orchestration. The fact that different styles of music require different vocal timbres for their proper performance indicates that the choral conductor must also be skilled in developing and employing opportunely the resources of what I shall refer to in this volume as the choral color-scheme. The special needs of *a cappella* singing furnish another field of inquiry.

The interpretative requirements of the conductor's technique include facility in the artistic application of the general principles of interpretation: such fundamentals as the proper reading of rhythmical forms, the choice of correct tempi, the use of rubato, the determining of dynamic intensity and the subtle art of enhancing aesthetic effectiveness by *crescendo* and *diminuendo*. These factors of interpretation must assert themselves variously in the various schools of composition. A definite erudition is required for each specific art-form. The structure of the many forms being academically different and the aesthetic intentions of classes of composers diverse, it is clear that a conductor must be well schooled theoretically and practically in the structure of the forms which he essays to direct. Gregorian Chant, Polyphonic music of the sixteenth century, madrigals and motets of the seventeenth century, Hymnody, Bach, Oratorio, Operatic choruses, modern Russian works, the choral opus richly embroidered with orchestral figures and the choral opus depending on its vocal content solely—all these and other types of choral music must be analyzed carefully, their distinctive features discovered, and facility in revealing these qualities with a group of singers achieved. The study of the art of choral conducting involves, further, at least an acquaintance with relevant facts established by the science of acoustics, for proper performance often depends upon a cognizance of these facts.

Altogether, the array of subjects of which a thoroughly qualified choral conductor must be master is formidable. His art is more complex than that of an orchestral conductor. The latter, generally, is free of the need to teach the players the technique of their instruments; the former faces the necessity of teaching the choristers the technique of singing as a primary and persistent demand. The choral conductor requires most of the information and technical facility of the symphonic virtuoso, plus a profound knowledge of some phases of music about which the latter can remain successfully in ignorance. In spite of this, the orchestral conductor is conceded a higher rank than his colleague of the chorus; perhaps, because "symphony" is the vogue, or perhaps because of the more theatrical and overwhelming musical moments over which the *chef d'orchestre* presides, or just perhaps because choral conductors have failed to acquire the broader musicianship and the greater technical equipment which would establish their pre-eminence. The noble oligarchy of professional critics may reasonably maintain a patronizing mien towards the choral conductor, for, generally he presents himself as the poor relation of the musical hierarchy, proving his poverty and *gaucherie* by ill-fitting musical habiliments and his clumsy knocking about of *objets d'art*.

The critics realize that the average orchestral conductor is a *graduate specialist,* and that the average choral conductor is not, is far from this. The modern choral conductor, generally, is unprepared for his office. Floundering about, he proves his lack of preparedness in every measure sung, in every idle motion of the baton, and most of all in the chauvinistic *fortes* which he supposes will successfully conceal the blemishes and inadequacies—if there be any!

Of course, there are some great choral conductors today whose profound understanding of their art and whose practiced control of the resources of choral singing elevate them to the fraternity of master craftsmen, but these constitute a very small minority. The majority has not been inspired with zeal to inquire into the technical demands which an artistic exercise of the baton makes upon choral conductors. Programmes frequently announce that the music to be sung is by Palestrina, Ingeneri, Gabrielli, Byrd, etc., but seldom is the music of these masters *actually* performed, the efforts of the conductor and chorus usually producing a counterfeit. The notes and the text may be those of Palestrina, etc., but the tone-quality of the ensemble, the lack of blend, the tempo, the absence of dynamic variations or the misapplication of them, probably all concur to neutralize the composers' intentions, distorting the effect and thus dissociating the music actually rendered from the conception of the composers.

A Tudor madrigal performed with the tone-quality and dynamic intensity proper to the choruses in "Faust" loses so much of its inherent personality in such disguise as to cease to be a madrigal. The programme may assign the number to Byrd or Morley or Wilbye, but the sounds purveyed in reality to the listener have no kinship with the music-fancies of the Elizabethan period.

Since the analysis of chorophony [1] to be undertaken in these pages is based upon the conviction that chorus singing is music's sovereign instrumentality of expression, it seems advisable at the outset to examine the premises from which such conclusion has been drawn.

The comparative effectiveness of each of the many instruments by which music discloses itself is determined by the ratio of its inherent powers of expression to the attributes of music as a whole.

Academically, music may be considered a science, related to both mathematics and physics; in practice, however, it is an art, involving relations with emotions and aesthetics. Therefore, music is a synthesis of the scientific and the artistic, and can function successfully only by a proper fusion of both the scientific and the artistic factors.

Music, being a means of expressing imagery, is a kind of language. But it is a language without vocabulary; for sounds, unlike words, cannot be defined univocally; they may mean many and different things, each individual listener determining his own interpretation. The effects of any single piece of music upon a group of individuals are admitted to be diversified and even contradictory. Likewise, the reactions of people to music generally are diversified, some people being profoundly moved and others reacting superficially. Occasionally, the extraordinary phenomenon of an individual who dislikes music is encountered, but the race as a whole is more sensitive to it than to any other of the Fine Arts. Music does not appeal directly to the intellect; its direct appeal is to the emotions and therefore its processes are subtle; they have not yet been comprehended.

Explain, for instance, why a specific style of music delights one while irking another.

Even upon persons of the same temperament and of equal culture the effects of music are frequently dissimilar.

The acceptability to earlier generations of scale-forms and harmonic

[1] The bibliography on the technical phases of chorus training and conducting being scant, the nomenclature of the subject is therefore meagre, and in order to escape the handicap of much paraphrasing, the writer presumes to coin such words as may seem desirable for clarity and brevity. Thus, "chorophony" and "chorophonic" will connote the choral art just as "symphony" and "symphonic" have come to connote the orchestral art.

relationships which are disturbing and in some instances abhorrent to modern ears, is not easily understood, and the explanation of the satisfaction experienced by almost all occidental peoples today in the major third, this interval being in the physics of sound one of the lesser consonances, is still subject for conjecture. The absence from general usage of so important a current factor as the leading-tone until the seventeenth century is perplexing,[1] while the ultra-discords, clashing cacophonies and quarter-tone progressions of the prevailing "new freedom" in music will long impress the majority as inexplicable deviations from aesthetic normalcy. It is clear that the faculty of discerning and enjoying beauty in music is an indeterminate disposition or predilection except to the extent to which culture may direct taste; it is equally clear that there are certain fundamental elements which concur to make music agreeable to the ear and affecting to the emotions.

However stealthy the actions and reactions of music may be, and however puzzling the personal affinities which it variously establishes with the biology and psychology of particular individuals, music must be said to have a nature, to be possessed of qualities essential to it, the absence of which would make it cease to be music, and the opposite of which would metamorphose it into an instrument of distress and positive pain.

It is obvious that all the means by which music essays to reveal herself are not equally endowed. There are single instruments and single voices; there are instrumental ensembles and vocal ensembles. Some single instruments are limited to meagre impressiveness by all three of the principal elements of music—pitch, dynamic energy and quality. Thus the bass viol, the tuba, contra-tuba, contra-fagotto, in the depths, the flute, piccolo, flageolet in the heights are handicapped by their very structure first, from functioning with notable effect through the range where the richest beauty may be reasonably said to lie for human ears,

FIG. 1

secondly, by confinement within narrow quantitative limits, and finally, by the monotony of their respective timbres.

According to an anecdote which serves for illustration independently

[1] The Bull of Pope John XXII, 1322, condemning its first appearance as prejudicial to the modal-consciousness of Gregorian music perhaps partially explains this.

of its authenticity, Mendelssohn was once asked:—"What is worse than a flute solo?" to which query he is reported to have answered: "A flute duet."

It is not the intention of the writer to satirize such instruments, for they are essential to orchestral ensembles, and, under certain circumstances are capable of delivering effective utterance in solo-passages.

But it is nevertheless true that there is disparity in the aesthetic worth of musical instruments.

In the family of instruments which are so constructed as to produce music effectively within the range indicated previously (Fig. 1) there is likewise inequality in the degrees of impressibility, due chiefly to difference in quality, although this is in some instances intensified by the difference in quantity. Thus, the string family, violin, viola, violoncello are probably the most highly appreciated single instruments because not only of lovely and variable qualities of tone, but because these instruments are usually heard in a medium dynamic compass—and art concurs with philosophy in approving the adage "In medio stat virtus." The brass family, comprising trumpet, horn, trombone and tuba,—and the reed family, comprising oboe, English horn, bassoon, and clarinet— would not be said by the majority to be as well endowed for general musical effect as the string family. And this, probably, not only because the timbre of the brass and reeds is less suited to the more frequently recurring intentions of music, but because, in spite of the lovely color which they sometimes contribute and in spite of the clarity, resonance, and partial-tone emphasis which they bring to the various orchestral lines, they cannot by their structure, produce as satisfying a tone as the string family.

In their turn, the strings must concede superiority to the ensemble instruments, such as piano and organ. For single instruments depend upon accompanying instruments for their efficacy. With the development of harmony and counterpoint, the human ear has come to require the consonance of several tones sounded synchronously for general aesthetic satisfaction.

People would quickly tire of listening to a violin played without accompaniment.

The ensemble instrument can draw upon the resources of harmony and is therefore more nearly equipped to exemplify the mystic art than any single instrument. The piano sings beautifully in the desirable range—it has an adequate dynamic flexibility and a beautiful timbre. However, the piano is a percussive instrument and therefore can generate only one tonal-color, albeit with many shades under the fingers of an artist. For this reason the piano cedes rank to the organ.

The pipe organ has a great plenitude of sonority, a diapason cathedral-tone for its own distinctive timbre, but it is also an imitative instrument, copying the tone colors of orchestral instruments. Time was, a decade or two ago, when some impresarios thought to replace the orchestra with the organ in theatrical performances. Their ambition was futile, for although the organ can approximate the instrumentation of a full symphony orchestra, therefore simulating its timbres, the simulation itself places the orchestra above the organ as the supreme vehicle of instrumental color. Likewise, two further considerations concur to emphasize the superiority of the orchestra; the impossibility of imparting real accentual stress to notes played on the organ: and the vitality achieved by the participation of so many individuals in the orchestra. Its diapason tone will always reserve the place of dignity for the organ in church music, but it can never attain parity with the orchestra as an ensemble of emotional appeal. There is only a single human factor revealed in the functioning of the organ, and this single influence, the organist, operates only indirectly, to the extent of choosing stop-timbres managing control-devices, regulating dynamics and releasing keys which allow air fanned by motors to do the actual sounding.

The symphonic ensemble, on the other hand, offers a human factor for each instrument played and for each note sounded. The contact of each player with his instrument is direct, and the vitality of the ensemble result is determined by the contribution of the individuals. The fervor or placidity, the impetuosity or calm of a hundred human beings speaks through orchestral music, while the organ is altogether a robot, a marvelous mechanism executing human intentions under the control of one operative.

But the orchestra, too, is in some degree a robot; it employs instruments of wood and metal. For this reason it cedes rank to the chorus of human voices. The chorus, by the fact of a human personnel making music without the medium of mechanical devices, can give intimation of mysteries captured by instinct and profoundly felt. Because it can appeal to the subconsciousness of listeners with the subtle expression of its own human experience, the chorus is the signally endowed interagent between absolute music and the emotions which, translating and qualifying it, relate it variously to memory or imagination.

Nor does the chorus lack any of the properties required for a convincing manifestation of the elements which the science of acoustics finds essential to music. It has all the colors of the musical rainbow; it can deliver itself of the most complex harmonic and polyphonic forms; its dynamic energy can be regulated to express any emotion or any degree of emotion; its sensitiveness is as capricious as the human imagination; it weds to melody the eloquence of words. It can blend in its crucible, by a fine alchemy, the most surreptitious forces of art, fusing in the heat of its flame temperaments, instincts, hopes and fears, aspirations and inhibitions. The chorus, finally, can worship, love, hate, plead, threaten and destroy only as human beings can, free from the irrelevance or the impeding influence of mechanical instruments.

The chorus today, generally, fails to show forth its endowment. But its ineffectiveness cannot reasonably be alleged against its possible worth. It is merely evidence that the chorus is not drawing upon its resources. While the art of the orchestral ensemble has been in the ascent, it has been natural to forget the richer art of the chorus, and in this forgetfulness to allow the technique of its development to be lost.

There have been, of course, brilliant flashes of choral splendor, from time to time and here and there. But they have not been brilliant enough or sufficiently long sustained to enlighten the multitudes of the profession as to the richness of the force they have been ignoring. For in metropolitan centers as well as in small towns, a disconcerting majority of directors still affects to conduct choral units in churches, concert-halls, school auditoriums, and radio studios with a minimum of knowledge of or discernible interest in the elements which differentiate chorophony from other kinds of musical exercise.

An aspirant to orchestral leadership can readily secure much information from the literature available; this is extensive; but the musician who would successfully take up the duties of the *Magister Choralis* must face the tedious task of discovering for himself many elements of his specialty. There is practically no bibliography of value on the subject, and the subject, in its entirety, suggests a long list of items for study, many of these presenting definite problems.

Those of the profession who have been engaged in setting forth anew the old ideals of choral virtuosity, have worked out the technical processes which they sponsor, largely by studying the structure of the chorus itself, by analyzing it into its many unsuspected components, and by relating these components to concepts of choral tonality which they have found hidden, like spirits striving to make themselves known, in the vocal scores of the centuries.

The importance of the mediaeval Scholae Cantorum cannot gratuitously be denied. In their unwritten codes of technique were the principles of high art which must again be discovered, understood, and applied. The student choirmaster must hie back to the polyphonic period, and by study, meditation and examination of the material found there, plus reasonable deductions, find the only basis upon which a modern technique may be built.

While the art of composition was expanding from the simplicity of the unison Gregorian Chants, through organum and discant to the complex polyphonic idioms of the Dufay—Palestrina—Tudor periods, there must have been a parallel growth in choral technique.

Whereas it is not possible, with the evidence available, to quote written records of the steps, principles, and the systems involved in the progress of choral expression from the tenth century's meagre needs to the faultless and dazzling virtuosity of the sixteenth, it is altogether reasonable to conclude from study of the extant scores of each succeeding generation, that greater demands were progressively made not only upon the technical facility of group-singers, but upon all the resources of vocal timbre, balance, and blend which the groups could develop.

The tonal loveliness, elasticity, buoyancy and the resulting mysticism required to reveal the beauty of a motet to the satisfaction of a Josquin des Pres, a Palestrina, a Vittoria, or a Byrd, were without doubt among the standard resources taken for granted in most of the cathedrals of Mediaeval and Renaissance Europe.

But such qualities of tone are not among the assets of the average modern choir,—cathedral, parochial, or secular. The harshness, rigidity and blare of the vocalism that assails the fair contour of Palestrinesque comeliness today would have inhibited the composition of most music of that style if they had been characteristics of the ensemble singing of the period. The very structure of the music itself indicates the genre of tonal effects preconceived by the composers. It would have been futile to compose music which assigned to each choral line the threefold independence of melody, rhythm and dynamic undulation, if the choirs available were not perfectly balanced units, the parity of quantity and the juxta-position of tone-colors being nicely adjusted between the sectional groups.

The homophonic style, however, requires no such fine adjustments. It is vertical music, the top part being usually the important one; and those below merely the harmonic support. This style indulgently permits some inattention to the graces of blend and balance to escape censure. It was the change from the mediaeval horizontal music to the vertical

style which has dominated music since the seventeenth century, that
marked the beginning of choral deterioration.

The gentle rise and fall of voices, trained to follow the restrained
melodic curve-lines of the earlier music was as essential to aesthetic performance as the singing of the correct notes. Today this refined undulation has been replaced by bold and noisy impacts with some phrases, and
unseemly hushings with others.

The aura, which the older *a cappella* style can create with such in-
definable effect, and in the absence of which this music is cold, awkward
and unfriendly, can be developed only as a corollary to the choral technique that effaces over-assertive vocal timbres and the advertising of
personal reactions by individuals of the ensemble. The incompatibility of
individual exploitation with the homogeneity conceived by the weavers of
the polyphonic choral texture probably impressed the *a cappella* singers
to the extent of restraining the expression of their dramatic consciousness.

The alloy of ego-vocalism took the chorus off the pure "gold standard"
in the seventeenth century, and the aura which had conserved to ensemble singing the even emanation of lustre that comes from the rapprochement of one choral line to another was dispelled by the displace-
ments of "dramma per la musica."

That through the "novelties" of the last two centuries and a half music
has come into an opulence of aesthetic wealth, no one can reasonably deny.
The symphonic, operatic and solo virtuosities have guaranteed the modern
exercise of music a fellowship with our richest influences. But we have
suffered an unnecessary loss. Perhaps during the *coup d'état* it was
necessary to subvert the old order. Revolutions usually banish or destroy
a dynasty. But the ostracism of the mediaeval and polyphonic criteria
having long since been accomplished, why not recall from exile the com-
mandant-principles of superlative ensemble song, and bid them flourish
again in affiliation with the symphony and the opera?

In some places, the old approaches to choral excellence survived for a
time; in some places they are being now revived; but generally a lesser
technique, a technique unworthy of the history of music, has prevailed.
The high achievement of the average modern chorus is mediocrity.

During the current generation, singing units have multipled steadily.
Even the smallest communities offer opportunities for vocal exercise and
experience. Everywhere, large numbers of men, women and children are
participating in the choral activities of the country.

Community singing is a splendid and highly commendable development in many parts of this country; it provides an excellent means of self-

expression to the multitude—its reaches being perhaps psychological or sociological rather than purely musical. Community singing, however, invokes only a minimum of aesthetic standards and exemplifies sparse qualities of artistry; yet, it supplies the impulse toward better achievements by qualified singers under competent direction. Good choral organizations do not spring over night fully equipped, from mediocrity to high excellence, and in this field the Art of Choral Conducting meets a challenge not to be disregarded.

The music-loving public is eager for lovely music and responds gratefully to the quality of instrumental performance. Choral music, as a rule, occupies a lesser place in the estimation of a critical public, but we cannot overlook the fact that instrumental soloists and orchestral organizations enjoying public favor are invariably of the highest professional standing, whereas practically all of the choral groups are made up of amateurs who sing for the love of singing good music under able direction. And here the choral conductor's responsibility is obvious and cannot be escaped. It is reassuring to observe the fact that amateur choral societies which give periodical concerts under skillful direction can count on large and interested audiences, and the size and continued interest of these audiences is usually in direct ratio to the ability and sincerity of the choral conductor. Three factors are essential in raising choral music to a high standard: quality, quantity and pitch, the three elements which determine the character of any musical sound; but *quality* is paramount and until conductors of choral music have become expert in developing tone-qualities that arrest the ear with pleasant sensations, they cannot expect to seize and hold the interest of the public.

The radio audience is showing itself to be moderately interested in ensemble singing. This is due, probably, to the increasing excellence of radio choirs. The conductors of some of these have been trying various devices to attract listeners, to assure them that their offerings are not tedious with the dull inertia of ordinary chorus singing. Some of these devices are inconsequential, some are charlatan; but the very fact that conductors realize that the customary style of choral singing is bald and tiresome to the people, is an earnest that presently they will discover some important truths, and the resuscitation of the old art will be made known. Competition for the coveted places on commercial programmes has become sharp, and "the survival of the fittest" is not a mere doctrine to the aspirants for radio eminence; it is a fact so well known to musicians that they are scurrying hither and yon, seeking knowledge of their artforms which will popularize their performances—and win contracts.

To offset the indications that too many masters of church choirs and choral concert societies appear to be contented with mediocre performances, one notes with satisfaction the establishment of certain institutes which are specializing in the improvement of church music. There are also courses in choral technique conducted in some colleges, these being of interest probably to future concert conductors. If, in these institutes and courses, emphasis be laid on the fundamentals of the choral art, if the horse be not allowed to assume his awkward and ineffective place behind the cart, which occurs when the study of repertory precedes and out-ranks the study of building a chorus of voices into a sensitive, vital and colorful instrumentality, and if the graduates emerge with as profound a respect for their specialty as the *chef d'orchestre* has for his, the churches and concert-halls may again resound with the irresistible loveliness of true choral music.

Supervisors and instructors of music in the Grade and High Schools are beginning to suspect that ensemble singing is a precise specialty, and that the feats of concerted ventriloquism which for so long have passed as choral singing, are an affront to the art. Already in many parts of the country, young protagonists of the new ideal are struggling bravely against the influence of the tories who fear to let go the ventriloquism, having nothing wherewith to replace it. When the former grow into a majority, the commendable results accomplished in recent years by a few High School choruses will become more general.

If choral music is to regain its rightful place among the arts, its promoters must be marshalled under the aegis of the old masters. Their spirit must encompass the neophytes and their insignia become the badge of honest competency.

To conclude: The modern chorus trainers and conductors must know the chorus as Mengelberg, Toscanini, Stokowski and the other scintillating stars of the symphonic empyrean know the orchestra.

Masters of tone-color they must be; of free, elastic, buoyant, dirigible intonation; of blend and balance and flexible control in all the dynamic panels from *pianissimo* to *fortissimo;* of discrimination in the selection of the proper choral timbres for the suitable performance of many diverse schools of composition.

Masters of repertory, too, they must become, so that no longer will a Gregorian Chant, a polyphonic motet, a Tudor madrigal, the Beethoven *Missa Solemnis* and the *German Requiem* of Brahms be set forth on one interpretative basis; so that no longer the *Miserere* of Allegri or the *Turn Thou Our Captivity* of Byrd will masquerade in the raiment of the *Carmen* choruses and no longer the *Dainty Fine Sweet Nymph of Morely* undertake her tribute to Terpsichore with the stiff and heavy tread of the *Soldiers' Chorus*.

The restoration of the true art of concerted song will be like the finding of a treasure-chest long hidden and then forgotten.

The secret skills of centuries are in some treasure-chest, with a benediction specially inscribed by the creators of a great art upon those who, finding the chest, open it generously to the world.

CHAPTER II

Three Primary Precepts

In order that the study of choral technique in this volume may be systematic and progressive, the subject will be viewed in five of its six principal phases:—

1. The vocal training of each choral line.
2. The development and use of the "color-scheme."
3. The blending of all choral lines into a unified ensemble.
4. The development of precision in attack and release, rhythmical accuracy, steadiness of tempo, rubato, and dynamic elasticity.
5. The cultivation of effective diction.
6. The training of choristers in sight reading.

A study of the principles of interpretation which must be applied in the conducting of the important schools of choral composition will follow in a second volume.

The first phase of the subject, the vocal training of each choral line, is concerned with three elementary purposes:

    (*a*) The correction of vocal abuses.
    (*b*) The development of positive qualities.
    (*c*) The establishment of accurate pitch.

———

A study of the correction of vocal abuses is thus the first step to be taken on the long road to choral virtuosity, and the student conductor must address himself to it as to the most important of the many important points in chorophony.

———

The majority of choral singers (and perhaps of soloists), with the possible exception of ultra-volatile lyrics, gives evidence of serious vocal abuse. Many have become so inured to bad habits of vocalism as to be probably incurable.

Vocal abuse, in the greater number of instances can be diagnosed immediately as an inevitable consequence of the "Quantity rather than Quality" philosophy of music. An excess of energy applied to the action of the vocal cords necessarily strains the delicate mechanism of the larynx, and a forced, unnatural phonation results. Chronic loudness in speech and singing concur to rob a voice of its natural flexibility. The throat becomes fatigued from overexercise, and the habitual utterance of *forte* and *fortissimo* sounds develops so much muscular contraction as to prevent the easy functioning of the larynx.

Many choral directors have favored this noisy vocalism, confusing loudness with resonance, and rigidity with sturdiness. They frequently refer to this unnatural tone-quality as a "fine, ringing, *natural* tone." Vocal studios, too, have contributed to the general tendency towards quantity, the studios which guarantee a speedy increase in loudness (the studio word being "resonance") having long attracted a large clientele.

The loud singing permitted and encouraged too often generally in the elementary schools, affecting large numbers of children, tends to focus their attention on quantity as a vocal asset. Some "standard" books of vocal exercises prove by the very structure of the vocalizes contained therein, that their authors found orientation in the same conviction. For a considerable portion of the exercises in these manuals cannot be used by average singers in their average way without injurious results. The vocal methods which are applied, knowingly or unknowingly, chiefly to secure amplitude of tone, before voices are "placed" naturally and throats reconditioned, are certain to confirm existing abuses and to initiate new faults. Such methods prescribe, at the outset, the use of the vowel sound *AH, forte* and upward progressions. Any one of these three features is sufficient to promote inflexible and constricted vocalism; when applied together over a period of months, the results are lamentable.

Faulty processes of tone-production are assisted to their unfortunate results by the constantly increasing noise of our modern cities. The din which, day and night, plays havoc with the nervous system, challenges every speaking voice to "talk it down." Taxis, trains, and trucks, motors, machines and megaphones, radio, rendings, and ringings, these and all other sources whence comes our ubiquitous noise, provide such competition to conversation that audibility seems to demand each year greater dynamic energy in everyday speech. Perhaps the overtaxing of the ear-nerves by the fanfare of sounds to which they are subjected, will ultimately lessen the sensitiveness of auditory perception. It is certain evidently, that this is an age of noise, and that the constant clangor is a factor in producing loud voices.

"Quantity" has found willing sponsors in other fields of musical exercise as well as in the chorus. The general level of dynamic strength at which music is performed seems unnecessarily high. Bands and orchestras play too loudly; pianists and organists cultivate a taste for grand *crescendos* and *fortissimos*. Many celebrated singers limit their dynamic variations to the area between *mezzo-forte* and *fortissimo*. The starting point in the scale of energy for a notable percentage of musicians is *forte*. Grand opera frequently degenerates into a conflict of noises, the participants in the orchestra pit, usually, although not always, out-clanging the singers. Probably the art of music generally will attain a greater aesthetic effectiveness, when musicians will have studied more assiduously the relation of music to the dynamic panels.

The effect of chronic, excessive loudness on singers is practically pathological. The condition of the whole vocal mechanism which has been disrupted by forcing muscles and cartilages to function beyond their natural limits, is a quasi-laryngitis. The vocal cords may even be out of their natural position; they may touch at their central points, which occurs when the *AH* or *EE* vowel sound, unprotected by a consonant, has been used extravagantly, or they may form an ellipse, which results from too much vocalization on the vowel sound *OH,* and inadequate attention to breath control.

The first prescription in the therapy of laryngitis is silence. Medical applications usually fail of their proper effect if the vocal cords are not permitted a temporary lessening of activity. And then proper methods of voice-placing and tone production must be applied.

The starting point in the technique of eliminating vocal abuses is the establishment of *pianissimo* as the invariable measure of vocal quantity to be used until the faulty production has been corrected. *Pianissimo* is frequently confounded with *piano,* and the first task of the student conductor is to learn to differentiate between these two dynamic panels. *Pianissimo* designates the softest sound-impulse that can be heard, and some composers, desiring to convey this degree of softness as requisite for the proper interpretation of their music, recognizing the latitude which performers allow themselves in determining dynamic intensities, are not satisfied to write *pp* but *ppp* and even *pppp,* as in the *All Night Vigil* of Rachmaninof.

The *pianissimo* which will be effective as an agency for correcting tonal abuses must be of the Rachmaninof order, a sound like Moore's "faint exquisite music of a dream."

Pianissimo vocalization is the choral conductor's most expedient stratagem in many choral needs, and pre-eminently in correcting faulty vocalism; with some other devices which will be discussed presently, it provides almost a panacea for vocal ills.

Pianissimo practice is the keynote of all the choral technique expounded in these pages.

The writer has never encountered a choral tone of superlative excellence, paralleling for instance the tonal excellence of the great symphony orchestras, where *pianissimo* has not been the principal factor in its growth. On the other hand, he has witnessed and directed experiments with this corrective factor by which large groups of ill-sounding voices have been quickly metamorphosed into units giving surprising intimations of latent tonal loveliness.

In the voices of boys, it will be generally conceded, the results of abuse are more flagrantly evident than in the voices of girls or adults. A boy is naturally a shouter. His instinct for affecting the bravura style, which he conceives to be a proof of masculinity, urges him to loud speech, placing a premium on vociferation, and delivers him to the choirmaster in a vocal condition grievously impaired. Any group of school boys, singing in their accustomed, unrestrained manner, will corroborate this to be most painfully true. Cohorts of excited college students, cheering madly at foot-ball games can hardly exceed the violent raucousness of one hundred small boys. The "acid test," therefore, for the efficacy of *pianissimo* as a vocal curative, is its immediate effect upon the vocalism of untrained boys. The writer welcomed an opportunity of making this "acid test" a few years ago, under circumstances which would assure the experiment fair challenge and severe inquisition.

During the course of a series of lectures at a celebrated conservatory, the writer had stressed the value of *pianissimo* so vigorously that much discussion and interested debate became current among the members of the faculty as well as among the student-body. To satisfy all concerned, the writer agreed to demonstrate the efficacy of *pianissimo* in a public hall. About forty boys were provided. Their voices were splendid specimens for such an experiment; full-throated, undiluted noise-tones; hardy, stentorian intonations; blasts of trumpets, couacs of reeds. The tonal abuse was excessive. After a preliminary statement of the principles of vocalism involved, the test began. The boys were requested to sing in their everyday manner, without restraint, "The Star-Spangled Banner." The noise was gratifying, the straining, heaving, gasping, reassuring; the strangling in efforts to get at the higher notes, sheer delight. Here indeed was a group of boys that would draw upon the full resources of *pianissimo* for a minimum of effect!

Presently, after a few breathing exercises and encouragement to relax,

a *pianissimo* hum at [musical notation] was introduced, and carried over into

OO. This was repeated several times, whereupon the same note was intoned *POO,* and carried down the scale. The same process was repeated, with extreme softness, at lower pitches. Then, the notes of "The Star-Spangled Banner" were sung to *POO* still at *pianissimo,* and finally the words of part of the verse were attempted, the boys being urged to copy the sound they had been making with *POO.* The success of the experiment was manifest at once. The stridency had disappeared as if by magic—the raucousness had given place to a quality of tone which with consistent development could grow into an instrumentality of aesthetic loveliness. The acid test was a triumph, not for the experimenter but for *pianissimo.* The writer has conducted many similar tests in different parts of the country, always with the same results.

In consonance with the practical purposes of this treatise, the writer urges all students to make similar experiments, so that by their own observations they may be more abundantly informed and convinced.

In lieu of boys, any group—provided they be of one category, soprano, tenor, etc.,—may be brought through the experiment with the same enlightening result. *PEE* or *PAW* should be substituted for *POO* with men's voices.

Pianissimo is like the photographer's dark-room in which the camera's films are developed; light destroys an untreated film and *forte* destroys an unplaced voice. The choirmasters of the great English Cathedrals, in the latter part of the nineteenth century were practically unanimous in rating *pianissimo* as the most important factor in eliminating faulty vocalism.

The writer's experience with thousands of singers confirms the soundness of their conviction. The value of *pianissimo* is not less notable with adults than with children. Boys are addicted to greater vocal misuse than adults, and if *pianissimo* can contribute so well to the correction of the greater defects, why not of the lesser?

The disembodiment of tone implied in *pianissimo* is recommended frequently in this treatise not only as a corrective element but as a positive agency in cultivating artistic features. For example a good choral *fortissimo* accrues from *pianissimo* practice of a passage rather than from much repetition in the loud dynamic panel in which it will be performed. Likewise, a convincing climax to a *poco a poco crescendo* is prospered by *pianissimo* rehearsing, the choristers merely *thinking* the increase of tone. And in the difficult matter of perfecting a choral blend the use of *pianissimo* is essential, so that the lighter tonal elements of each choral line may float about, encounter and merge with the partial tones of the other lines.

A few writers in recent years have derided the use of *pianissimo,* associating it with the anaemic vocalism affected by the "crooners" of the radio. Referring to it as "building on the soft," they caricature it as an ineffectual exaggeration. The writer at once concedes the futility of *pianissimo* for correcting poor tone-production, *if the vocal exercises begin in the middle register or proceed from low to higher notes.* In fact "building on the soft" in the middle register is not only useless, it is practically impossible, because the swollen condition of the membranes and sometimes of the cords as well, resulting from misuse, prevents the utterance of pleasant soft tones in the middle register. One of the indications of the progressive harm of incorrect tone-production is the difficulty which singers experience in attempting such tones.

Frequently, the cords are found to touch each other during phonation, thus developing in their middle portions an attrition which obstructs *piano* and *pianissimo* intonations in the middle register.

The late Dr. H. Holbrook Curtis, a most distinguished laryngologist and the highly esteemed throat physician of the Golden Era of the De Reszkes, Melba, Eames, Sembrich, Caruso, Homer, etc., at the Metropolitan Opera House, New York City, has presented the case clearly and briefly. In his book "Voice Building and Tone Placing" (p. 136) the Doctor writes:— ". . . as the muscles of the larynx tire, there ensues a lack of perfect equilibrium, and the tones are produced by forcing, in an attempt to overcome the uncertainty which one always feels as the result of loss of tension from muscular fatigue. We often observe in the laryngoscopic mirror, after the singer has overstrained them, a dusky congestion of the cords and a slight bulging of their middle third. If one looks closely and asks the person to sing a note in the medium, it is remarked that the cords touch one another in the bellied position. . . . The subjective symptoms are these: pupils complain that they are losing their *piano* notes, and it is difficult to sing *mezzo-voce.*"

A few more words from the pen of this international specialist will serve to indicate the method of employing *pianissimo* to advantage:

"The voice (p. 167) should be trained from the *head register down,*—that is, the timbre of the head tone should predominate the scale and should be brought as low in pitch as possible." And (p. 171) "The scales should be sung *piano* and *leggiero,* with as little effort as possible. There should be, as yet, no attempt to produce intensity of tone. The great masters of all instruments (with the exception of a few Germans) now insist upon the light touch to begin with. So with the voice, the first exercises should be gentle, and should be sung *mezzo-voce.*"

Downward vocalization is the second agency in establishing free tone-production. This practice was adopted by the English choirmasters as an indispensable associate of *pianissimo.*

"Building on the soft" usually connotes in the practice of its advocates, the attempt to vocalize softly in the middle register. This attempt has been shown to be futile and frustrate. But the scheme advocated by the most successful chorus directors of many generations of initiating vocal exercise at a pitch which it is easy to sing a light volatile tone, and of extending this quality downward through the middle and lower registers, commends itself as thoroughly compatible with and prospering the natural functions of the tone-making mechanism.

Downward vocalization, *pianissimo,* from a point above the middle register, will gradually endow the middle and lower registers with some of the lightness, elasticity and buoyancy of the upper notes. It is clear, on the other hand, that loud vocalizing, beginning in the lower register and progressing upwards, will invariably tend to constrict the upper register, carrying up at the same time the objectionable elements of weight, throatiness and inertia.

The lower and middle registers, principally the latter, are more frequently used and therefore more frequently misused than the upper. Bad quality must be purged from the middle register and this can be accomplished only by cultivating the higher register first, and the *downward* application of this cultivation to the middle and lower registers.

Downward vocalization and *pianissimo* are important factors not only in clearing away abuses, but they serve effectively in keeping properly trained voices flexible and accurate to pitch. As a "tuning-up" process at the beginning of rehearsals and as correctives during rehearsals, they have no substitutes of equal value.

There are some fundamental points to be developed in connection with the application of these principles. These concern the general scheme of pedagogy to be adopted, and correct breathing, upon which all satisfactory vocalism ultimately depends.

The processes of choral training sponsored in this study comprise a sequence of steps which cannot be successfully broken. The procedure is literally a "translation" i.e. the "carrying over" of a good quality or condition to the nearest weak spot which its beneficent influence may repair and strengthen.

It is important, consequently, to seek a pitch for a starting point at which some good qualities may reveal themselves or be readily created.

Sound pedagogy rests upon starting right and upon *gradual progress*.

The last theorems of Euclid are relatively simple to the student who has followed the unfolding of geometry step by step, conclusion by conclusion, corollary by corollary. But to the "jumper" these are as unenlightening as the "curvature of space" to the general public.

The text book of contrapuntal composition which dominated the educational system for several generations was the "Gradus ad Parnassum" by Johann Joseph Fux (1660–1741). The complete subject, consisting of the theory and practice of counterpoint, discovered itself *per gradus,* literally, *by steps* from the simplest musical truism to the most complex contrapuntal intricacies. Mozart and Haydn built their polyphonic technique upon it, and Cherubini as well as Bellermann found in it the well ordered exposition of the subject upon which to base their more modern treatises.

The "Gradus ad Parnassum" of choral technique involve the same gradation of advancing steps as Euclid demonstrated necessary for geometry and Fux for counterpoint.

The writer has seen many choirmasters grow restive with the monotony of the preliminary measures of choral training, and hoping meticulous attention to these to be unnecessary, hurriedly advance their choruses to points for which they were altogether unprepared. If the ideal be a superlative manifestation of the choral art, the progress must be *poco a poco,* choristers must be drilled to perfection in the fundamental requirements of good singing, and thus become habituated to artistic practices. Without patient willingness to "make haste slowly" a choirmaster does not merit more than mediocre results. Quintillian's epigram "the perfection of art is to conceal art" is a sound dogma of aesthetics, bespeaking relentless refining of the minutiae of which such perfection is the synthesis.

Reference was made in passing to correct breathing as a prerequisite to vocal grace. Teachers are wont to discourse of this as the "art of breathing," elaborating various and complex systems for its mastery. But the *act* of breathing is a primary instinct of all living animals and men, dictated by a physiological necessity over which volition has no domain. There is no "art" involved in breathing, except in so far as the misnomer may be popularly associated with "control." Is there art in the functioning of the heart, in the primary acts of seeing and hearing? Medical science assists in regulating irregular hearts, eyes can be trained to observe more and understandingly, and ears can be cultivated to distinguish nuances of sound, but with the physiological performance of heart, eyes and ears, "art" has absolutely no connection. Likewise the pulmonary functions of the human body are altogether independent of any and all canons which pedantry may contrive for them. If by the "art of breathing" something not accurately an art is signified, a mere summary of the natural processes by which the lungs are filled with air and the blood oxygenized, the writer will not challenge the caption, but if the "art of breathing" involves a technique to be learned and practiced like the rules of a craft, he argues that it be eliminated from choral nomenclature, for it is confusing and misleading.

A normal infant breathes correctly, according to natural laws ordained by God. So, too, a sleeping man breathes easily and adequately without the application of acquired technique.

When one is self-conscious or nervous—as singers and speakers are wont to be—one is likely to perform natural functions in an unnatural manner, but there is no "art" needed to restore the functions to normal. Habits of inadequate breath-control are often developed through carelessness, also, but the mere insistence on giving nature full opportunity to fill the lungs properly is all of "art" that is required.

A person who performs natural acts hundreds of times each day in a perfectly natural manner, will frequently perform the same acts awkwardly and unnaturally if suddenly called upon to give a demonstration in public.

A fluent, even garrulous parlor conversationalist often loses control of his facility in expression before a formal audience, and the vast majority of persons who are accustomed to breathe properly under ordinary circumstances, will at first inhale and exhale in a signally unaccustomed and unnatural manner when requested to stand and to take a sudden, deep breath before observers. Their *natural* easy methods are replaced by efforts, and efforts connote the idea of unwonted exertion which in physical acts may be prejudicial to natural processes.

Innumerable monographs and dissertations have been written on this alleged "art of breathing" and a novice is justified therefore in suspecting that much erudition and acquired skill are needed before the lungs can fulfill their part in vocalism. The novice's increasing experience, however, will not confirm the suspicion. In some studios a regular course in "breathing" is given as a preliminary and almost independent department of expensive instruction. The average child and adult generally breathe correctly, otherwise the human race would long since have become extinct. But under the stress of self-consciousness, both children and adults are likely to show two faults: first, they raise the shoulders while inhaling; second, nervously or through inadvertence, they permit the breath to be exhaled too suddenly. Perhaps a third fault may be noted among individuals of the phlegmatic type, i.e. indolence in filling the lungs to the capacity permitted by the breathing-space. But no canons of art are necessary to correct these faults. The majority of intelligent people is surprised to learn of such defects, and it is a simple matter to eliminate them.

Pedagogy prescribes nothing more complex here than the indication of the breathing process—in and out—established by nature with short periods devoted to the practice of this process. Emphasis of course should be laid on the advantage of breathing as deeply as possible and of exhaling as conservatively as possible, in order to assure steady wind pressure to all the notes of a phrase. It is easy to show a group of children this process. With boys, the writer proceeds in the following manner: having requested them to take a quick deep breath, and having brought to their attention the fact that they have all raised their shoulders, he places a boy on the top of a table. The boy is directed to lie on his back with hands crossed loosely over the diaphragm. Upon being bidden to breathe deeply, he and the other boys are asked to observe, first that his hands are gently lifted and second that his shoulders remain equivalently motionless.

Upon the application of this information to the class, standing with hands similarly folded, all will notice that these are pushed out if the shoulders be kept down, and drawn in with the diaphragm if the shoulders be raised. Therefore a simple precept is announced which will serve all the needs of vocalism. *Keep the shoulders down and breathe as deeply as possible.*

The second fault is even more easily corrected. The tendency to allow too speedy exhalation of breath can be checked and presently eliminated if the choirmaster insist that the lungs be emptied slowly while he counts a given number.

These simple practices if made the first step at each rehearsal will guarantee a breath control adequate to any singer's legitimate needs.

The pedagogy in this matter may be applied, with appropriate modifications, just as successfully to adults. Following these practices, which were emphasized by the celebrated choirmaster of Boston, Samuel Brenton Whitney, the writer has experienced no difficulty in developing breath control among choristers which at times has seemed prodigious to observers, but which in reality was only a carefully exercised normal power, easily matched by any who would apply the same means. Of course, there is more to be discussed about the use of breath in singing and these points will present themselves subsequently, but in the matter of inhaling and exhaling there is nothing more involved than has been argued here. It seems desirable to breathe through the nose, when possible, this organ being designed by nature to sift and moisten the breath, but there are many occasions where oral breathing is necessary as well, if the sixteenth and eighth beat rests are to serve as "filling-stations."

Each rehearsal should begin with breathing exercises, chiefly as a limbering-up measure, and in order to remind the singers to avoid the faulty affectation of raising the shoulders. It is desirable, of course, that the practice room be well ventilated. The writer never fails to devote a few minutes to this beneficent practice at rehearsals, in tuning-up periods before services, and backstage before concerts. For hygienic as well as vocal ends, it is profitable to encourage deep breathing through the nose, while the choiristers are out-of-doors.

When the great epidemic of influenza gripped the country in the autumn of 1918, the Paulist Choristers had just returned from a difficult war-pilgrimage of six months. The boy-sopranos were fatigued and in such physical condition as to be ready victims of the disease. Many boys were stricken by a violent form of the infection, but all convalesced. Doctors in attendance were unanimous in the opinion that their extraordinary pulmonary development was an important factor in their recovery.

This "extraordinary" development was merely ordinary capacity expanded by extraordinary fidelity to routine exercises.

Like breath control, tonal control can readily be reduced to simple elements. For like breathing, speaking and singing are natural faculties of the primary physical order. Therefore, it is unlikely that the manner of their correct functioning would be hidden behind esoteric information, comprehensible only to the erudite.

Tonal expression is a facile experience to which both physical and mental factors contribute their share. The former must be relieved of encumbrances and allowed freedom to produce the sounds natural to a throat. Anatomy and the physics of sound concur to determine what tones are producible. The expedients most useful in ridding the voice-mechanism of obstructions are simple in themselves, and, if followed in logical sequence, will generally be successful. The mental factors contributing to artistic singing are commonplace, and can be readily fostered by the application of elementary principles of psychology. These will be discussed in due course.

All of the technical precepts which will assemble themselves in the first phase of choral training, i.e. the vocal training of each choral line, will be seen as directed to the end of helping a singer's larynx, vocal cords and resonance chambers to operate in a natural manner, so that potential vocal beauties may be revealed.

The writer offers five stages of corrective training in an ensuing chapter, which by long experience have been found abundantly successful in preparing voices for the more positive treatment by which the polychrome effects of chorophony may be attained.

The five stages constitute an orderly sequence of steps required by foregoing considerations and are *applicable to all voices* with such modifications as will be noted in their proper connections. They proceed naturally from a safe starting point in the manner of "translation" already indicated.

The student must realize at the outset that the five stages will not complete the vocal training of any choral line, least of all the soprano line, but that they are measures necessary to prepare the voices for the elegances of tonal color which in many lovely tints may be readily cultivated—later!

The "Five Stages" are offered also as a prophylactic and therapeutic treatment for voices already well placed, but needing a tonic or an aperitif to clear away "throatiness" and other vocal indispositions which commonly embarrass a singer. The writer in his personal work endeavors to exemplify the entire span of the five stages in quick succession at the start of every rehearsal even with thoroughly conditioned choristers.

Chapter III, then, offers the writer's "bag of corrective tricks." These will be set forth in their many particulars, pitched and vowelled primarily for sopranos, particularly boy-sopranos. The modifications required for mezzo-sopranos, contraltos, tenors, baritones and basses are indicated in Part II of the chapter. The special needs of the changing voice during its cultivation as alto-tenor will be discussed in a separate chapter.[1]

But it is important to note again that these Five Stages are the prescrip-

[1] See Chapter VIII.

tions of a vocal therapy which is applicable to all voices except the alto-tenor, from highest soprano to lowest bass.

In summary of the considerations offered in this chapter, it may succinctly be stated that the "Five Stages" expand gradually from three primary corrective precepts of choral technique:—

Precept No. I.   Pianissimo.
Precept No. II.   Descending Vocalization.
Precept No. III. Shoulders down!

CHAPTER III

The Five Stages

Part One—Boys' Voices

The First Stage

Since the application of these ensuing stages to boys' voices must be made with special care and alert attention at certain points which need less emphasis with adults, I shall present the material as suiting the vocal and mental states of a group of untrained boys, eleven or twelve years of age.

With boys, all exercises and steps must be *made* to take effect by the teacher.

Until their aesthetic reactions to good singing have been wakened, boys contribute little to facilitate progress. They do not concentrate; the restraint put upon their normally loud utterance is annoying; they have no sympathy with a monotonous and seemingly meaningless routine of vocalizes. Their minds are constantly straying to thoughts of athletic adventure and, being frequently fatigued in body after a day in the class-room, there is a minimum of spontaneity in their vocal efforts.

Just as truly as Horace's poet must be born and cannot be made, the modern choir-boy is not a natural but a manufactured product.

Furthermore, the first three stages, being altogether remedial, affect small boys as all disciplinary and corrective measures affect them; they don't like them and are anxious to escape submitting to them.

Therefore, the choirmaster must attend well to his pedagogy. He must invent means of interesting the boys in the practice periods of the stages, and by dividing the periods between vocal exercise and practice in sight reading, etc., lessen the monotony of the rehearsals.

After having discussed the vocal exercises of the first stage, I shall make some suggestions as to a profitable division of rehearsal periods.

About ninety percent of boys between the ages of ten and twelve years will generally be found suitable for choral purposes. Not more than one or two percent as a rule, however, can be developed into *solo-boys* of the first rank.

During thirty-five years of experience with boy-choirs, I have failed to notice any difference in vocal endowment that could rightly be attributed to racial factors. It was a common fallacy some years ago that boys of Latin and British parentage were much more richly gifted vocally than sons of the northern and central Europeans. In London, a most distinguished choirmaster once insisted to me personally that it would be impossible to train American boys to sing as well as English boys. But I have found them all alike,—the sons of Italy, Erin, England, Germany, Poland, Russia—just so many pounds of restless wriggling boyhood, to be conducted to a high plane of artistic effectiveness only by assiduous application of definite processes, and the exercise of a signal degree of patience.

Before ten years of age, boys are not mentally re-active enough to be ready for serious vocal progress, and after twelve years of age, they are too old to begin the stages, for by the time these and the processes that follow the stages will have taken effect, their voices will begin to change, and many calories of the choirmasters' energy will have been wasted. Generally, it is not profitable to have many boys under ten and a half years of age in the senior choir. The younger boys should be assembled in a choir of probationers and be given separate rehearsals.

If fifty boys were to present themselves as candidates for a choir requiring thirty, the twenty whom I would reject, other things being fairly equal, would be the twenty most phlegmatic.

The nervous boy makes the best chorister, being more likely endowed with the artistic sense. This fact is at the base of many of the choirmaster's woes, for the nervous boy is the one who requires the greater amount of watching and disciplining. Some of the best solo-boys of the Paulist Choristers were the outstanding rascals of the organization, contriving all sorts of mischief to disrupt the order of the choir-hall, sanctuary and concert stage. Notwithstanding this, the boy with temperament nets better musical results than the better ordered but less imaginative boy.

The ten percent of candidates unlikely to react readily to vocal instruction includes boys suffering from chronic laryngeal or nasal disorders as well as a few who seem to be practically tone deaf. Theoretically it is possible to improve the sense of pitch of the latter, but the undertaking imposes an extra and unnecessary burden on the choirmaster.

Given a wide choice of candidates, it is clear that the selection should fall upon boys whose speech is the more refined and whose manners reflect the influence of gentle parents. It should be noted, in this connection, that frequently boys from families poor in material resources, reveal more qualities of the gentleman than their more opulent fellows.

In the selection of singers, music-teachers in the public and parochial schools have little choice. Generally, they must include all the pupils—even those with changing voices—in the singing ensemble. This requirement handicaps the development of artistic standards in school singing. But since the purpose of teaching music in the schools is much broader than the training of selected pupils to sing beautifully together, most teachers are reconciled to the disadvantage of dealing with some impossible voices.

Therefore, the application of the Five Stages in their entirety in school music generally is neither feasible nor desirable. But the fundamental principles can be easily applied.

For the choir-conductor, however, except in extraordinary cases and with expert application, an epitome of the Stages will not suffice to eliminate abuses and defects and to prepare the voices for their *positive* development. The soprano-boys must be made ready for a rich repertoire which demands uncompromisingly, as the first requisite for its performance, a vocalism free from faults and delicately attuned to mystic intimations.

With *Precepts I, II* and *III* (see preceding Chapter) as the basis of the plan, the First Stage should be applied as follows:—

At the initial rehearsal the boys must be immediately apprised of the tone-quality which is to be abandoned. This is readily accomplished by having them sing a familiar patriotic anthem or hymn-tune with as much stentorian gusto as possible. There is probably no group of untrained boys anywhere in the world today which will fail to produce so execrable a quality in these circumstances as to merit to be styled "the horrible example." The choirmaster should then make appropriate remarks about the quality, emphasizing its lack of pleasing elements, its harshness, and in general, its unmusical character. The boys may not perceive for some time where the choirmaster is piloting them, but with so practical a demonstration furnished by themselves, they see clearly and at the very first lesson whence they are being led. If a pipe-organ be available, one can develop the illustration to further advantage by playing the anthem or hymn-tune first with a loud reed-stop, a cornopean or trumpet, the expression shutters being open, indicating this to be the "horrible singing tone," and then with a *stopped* diapason or light eight flute plus a faint string (aeoline), declaring this to be the quality hereafter to be sought and cultivated.

The boys must now be exercised in correct breathing (see preceding chapter). Breathing exercises should constitute the first step at every rehearsal and tuning-up period.

Having taken a deep breath, the boys, standing upright, but without muscular tenseness, should hum

Fig. 1

for approximately eight *moderate* beats.

As to their posture:—it is important to inculcate early the habit of placing one foot slightly in advance of the other in order to give good support to the abdominal muscles which together with the muscles of the legs will absorb any general bodily tension that the act of singing may entail. The boys readily understand the importance of this when the stance of the professional pugilist is referred to as an important asset. Adults recall readily the position of the feet assumed by the celebrated opera stars, who, not uncommonly, sacrifice the grace of a posture more appropriate to the scene enacted to secure a reliable fulcrum for their vocal movements.

The usefulness of correct humming for inducing relaxed production and nasal resonance has long been understood by specialists.

Faulty use of the hum is not only profitless, it is injurious.

For several years in the early part of my professional life, I opposed the hum, finding that it intensified the rigidity of production which it was presumed to cure. But I had not learned the proper method of humming. This I learned later from Dr. James Bates, of the London College of Choristers, Paddington. He made clear its efficacy as a preliminary step especially with boys. I attended many of his rehearsals, observing the great value of the device, when the hum is produced with the tongue resting lightly against the lower teeth (until its completion when the tongue necessarily touches the upper teeth) the lips slightly apart, the sound simulating a prolonged —N— rather than —M—. If a slight tickling sensation is experienced at the tip of the tongue, the humming may be judged to be almost effortless and therefore a *good* sound which can safely serve as the starting point for correct vocal development.

Therefore, I establish the *pianissimo* hum as the initial expedient to be employed. The advantages which soon accrue can be readily translated into the production of vowel sounds which will be the next step forward.

The note given in Fig. 1 may in some cases seem to be a semi-tone too high or too low for the first experiment. The choirmaster can quickly decide, for the proper note must be that which is most easily sounded. Some groups of boys sing $E\flat$ and even D with less effort, others F, but the starting point must be in this limited area, for the volatile lightness of a note above the middle register must be clarified, steadied and eventually brought down through the middle register to modify and temper to elasticity the thick harsh vocalism heretofore employed there by the boys.

Three defects will be immediately apparent when the boys hum Fig. 1.

The first defect is the fault of approaching the note from below, "scooping," and unless eliminated early will prevent pure intonation and accuracy of pitch in ascending intervals. It will also promote sluggishness in rhythmic movement and general vocal slovenliness.

"Scooping" conveys the impression of inertia; it carries up the weight of notes below and subtracts vitality and lightness from the note itself.

The boys must be taught to "think down" to a note, regardless of its position on the staff. I have cured many hundreds of boys of this serious shortcoming by assuring them that all supposedly high notes are in reality much lower than they imagine, and by drawing this diagram on the black board:—

Fig. 2

saying, "if you still think the note is high, go up the dotted line in your mind to X and then drop on the note."

Unfortunately, the habit of unconscious portamentos, "scooping," is general among adults as well as among boys. Sliding into notes is almost a universal fault, particularly when the intervals involve wide upward flights. Sliding down into lower notes is also a common tendency needing correction, even if its effect be less pernicious than upward "scooping." Performances notable for technical virtuosity and interpretative intention are frequently marred by the indefiniteness due to habitual portamentos. This inelegance of intonation is observed in all the choral lines, including the bass line, and should be attacked as a choral defect of primary magnitude. In the soprano and bass parts, "scooping" is fatal to even a minimum of choral effectiveness.

Boys are quick to appreciate the faultiness of "scooping" and will readily outgrow it, if the choirmaster calls attention to its every recurrence.

Good or bad habits of vocalism take root at the beginning, and as the law of habit is one of the most powerful dictators of human acts, the habit of clean-cut direct intonation of every note must be inculcated persistently.

The second defect observed in the first attempts at Fig. 1 is lack of breath control. Self-consciousness and the mental effort of trying something new under critical surveillance cause the breath to escape altogether almost at the instant of attacking the note. Therefore a tremulous and uncertain tone continues, if, indeed, it can be sustained at all after the impact.

This tendency will always reveal itself even in highly trained choristers, for impact with first notes of phrases and accented notes seems to suggest to their subconsciousness a warrant for squandering breath. The effect of such squandering is not only to alter the tone-quality of the ensuing duration of a single note, or the several notes of a phrase, but also to interfere later on in repertoire with the graceful finesse of execution which requires that all notes be sounded alike, *except for definite reasons of interpretation*.

This fault will gradually decrease in degree, as the choristers gain control of their breathing.

In this stage, it is my custom to ask the boys to exhale without humming while six beats are counted. Having thus exercised them in gradual exhalation I ask them to apply this at Fig. 1. Using graphic pedagogy with simple devices, I have found value in this instance in telling the boys to "sing the note in a straight line at all points the same, without wavering," the while running my finger across the flat surface of the piano. I have often observed the eyes of all the boys intently watching the unwavering progress of my finger surreptitiously bringing to their humming a notable degree of evenness and steadiness.

The third defect is the proclivity of untrained singers to fall off pitch at the instant of release. The lack of breath control explains this as well as the preceding fault. Also, a natural proneness to be *careless about finishing things well* contributes to the inexactitude. It can be eliminated almost immediately by drawing the attention of the choristers to the necessity of a keen, accurate and well defined stop, synchronous with the choirmaster's signal.

The group must be trained from the first rehearsal to start and to stop precisely together, as one voice.

One must not expect speedy results in correcting defect No. 2 for the proper application of breath to notes and phrases will come only when repose has been acquired, after carefully tutored experience. Rigidity is hostile to the nature of music, wherefore it is incumbent on the tutor to recommend complete relaxation of mind as well as muscular ease frequently during the practice periods.

I recall a distressing half hour with the sopranos of the Paulist Choristers who were assembled to "tune-up" before an important recital. The boys were very tired, having traveled much and sung several times during the preceding week. The programme was a request programme, opening with a number in the minor mode, *a cappella* (always a hazard)! The boys' tone was tight, rigid, and slightly off pitch. I knew that the minor *a cappella* number would be a failure and thus create for the boys a state of mind fatal to the artistic performance of the ensuing numbers. I tried many and various devices to lighten their voices, but without success, finding myself in a situation almost as droll as that of a celebrated. English choirmaster who complained with exasperation: "I don't know why that boy continues to sing flat, for I have vigorously boxed his ears." Although omitting that gentleman's inept experiment, I did contrive to increase the tenseness of the boys—vocally and mentally—by too much rebuke. Suddenly a young baritone of the chorus, who had been observing the proceedings, said to me "why don't you make them smile? It's the only thing that will help now." Finally, I had them smiling—and relaxed.

The performance of the minor number and therefore the rest of the programme was easily accomplished with gratifying effect.

I applied the same treatment to a solo-boy who was nervously about to undertake the extraordinarily difficult soprano part in the Abbellimenti of Allegri's "Miserere" at the Metropolitan Opera House, New York. He had been singing the top notes sharp at rehearsal. In my dressing room at the Metropolitan, I talked baseball and similar subjects to him—we joked together. When the signal came to go on stage, he was smiling! His mental relaxation and therefore his muscular resilience thus contributed to an easy achievement of the string-harmonic effect which makes the high C of the Abbellimenti so incomparably beautiful, if in strict tune.

A recent writer on voice production vigorously condemns relaxation as deleterious to the muscular activity upon which singing depends. If he defines relaxation as languor, supineness or inertia, I agree with him, but in the Oxford Dictionary's definition of the word, viz: "diminution of tension"—I find a recommendation essential to proper vocalism. The only tension required for vocal utterance is the relatively slight effort with which the air is pressed against the vocal cords and the simple tension applied by the arytenoid cartilages to establish pitch.

The first lessons in piano technique aim to relax the fingers. It is inconceivable that dexterity in playing any keyed instrument can be achieved while the muscles of the hand and fingers are tense. For sturdy effects in Liszt, of course, the concert artist must develop a muscular power in the fingers, but the accepted basis of successful technique is ease of muscular action.

And so, too, says the golfer who likes "par."

The application of the same doctrine must be made to put singers at ease, freeing them from mental hazards and diminishing unnecessary tension of the thyro-cricoid muscles. It may be stated thus as *Precept No. IV*—

"Keep the Choristers relaxed and in good humor."

Having been directed to observe and understand the three faults in their first experiences at Fig. 1, and having repeated the note a sufficient number of times to perceive the correct manner of utterance, the boys are ready for the next exercise. . . .

FIG. 3

These notes should be hummed, care being taken to correct the defects already revealed in the first effort at Fig. 1. Each note should be well separated from the next, to give opportunity for reiteration of attack and release. The use of *legato* in these descending notes of the first stage is not recommended. In order to assist the pupils in overcoming the defect of involuntary portamento, it is advisable to practice all notes separately. In fact the frequent use of *staccato* in vocalizations with well placed and highly cultivated voices has been found to be most helpful in maintaining the free mobility of production which is an essential of artistic singing. Therefore, *Precept V*—

In the preliminary exercises, keep the notes detached. The frequent use of staccato even after voices are well placed is helpful in maintaining clear address.

The choice of semi-tonal descent is due not only to the plan in these stages of carrying upper lightness gradually down to the lower registers, through every intervening note, but also to the opportuneness of inculcating intervallic accuracy in the beginning. Descending semi-tones are the *bête-noire* of many accredited artists, some of these being quite unable to sense the exact distance from an upper tonic to the leading-tone. Coloratura and light lyric sopranos, having less of color than of limpid transparency in the timbre of their voices, are detected more quickly in this uneasiness than the robust types of voices. Boys' voices being essentially free from the pigments of dramatic semblance and personal agitation, are almost diaphanous, and only their purest intonations are tolerable. Madame Blanche Marchesi (Baroness Caccamisi) accounted for the strange ineffectiveness of a highly cultivated English choir, by the inability—upon analysis—of the boy-sopranos to sing a descending half-tone true to pitch. Study of this point of view, and the application of it over a period of years, has produced conviction that the inclination to sing these descending close intervals flat, must be a point of vigorous attack. And so in the initial stage of training, boys should be given abundant chance to overcome the tendency.

Having hummed through the exercise at Fig. 3 a half-dozen times, the boys should again hum the note at Fig. 1. Translating it without break into the closed-vowel sound *OO,* and reverting to the hum, release the note with POO, as follows:—

Fig. 4

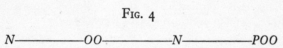

In order that the net result of the humming exercises, and their efficacy in light production may accrue to the formation of this first vowel-sound, the choirmaster must achieve an unbroken continuity between the —*N*— and the —*OO*—. The exercise at Fig. 4 is worthless save as a means of transferring the relaxed correctness of the hum to the vowel-sound. One must be alert here to detect and correct a dipping down from the pitch and a consequent "scooping" to the *OO* sound.

When presently boys show fair facility in this exercise, the same alternation of hum and vowel-sound should be carried through the notes of Fig. 3. These items constitute the vocal menu of the First Stage—a meagre but curative diet—and may not safely be enlarged upon or altered essentially until the boys have given evidence of definite accomplishment.

The period of time which is required for acquiring facility in these simple forms varies according to the number of rehearsals each week, and is determined as well by the seriousness of the handicaps on the outside, which the choirmaster must combat. If the boys come from homes of refinement, the obstacle of loud talking and unrestrained shouting will be less grievous than if the boys are gamins of the noisy streets.

In most choirs the first stage should extend through three weeks, but if daily rehearsals are practicable, the steps of the second stage may be introduced at the conclusion of a fortnight. The choirmaster who is intent upon establishing a solid groundwork will probably discover that three full weeks will be the minimum required in the first stage.

The rehearsals should not be prolonged beyond one hour. In the early stages, much variety of activity must be employed to distract the boys from the uninteresting drudgery of elementary voice placing. A rehearsal-hour in the first stage might be divided advantageously as follows:—

The first fifteen minutes: breathing exercises and practice of Figs. 1, 2, 3 and 4.

The second fifteen minutes: instruction in reading music, beginning with the time values of notes written on a blackboard.

The following fifteen minutes: the pronunciation and enunciation of

(*a*) English
(*b*) Latin

The final quarter of an hour: repetition of the exercises of the first period, and an urgent request of the boys to temper the intensity of their vocal utterances at play and in ordinary conversations.

The first and last periods of the rehearsal in this Stage have been discussed; there is much to be gained from judicious use of the second and third periods. I recommend the immediate introduction of sight reading for two reasons; first, because the average choirmaster dislikes teaching this very important subject so heartily that generally he will grasp at any disingenuous excuse to postpone the undertaking, and many neglect it altogether. Desultory or unsystematic attempts bear no fruit, and if the choirmaster's intention to produce a superlative choral unit be *bona-fide,* he cannot escape the necessity of introducing at the outset a carefully thought out plan of developing accuracy and facility in reading music. The second reason for introducing the subject in the First Stage is the *receptivity of the choristers at this period.* Lessons in sight reading come as a diversion from the vocal exercises, and while the first principles of correct vocalism are being learned, it is opportune and easy to open their minds to the rudiments of music-reading.

I have recommended the time-values of notes as a good starting point, because rhythm, being of the essence of music, appeals to natural instinct and boys give their attention to it without ennui. At the conclusion of the Five Stages, the choristers should be adept in interpreting all the various time symbols used in modern music.

It will be noted during the progress of the Stages that rhythmic accuracy is inculcated as an additional objective in all vocalizations.

The application of the third quarter of a rehearsal period to the demands of pronunciation and enunciation recommends itself without much debate. Diction and phraseology constitute an important phase of chorophony and the proper articulation of vowels and consonants should be undertaken immediately. An excellent manual of the technique of enunciation—"Tongue and Lip-Training" by E. Thornfield[1] should be on the desk of every director whose choir is to sing in English. Practice of Latin pronunciation should be postponed until the boys have acquired a degree of clarity if not of elegance in English diction.[2]

The Second Stage

In each succeeding stage it will be easy to increase the compass within which to apply the vocalizes of previous stages.

The first advance will be the extension of Fig. 3 to read:

FIG. 5

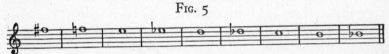

A further step forward will be to introduce the *legato* in this descending series, guarding against an inclination to anticipate ensuing notes. An advantageous variation here will be found in a whole-tone descent, alternating with the paradigm. A gradually longer sustaining of notes throughout the entire compass of Fig. 5 will serve to indicate the progress of the boys in breath-control.

No variation in dynamics should be permitted, *pianissimo* being still the sentinel of progress.

Another progressive feature of the Second Stage is the addition of the attack of vowel sounds without the preparatory hum.

A careful recapitulation of all the instructions of preceding practices is the proximate preparation for advance. Proximate as well as remote preparation for new ideas or experiments is a counsel of sound pedagogy.

The prefixing of a consonant to the vowel sounds will be found helpful in giving a forward delivery to the tone. It is, in fact, extremely hazardous to permit, at anytime, much vocalization of the vowel sounds *AH* or *EE* without the protection of an initial consonant.

The tendency to "swallow" tones is notable among beginners. The unnecessary constriction of crico-thyroid muscles results in a "throaty" tone which is defective acoustically as well as aesthetically. Whatever

[1] Published by Cary & Co., 13 Mortimer St., London, W. I. (Edward Schuberth & Co., New York City, Agt.)
[2] See Chapter XIII, "Diction."

interferes with a free production of a tone distorts its quality, preventing it from moving freely to the resonance chambers and robbing it of the important partials which are needed to establish its natural character. Therefore, habits which promote distortion must be corrected. The writer adverts here to the exception which, in this connection, must be made in the development of the counter-tenor voice (alto-tenor)[1] or falsetto substitute voice created by the exigencies of ecclesiastical canons for the alto line in liturgical choirs, and recently in vogue as a substitute tenor in high school choruses.

While it is true that the only muscles employed in the actual production of a tone are the arytenoid and crico-thyroid, and furthermore, that their action cannot be controlled by any other physical action of the singer, it is equally true that the muscles of the face and tongue may be employed to prevent excessive constriction. Consonants may be used profitably to relieve the laryngeal "squeeze," because they prepare a tone for its final emission by giving it a focal point in the mouth. Acoustically the tone is made in the larynx by the pressure of air against the vocal cords which are thus set in vibration, but physiologically, the tone receives its direction, as it were, from the muscles of the face. For instance, the vowel sound *OO,* or any other vowel sound, may be easily and unwittingly "swallowed" if expressed without a consonant, but a deliberate act of the will is required to produce a throaty quality if the vowel be articulated with a labial, dental or lingual consonant. *B, F, P, V,* in effect, impel the tone outward as from the lips, while *D, N, T* energize its emission from the tip of the tongue against the teeth.

Psychologically, the reaction of the singer to frequent vocalization with consonants is to seek the same feeling of muscular freedom in the larynx when singing unprotected vowels. After much experimenting with the consonants, I am convinced that *F, P* and *M* are the most useful for the purpose here considered.

The function of the consonant, in the practice which I am recommending, is to compress the air in the mouth rather than altogether below the cords. The letter *K* is of course a great clarifying agency in the alphabet, but in the initial stages of voice-placing, it is unwise to make use of it, for it places the focal point of its emission too near the vocal cords. All consonants stop the breath at some point in the mouth, and it seems desirable to stop the breath as far forward as possible. For by giving sounds a forward placing, one in reality is merely guarding against un-

---

[1] See Chapter VIII, "Changing-Voice, Counter-Tenor."

necessary tenseness in the region of the larynx. The letter *P* seems efficacious to this end. But it is too explosive for beginners, who must be aided in conserving their breath supply. After the initial Stages have been completed, I recommend the use of the letter *P* as an important agency. In fact, as will appear later, this labial consonant can be made to serve as one of the most effective instrumentalities of the choral tutor.

In these early stages, however, I recommend the use of the letter *F*, for it is a labio-dental consonant. If the reader will speak aloud the following alliteration, he will find in it demonstrative evidence of the efficacy of the letter *F*, for *F fluent, facile favors forward focus.*

The use of the consonant *M* is invoked to stimulate the singers' impression of resonance, for, fashioning another alliteration, *M magnetizes muscular motion masqueward.*

Dr. Holbrook Curtis suggests this experiment (p. 141, "Voice Building and Tone Placing"): "First, place the tip of the finger upon the larynx or Adam's apple, and sing the words *Mama, Papa, Baba, May, Pay,* and *Bay,* and then sing the vowel *E,* pronounced as in *ear.* We observe that there is more commotion under the finger when *E* is sung than when *Ma* or *Pa* is attempted, and the origin of the vowel is in the larynx. The same will be found true of *Ah.* This production is known as the stroke of the glottis. We find that by prefixing a labial consonant, *M, P* or *B,* that the shock is reduced to a minimum. Hence, *Ma* or *Maw* should be the word to use in practice, and almost never *Ah,* and never *E.*"

The present writer postpones the *Maw* and *Mah* sounds until the gentler *Moo* sound has been practised for a number of practice periods. The *E* sound, freed from its deleterious effects by the prefixed consonant may be used here to advantage, since it simulates the string-tone, which in conjunction with the flute tone (*Moo*) must be cultivated as the primary tone-colors of the boy-soprano voice.

The procedure in the Second Stage, then, will be to employ *FOO* and *MOO, FEE* and *MEE* in the same juxta-position as the hum and *OO* in the exercises of Figs. 1, 3, 4, 5.

FIG. 6

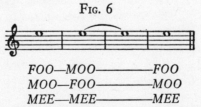

FOO—MOO————FOO
MOO—FOO————MOO
MEE—MEE————MEE

Precept No. VI. Prefix a consonant to the vowels in vocal exercises.

Should the choirmaster suspect that the compass of Fig. 5 is too ambitious for this exercise, he should be conservative and apply to the highest notes only the *N—OO* formation, until he is definitely certain that the consonant-vowel attacks will cause no straining. These paradigms are all given with average possibilities in mind, and only an approximate compass is suggested.

The boys must be kept in the exercises of the Second Stage until the *FOO* is quite free from murkiness, probably for a period of six practices. If they cannot sing *MEE* without a slight increase of quantity, this sound should be postponed to the Third Stage.

Precept No. VII. Notes above   *should be attacked with the chin slightly lowered.*

Boys show, as a rule, an inclination to thrust the chin forward, with tightening of all the surrounding muscles as an inevitable consequence. A favorite prima-donna brought the value of *Precept No. VII* dramatically to the attention of the profession, when at the moment of scaling the heights to a rarefied altissimo, reaching downwards, she caught up the train of her gown.

The professional critics were astonished at the feat!

But examination of the physiological reaction to the throat of her downward movement suggests that the prima-donna was more ingenious in her art than the professional critics had suspected.

The Third Stage

It may be assumed that the choirmaster realizes fully the necessity of applying the chief forms of earlier Stages at the beginning of each rehearsal. The compass for the exercises for the First and Second Stage may be extended at this juncture to these termini: A♭ above the staff down to F, first space.

During the weeks which will have elapsed before entering the Third Stage, the boys should have acquired ease in breath control, and facility in the light production of the *FOO* and *FEE* sounds.

If this ease be still wanting, the choirmaster will probably discover that he has insisted too little on one or more of the elementary factors, notably, perhaps, diaphragmatic breathing, and laryngeal relaxation, both in the *hum* and in the *OO* sound.

Before proceeding further, he must review the elementary principles with great care.

The particular step forward of the Third Stage is the passing along of the correctly placed *FOO* and *FEE* sounds to other vowels. The open vowel sound *AH* must be postponed to a more advanced stage, but *O, A* (as in *pay* and *pat*) and *U* (as in *pure*) may safely be introduced here. Just as in the preceding stages, these new vowel sounds should be assured correct production by the sounds already well poised, thus:

```
FOO——FO——FOO——FEE
FOO——FEE——FOO——FO
FO——FOO——FEE——FAY
FEE——FAT——FOO——FO
FOO——FEE——FU——FOO
```

It is opportune also, here, to introduce a variety of descending intervals and rhythms, first to mitigate the tedium which the singers are experiencing, and, secondly, to put into service a system of vocalization which will not only accomplish the definite purpose of developing the voices but also effect by-products. There is so much to be accomplished in the practice periods that the concomitant development of as many artistic virtues as possible is imperative. The by-products readily promoted at this Stage are rhythmical accuracy and a sense of melodic cadence.

The type of vocalization which will include as a collateral effect the development of the complete melodic sense cannot be safely introduced until the Five Stages will have been completed, for the arsis and thesis of melody obviously require ascending as well as descending progressions with dynamic variations.

FIG. 7

The employment of melodic fragments provides an escape from the monotony of practising consecutive tones and semi-tones, but care must be taken lest such exercises degenerate into mere tune-singing.

In adopting melodic vocalizations, first attention must be given to the vocal results, the choirmaster keeping clearly before him the purpose of the Five Stages, viz.: the correction of vocal abuses.

Concurrently he may advert to the rhythmical and melodic forms of the exercise.

Since there is an almost universal disregard of proper accentuation and undulation among musicians through inadvertence or failure to appreciate rhythmical structures with their implications, it is expedient for a choir-master to inculcate early so high a regard for this important feature of music, that the choristers will later need but little coaching to deliver rhythmical forms properly.

Obviously, the rhythmical defects in the four exercises of Fig. 7 will be:—

In exercise *A,* the addressing of the first and second beats with the same accentual stress.

In exercise *B,* the application of undue stress to the second and third beats.

In exercise *C,* the reduction of 4/4 time to 2/4 by imparting a strong accent to the third or weak beat.

In exercise *D,* the equalizing of the up and down beat accents.

Control of accentuation is essential to all musical performers—if their ideal of performance be worthy—and to choral singers, especially in the polyphonic styles, lack of such control is as serious a handicap as defective vocalism.

The undulations, verbal accents and logic accents of the Palestrinesque idiom require a perfect technique in this matter.

Therefore, the choirmaster must be vigilant from the start to prevent slovenliness and inadvertence to the niceties of rhythm.

The defects are cured by following this precept:—

Precept No. VIII. Keep accents off the wrong notes.

One must guard against stressing the strong beats too forcibly, for such practice develops an unbalanced form which is equally mischievous if not more mischievous than the failure to distribute the strong and weak beats.

The formula recommended in this connection is *"Accentuation by Diminuendo"* which will be expounded fully in another volume. The application of this formula in the Third Stage is embodied in the precept itself.

The sense of melodic progression, under cultivation here, does not require much attention from the tutor at this juncture; but it is well to insist first upon a steady tempo and then to introduce *rallentando* and *accelerando,* asking the choristers to tell their reactions to these variations.

The early introduction of these resources of interpretation will awaken the aesthetic consciousness of the new singers to their importance.

The choirmaster will already have observed the juxta-position of *staccato* and *legato* in the exercises of Fig. 7.

While the aim is to produce a smooth *legato* style, the use of *staccato* will be found serviceable in correcting the rigidity against which the Five Stages are directed.

This juxta-position will be treated in the following Chapter under the caption "The Positive Development."

It will be advantageous to alternate enunciation of vowel sounds with humming at Fig. 7, and to follow such vocalizations by the simple exercises.

Occasionally, I have found boys who, in this Stage, cannot be trusted with the tunes, sensing so much of agreeable jingle in them as to be distracted from their curative purposes.

In this circumstance, the tunes must be postponed.

Progress in the elimination of bad vocal habits will now be more rapid, and a few rehearsals should prepare the boys for the next Stage.

The Fourth Stage

The approximate compass now includes ♯ at least for the simpler exercises. It is doubtful if the boys can profitably attempt a variety of vowel-sounds on the top notes until later. Eagerness to secure immediate fluency in the higher register may be responsible for a later shrillness, which one will be hard-pressed to overcome.

The forward steps of this stage include (1) a broader use of consonants, (2) the diatonic scale, (3) difficult intervallic skips, and (4) variety of rhythms, tempos and quantity.

(1) Consonants are introduced more generously now in preparation for the articulation of phrases which will be undertaken in the Fifth Stage. Such combinations as *food, flute, fruit, brute, fob, frog, feat, fleet, meat, mode, moor,* etc. will be found effective in producing distinctness of utterance, and in promoting resonant forward delivery. These words should be sung very slowly.

Fig. 3 is the safe paradigm for such exercises, the melodic forms of Fig 7 being too complex for effective use here.

While the choirmaster must be alert here as always, to prevent any deterioration or sacrifice of tonal quality, an exaggeration of the articulation peculiar to each consonant should be suggested.

(2) The practice of the complete diatonic scale (in descent, of course) will be welcomed by the choirmaster as a sign of definite accomplishment, for it means that the volatileness of the head voice has been successfully superimposed on enough lower notes to complete a gamut without a break in quality.

Beginning at the accustomed point ♯ descending scales should be sung to the vowels already in use.

It is well at first to separate the tetrachords, in order that the choristers may mentally warn themselves to address the lower notes with a quality like that of the upper, thus:

FIG. 8

Foo_____   Foo_____
Fee Fee Fee   Fee   etc.

The scale should finally be sung in its normal descending form in one breath.

Although the greater part of the average choral repertoire is based upon the scale of two tetrachords, the choirmaster will serve the needs of Gregorian and 16th Century music, if he divide the scale into the fifths and fourths which constitute the modal structure of these styles—e.g.:

FIG. 9

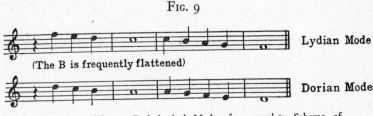

Lydian Mode

(The B is frequently flattened)

Dorian Mode

(See any article on Ecclesiastical Modes for complete Schema of Gregorian & Palestrinesque scales.)

A few faults will probably assert themselves: excessive use of breath in approaching the cadence of the scale; a too ample distancing of the intervals; unnecessary change of mouth and lip formations. Unconsciously, boys, and adults frequently too, are thrown off guard by initial success, and become unknowingly careless at the finish of things. A good start is essential, but only as a means to an end; the end here being a complete scale, homogeneous, and therefore equal tonally, in each of its consecutive steps.

The corrective to be applied is merely this: insist that maximum care be given to the concluding notes.

An inclination to amplify the distance between descending intervals, while causing particular difficulty with semi-tones, sometimes operates so actively as to cause whole scales to be sourly out of tune. This tendency no doubt is due to an unsuspected eagerness responding to a quasi-law of gravity, as it were, to be drawn down.

An advice then frequently to be reiterated is:

Precept No. IX. Keep descending intervals close together.

The converse of this is:

Precept No. X. Keep ascending intervals far apart.

(Precept X will not be invoked until the completion of the Five Stages.) The director should choose a simple gesture by which he may remind the choristers to apply Precept No. IX. The writer uses the thumb and forefinger of the left hand, moving rapidly towards and away from each other to accomplish this purpose. The use of appropriate gestures for signalling to the chorus will be elaborated in Chapter XV.

Shaping and reshaping the aperture during vocalizations in which a uniform vowel sound is desired, is a whimsicality of boys, originating perhaps in the suspicion that the same vowel requires different lip-formation at different degrees of the gamut. The choirmaster must be urgent in his correction of this disposition, lest stability of utterance surrender to caprice.

(3) The increasing flexibility of the voices should now be directed to the proper intonation of more difficult intervals, thus:

(a)   FɪG. 10

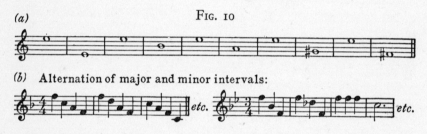

(b)   Alternation of major and minor intervals:

Two tendencies will be manifest here—*(a)* to "scoop" from a concluding lower note to the high note of the ensuing measure and *(b)* to waste breath in the accomplishment of a descending octave or fifth, these progressions stimulating the sense of precipitation. The troublesome "scoop" has been discussed; to allow the latter tendency to prevail is to leave voices which may have excellences of tonality, correct placing and resonance, wanting in regulation in much the same fashion as an organ-builder would fail with a rank of pipes voiced perhaps to the most delicate nuance of distinctive timbre, through unevenness of wind application.

(4) Without employing other vowel-sounds than those already in use, still maintaining the *downward* character of the exercises, the choirmaster may in this stage compose vocalizes of greater variety than those already suggested.

By this time, he has learned the particular needs of his choristers, and the vocal exercises should be written with these in mind. It is rarely profitable to have recourse to books of vocalizations for these are designed after general patterns and may or may not contain the elements needed for a particular group. Further reference, in detail, will be made to the widespread but unwise use of "patent-medicine" vocalizations.[1]

[1] See Chapter XIV, "The Art of Vocalization."

In this connection, it is proper to emphasize that the vocalizations offered in these pages are suggested forms only, and that each choirmaster should, if possible, write his own exercises, seeking to promote the same ends as the forms herein printed.

Vocalizes from this point on should exercise the voices in many things at the same time. *Legato, staccato,* sustained sounds, attack of distant notes, *arpeggios,* quick passages, these and other forms should be assembled in a few exercises in which the melodic as well as the rhythmic content is an arresting element. The pupils are being trained to sing melody; why then not vocalize them to real melodies, in place of the dull collocations of intervals which have become almost standard? Here are a few suggestions:—

FIG. 11

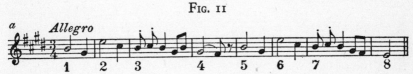

And through the keys of the acquired compass

In vocalizations of this type, the tutor should advert to the following details:—

Exercise No. 1

(*a*) No second or third beat accents.

(*b*) No *crescendo* on the *E,* 2nd and 6th measures, keeping evenness of quantity in mind.

(*c*) A real difference between *staccato* and *legato* in 3rd and 7th measures.

(*d*) An excellent opportunity for inculcating "accentuation by *diminuendo*" in 4th measure, $G\#$ *diminuendo* to $F\#$.

(*e*) No *crescendo* on approach to cadence in 7th measure.

All vocalizations should be practiced first, at a steady tempo, *rallentando* and *accelerando* being *applied later upon direct signal.*

Exercise No. II
(*a*) Watch for correct accentuation.
(*b*) *Chins down* for the top *F* in 1st measure.
(*c*) Accuracy of pitch and identity of tone-color on accidental in 3rd measure.
(*d*) Avoid *crescendo* on *A* and the approach to it in 6th measure.
(*e*) Avoid *staccato* and *crescendo* on eighth notes in 7th measure.

Exercise No. III (minor mode)
(*a*) Avoid thickening of tone-quality often induced by minor harmony.
(*b*) Correct the first note, which probably will be sung as a sixteenth note by the majority.
(*c*) Observe the rest in 1st measure.
(*d*) Apply *b*/ and *c*/ in 4th measure.
(*e*) Avoid crescendo on *G* in 5th measure.
(*f*) Listen for intervallic accuracy and steadiness of tempo in 7th measure, the tendency in such a form being to stray from pitch $D\#$ to C natural, and to retard the minor cadence.

The temptation to abandon the simpler forms altogether will now allure, but the choirmaster who yields will presently have sacrificed the fruits of much labor. I have known many personally who, adhering faithfully to the monotonous processes of the Stages up to this point, became deceived by the signs of progress. Rating the progress too highly they ceased to apply the rigorous curatives, and, of course, in the end failed to develop artistic ensembles.

The insistences and forms of the first Three Stages may never be minimized, and regardless of the later growth of the voices, they must be exemplified, at least in epitome, vigorously and conscientiously at all rehearsals.

A slight increase in volume of sound may be allowed towards the end of this Stage. The choirmaster as well as the choristers will long since have felt the desire to bring the newly found voices out into the open, as it were, but successful repression of this eagerness may be considered a criterion of the choirmaster's steadiness of purpose.

The *crescendo,* which safely may be permitted now, is limited to a gradual increase on sustained tones only, and in the moderate compass of Fig. 3 from *pianissimo,* through *piano,* to a meagre *mezzo-forte.*

Conservatism in this operation is imperative.

Pianissimo has been the dark room of the developing process, and a sudden effulgence of light may delete entirely the impressions as yet not secure on delicate plates. The whole fabric of voice production which has taken months to build, may come tumbling down in irreparable fragments, if quantity suddenly becomes an active influence. The old slogan of English choirs *"Quality not Quantity"* must be invoked at all times, and perhaps never more urgently than at the moment of experimenting with the *crescendo.*

The qualities of the good *crescendo* are of course a *gradual* increase and imperceptibility of the greater exhalation involved. The technique of good *crescendo* and *diminuendo* will be given later.[1]

Each *crescendo* should be followed immediately by a *diminuendo* and all exercises of this sort should be concluded by several vocalizations sung at a most tenuous *pianissimo.*

The Fifth Stage

In the last Stage of this preliminary training, the range of the boys' voices should be made to include two full octaves:—

Caryl Florio, many years ago, referred to the voice of the boy as "having no top." Boys can sing very high notes. With great ease, the compass of almost any properly trained boy can be extended to the rarefied regions of *altissimo,* but until quality and flexibility have been perfected within the two octaves, there is little to be gained by extravagant flights beyond the range indicated. The usefulness of boy-sopranos is confined to a limited range, rarely exceeding the high *B* flat, and higher notes are sought chiefly in practice for purpose of clarification.

Occasionally, it is true, compositions call for unusual fluency in the uppermost register, but the dignified, impersonal, spiritual styles of music which boys congruously may sing, rarely stray beyond the first leger line above the staff. Now and again the public is invited to observe the aero-planing of small boys near the clouds, but such capitalizing of vocal aptitude is a frivolity rather than a legitimate exercise of art.

The long postponed introduction of the open vowel sound *AH* should be made in this stage.

Just as in the First Stage the *N* and *OO* are related by unbroken continuity, and in the Third Stage, the *FOO–FO–FEE,* the *AH* here must be prepared, thus:—

FOO————————*FAH*————————*FEE*		
MOO————————*MAH*————————*MOO*		
MEE————————*MAH*————————*MEE*		

[1] See Chapter XII, "The Control of Dynamics and Tempo."

This exercise and all the forms in which the *AH* will be practiced should be done *pianissimo* with frequent reversion to the *HUM* as a corrective.

AH involves an opening of the mouth wider than other sounds, and in delivery receives but little assistance from the muscles of the face. Naturally, these facts predispose to a less forward placing than is readily achieved with the other vowels. For this reason the use of *AH* has been discouraged until the singers should have become quite accustomed to singing on the lips. For many years I allowed the choristers to sing the *AH* sound by itself in this Stage and during their later development, but I have more recently insisted upon the habitual prefixing of a consonant.[1]

The prefixing of *F* and *M* to the *AH* will tend to compensate for the lack of muscular attendance.

The *crescendo* may be amplified to a greater extent during this Stage, provided, of course, the elementary use of it has been adequately guarded.

But the *crescendo* should not be applied to *MAH* until the placing of the sound has been made uniformly correct in both high and low registers, and then only moderately.

The singing of scales, etc., may now be safely attempted at the various degrees of quantitative expression. But the corrective *pianissimo* must always be at hand to neutralize the tendency to force which is usually a concomitant of early efforts at *mezzo-forte* and *forte*.

Fortissimo should be postponed to a later period.

Demands upon breath-control should be increased, both in an extension of sustained tones and in an increase of phrases to be delivered in one breath.

A fruitful plan is the alternation of sustained notes and quickly moving phrases, both *legato* and *staccato*.

Sluggishness, which impedes rhythmic precision, should be watched for, particularly in forms offering up-octave skips on unaccented beats. This last observation must not be interpreted as connoting the idea that upward vocalizations have been introduced, but only as in reference to exercises which are in accord with the suggestions at Fig. 11, and in the accompanying context.

Rapid *chromatic scales* (alternately *legato* and *staccato*), with a long sustained final note upon which a *crescendo* and *diminuendo* may be made, will be found an excellent means for developing flexibility.

Opportunity must be made also for practicing difficult intervals, so

[1] See "Second Stage."

that facility in placing the correct quality of tone on notes in chords out of thought with or diametrically opposed to the key-tonality may be attained.

Minor scales will be employed with more academic correctness later, when the use of upward vocalization permits them to be sung in all forms.

Extending the paradigm Fig. 5 to *C* below the treble staff, the master should direct the boys to sing words and phrases, on each of the notes consecutively.

In view of the difficulty to which both the physics of sound and the vagaries of English enunciation [1] contribute, the choirmaster must set the highest possible standard before the choristers.

The best point of attack seems to be the final consonants, those elusive *B's, D's, F's, G's, P's,* and *T's,* which conclude so many words of English vocabulary.

Sentences should be assembled from words containing a variety of these, and practiced both in recitation and to simple vocalizes. Exaggeration will be found to be a necessary principle in the rehearsing of such sentences, just as the actor is guided by it in the technique of dramatic speech. Attention must be directed also to an unhurried pronouncement of sibilants, postponing the hissing element to the last fraction of the second. The swirling and swishing of *S's,* soft *C's* and *T's* through the multiple parts of an "a cappella" chorus are as distressing a factor as the prolonged ciphering of a querulous note in an organ.

Four or five months of assiduous application of the vocal rudiments of the Five Stages should find the boys altogether free from the harsh tone-quality with which they sang at the start and which they now recognize as undesirable. In effect, if the advance from one point to another has been orderly and careful, they should now possess an abundant breath-control and be able to sing any form of descending vocalization with uniform quality, from the high *C* to the *C* below the treble staff. Relaxation, lip-focus and quiet vibrancy should now characterize the whole range. There should be no evidence of a "break" between the upper and lower registers. Although quite flaccid, the tone-quality should now have begun to give intimation of that potential content of beauty, tranquility and spirituality, which it will be the present responsibility of the choirmaster to bring to maturity. Resonance, breadth, timbre and other positive vocal virtues will develop readily by the application of the technique set forth in the following chapter.

[1] See Chapter XIII, "Diction."

The Five Stages—Part II

Adults' Voices

The precepts established in Part I of this Chapter for correcting the major abuses of boys' singing must be applied similarly to the voices of girls and adults. The principles of physics do not prescribe one acoustical process of tone-making for juniors and another for seniors, nor does anatomy indicate different processes. In the construction of organ pipes, the same basic cause and effect principles which are heeded in fabricating sonorous and deep-toned pipes are applied in the structure of the lighter and higher pitched pipes. And so with the making of sounds in the human larynx, there is but one continuity of cause and effect principles for sopranos (juniors and adults), mezzo-sopranos, contraltos, tenors, baritones and basses. Certain modifications and variations of the exercises of Part I must be observed in the application of the rudimentary principles to voices of different timbres and categories, just as the "voicing" processes for flue and reed pipes vary in organ building, but the considerations which have been advanced as essential to the proper delivery of singing-tones in general cannot scientifically be altered. All vocal sounds are made in the same manner, fundamentally. The larynx is a pipe standing on a wind-chest with the vocal cords functioning as reeds. The pressure of the air against the cords causes them to vibrate. Greater or lesser tension of the cords produces faster or slower vibrations, thus determining the pitch. The air waves move to the resonance chambers above and below the glottis, and by impact with the membranes of these (the sounding board) a musical tone is produced. Thus the free action of the cords and the resonators must be conserved in the production of all singing-tones of children or adults. The faults which prevent the natural functioning of the vocal factors of boys and girls cause the same difficulties for their seniors.

The following modifications are recommended in applying the Five Stages to the voices of adults.[1]

No modifications are required in the use of the Stages with girls up to the sixteenth year.

The First Stage

The pitch (approximate) at which the exercises of this and ensuing Stages should begin, is for the various voices:—

[1] See Chapters VI, VIII, IX for the special development of adult voices.

Soprano, lyric or dramatic

Mezzo-Soprano

Contralto

Tenor, lyric or robust

Baritone

Basso-cantante

Basso-profundo

Since the starting pitch for vocal exercises throughout this treatise is indicated for soprano, the student should refer occasionally to this page for the relative pitches suitable for other voices.

The translation of the hum to the ensuing vowel sound should be modified thus:—

For Mezzo-sopranos	N————————OH————————N
For Contraltos	N————————EE————————N
For Lyric Tenors	N————————OH————————N
For Robust Tenors	N————————EE————————N
For Baritones (round)	N————————O O————————N
For Baritones (string)	N————————EE——O O——N
For Basses, cantante and profundo	N————————OH——EE——N

Adults should be urged to confine their singing to the practice-room, until the chief faults have been eliminated. Soft speech in conversation should be recommended, and frequent exercises in deep breathing. Generally, children will not follow these suggestions, but a large percentage of adults will profit by them. The breathing exercises should include not only the normal and slower than normal inhalations, but the quick breaths which later will be required in the repertoire.

The Second Stage

No modifications are indicated. In all Stages, however, the director should favor the use, primarily and generally, of the vowel sounds most suited to the development of the various classes of voices. See table above.

The Third Stage

It is safe, usually, to allow adults to include the *AH* sound if its emission be safeguarded by the consonants, *F, P* or *M*.

The director must be conservative, however, and if an increase of quantity is required for the sustained *FAH, MAH,* or if heaviness, huskiness or roughness be in any degree present, the use of the *FAH, MAH* must be postponed. As noted in Part I, children should not be allowed to experiment with this vowel sound until the Fifth Stage.

The Fourth and Fifth Stages

No modifications are indicated.

CHAPTER IV

The Positive Development

The Five Stages furnish practical measures, carefully graded in sequence, for the elimination of faults in tone-production. Concomitantly they promote a vocal technique which permits a natural and extensive growth of tone-color, resonance, and nuance. But the Stages are primarily a negative process, and must therefore be complemented by positive expedients, the judicious application of which will effect a more finished blend of the vocal registers, increase flexibility, and bring under control all the factors which contribute to the art of effective singing.

At the conclusion of the Stages, voices usually lack color and strength in the middle and lower registers. These registers have been thinned out by the unvaried downward vocalizations. But since the middle register comprises the notes of the most effective vocal area, it must be restored, amplified, and permitted to function to the full extent of its natural endowment.

The remedial measures adopted in the Stages require the temporary discontinuance of normal vocalism in the middle and lower registers. The aid of the volatile vibrations of the higher register is invoked to assist the larynx to function with ease in the abused area of the middle and lower registers, but the adage, "physicians mend or end us, *secundum artem,*" should be written "mend *and* end us" for singing masters who stop at the mending process. The mending is only a means of unencumbering voices, a system of healing by which they are made ready for positive development.

The ultimate purpose of each step in the Stages is the eventual expression of voices in the fullness of their potential beauty.

Some choral directors seem to be guided by the impression that the vocal training of the single lines is complete when faults have been corrected. This is unfortunate, for many who have done excellent preliminary work and might have developed a convincing choral tone, have failed to bring their organizations to a high level of artistry because of that point of view.

It is imperative that the director comprehend the totality of vocal resources. If the curative exercises of the Stages be not followed by constructive, broadening and timbre-enriching expedients, the tone quality will be altogether inadequate to the lyric and dramatic demands of the choral repertoire. Such tone-quality lacks lustre and vitality; it is placid, smug, neutral, and generally dolorous. At least, it is unconvincing and therefore futile as a medium of artistic value.

Boy-sopranos will develop a definite hoot if the scheme of the Stages be not supplemented. The hoot is, of course, a distressing sound which not only imparts a mournful monotony to the singing but also constitutes an insuperable obstacle in the way of clear enunciation. How often, in the great cathedrals, one hears the choristers hooting through motets and anthems like surpliced owls ululating in the chancel! Such ululation is but little less an affront to aesthetic propriety than positive ugliness. Boys' voices are notably impersonal and when their natural pallor becomes moist with the tears of an unknown sorrow, the effect is most depressing. I have personally felt myself slipping into the doldrums, on many occasions as the spiritless intonations of boys, singing without natural middle registers, drifted through vaulted arches seeking something to be unhappy about.

An altogether untrained boy-choir is, of course, the monstrous ogre of music—and a hooting boy-choir turns a church into a cave of Trophonius. There must be color in the voices. The moaning and "whooing" of Alleluias, the lamenting of the Te Deums and the reluctant exultation of Magnificats are certain to depress, and since it is the function of music as well as of the liturgy to stimulate and raise, the hollow dejection of such singing must be excluded.

Such methods must be amended.

Likewise, the coloratura and light lyric soprano voices of women need positive development. For these voices take on a chronic paleness if a progressive system of vocal exercise be not applied to the middle register. The *whiteness* of such voices is the characteristic generally noted by critics in disapproving them. The hoot of the boy and the whiteness of female lyrics are due principally to the same cause, i.e., lack of attention

to notes of this compass:—

Constant and unvaried use of *who* (traditional in many choirs), drawing in the cheeks and pursing the lips, precludes the development of other clear vowel sounds and the timbres associated with them. It also fixes upon the voice an emptiness which boys cannot usually remedy after twelve and a half years of age.

The whiteness of lyrics can be easily activated into livelier tints by broadening the quality in the compass indicated above. The prevention of the hoot in boys and the broadening of the tones of female lyrics will be studied together, for these undertakings are accomplished by virtually the same technique.

The procedure in this technique is the converse of that prescribed in the Stages.

A *volte face* is indicated, but this does not mean that quantity now becomes the standard or criterion of progress or that attention may be safely directed away from the factors which were instrumental in correcting abuse. On the contrary, quality in its many attributes becomes even more insistently and directly the goal of effort.

Quantity will be employed only as a medium by which *quality* may be broadened to its *natural* extension.

As a resource of dynamic expression, quantity will be studied later, but the writer avers here that there is more of dangerous menace to vocalism and to interpretative temperance in the *forte* degrees of quantitative amplitude than in any other phase of musical expression. But the economy of progress here does imply the employment of ample *crescendos* and the exercise of the voice at louder degrees than were consistent with the purposes of the Stages.

Upward vocalization and *broad dynamic changes* must be undertaken only in conjunction with their opposites (the formulae of Chapter III), and this juxta-position must be so painstakingly maintained that while a voice is acquiring an increase of resonance and colorful vibrancy, it is never in danger of breaking again into irregular fragments or of reassuming the noisy blare against which so much effort has been directed.

The safe and effective scheme to be adopted is herein elaborated according to what appeals to the writer as "the principle of apposition." There are two aesthetic responsibilities included, one involving productive measures, the other protective measures. The vocal exercises must, therefore, henceforth be appointed with this apposition in mind. There are other phases of chorophony also in which the principle of apposition must be a guiding influence, as will appear later in this Chapter.

The following exercise is an example of the apposition of the *productive* and *protective* processes. It is obvious that the latter are the renamed *corrective* measures of the Stages.

FIG. 1

The productive value of the first two measures (*a*) with the upward progression, open vowel, and crescendo to a *forte lunga* is evident. But there is risk that beginners, especially, and even many cultivated singers, will sing up to each succeeding note, thus inducing thickness, and force the *crescendo*. The ensuing measure (*b*) sung at *pianissimo staccato,* with the less open vowel *EE* protected by the consonant *P* which focuses the sound directly on the lips, immediately compensates for the possible harm at (*a*) and frees the voice for the safe and profitable singing of the next measure (*a*). In the fifth measure both *productive* and *protective* factors are invoked simultaneously, the upward progression with its *crescendo* being in the safe custody of *MOO* and *staccato,* the *diminuendo* and *lunga* in the sixth measure furnishing further protection. The seventh measure (*a*) provides opportunity for broadening with the direct attack of *MAH* at *forte,* the while keeping it under the gentle restraint of a *descending* progression, yielding it for a final elimination of dangerous symptoms, developed enroute to the *diminuendo* with *POO* to *pianissimo*.

The foregoing exercise illustrates an effective co-operation of both productive and protective factors.

The following paradigm, however, is safer for voices which have responded sluggishly or only partially to the corrective formulae.

The protective factor is put into operation at the outset, thus

FIG. 2

preparing the voice proximately to meet the hazards of Fig. 1, which should now be attacked, in continuity with Fig. 2.

The forms given in Fig. 1 and Fig. 2 are offered only as the picture in the writer's mind of an agreeable collaboration of two opposite processes. They are presented only as the basis for a developing plan.

It would be a mistake for the student to assume that the above paradigms represent an epitome of the complete strategy involved in guiding voices to their mature estate.

There can be no doubt that some plan of preventing the growing voice from relapsing into former bad habits or acquiring other defects must be devised and followed with fidelity. In the experience of the writer, the scheme of employing the two opposite processes as closely together as possible, has been fruitful of gratifying results. Therefore he establishes as

Precept No. XI

All measures prescribed for the broadening of vocalism must be exercised in strict apposition to the protective measures of the Stages. Forte *must be safeguarded by* pianissimo, *upward progressions by downward progressions and* legato *by* staccato.

Here follow a few exercises constructed according to *Precept No. XI* They promote resonance, amplitude, color and other vocal virtues. They are not designed specifically, however, for the cultivation of the chromatology of all voices. Such specifics are suggested in the Chapters concerning the different types.

The student should note again that the primary purpose here is safely to restore and amplify the middle and lower registers.

The writer will recommend in a later Chapter [1] that these patterns and all subsequent specimens be used as norms only and that the actual exercises employed in the choir-hall be composed by the choirmaster himself, exemplifying the particular principles or precepts involved:

[1] See Chapter XIV, "The Art of Vocalization." The accompaniment of vocalizes is also discussed.

THE ALPHABET

Many similar patterns could be supplied but to no practical purpose, since the main points in the amplifying process are exemplified in the series given. All vowel sounds, with a variety of consonants should be used, and the exercises should be practiced at all pitches comfortable for the voices. Since the aim here is the broadening of the tonal resources in the middle and lower registers, it is plain that vocalizations should be devised with *crescendos* indicated in these registers.

The idea involved in Precept No. XI seems to require an apposition of singers as well as of processes, i.e. those with softer voices should be stationed near those with the louder, so that the voices needing amplification may borrow from and copy voices more developed, and the latter be restrained by the delicacy of the former. In a choir of boy-sopranos, it is a fatal mistake to station the developed voices together. Their natural tendency, it must be always remembered, is towards the *more noisy,* and a vocal conspiracy against the lighter elements which conserve the *quality* of vocalism, always establishes itself in the section of a choir where many sonorous big voices sing together. The necessity of careful allocation of the boys from this point of view sometimes escapes the choirmaster, and especially the necessity of frequently revising the allocation. Boys develop quickly, physiologically and vocally. They change each succeeding day. The approach to adolescence is necessarily gradual and a boy's throat shows *gradually* increasing symptoms of this phenomenon. Therefore boys who at the start of a season were properly grouped together, should perhaps be arranged in different squads at Christmastide, and at Easter be again rearranged. A safe grouping may be secured in the ratio of two light voices to one notably broader voice.

During practice-periods, the arrangement of the boys in such fashion is always feasible; at services and at other public performances this apportionment may be more difficult, since choirmasters feel a benefit in keeping the lead-boys together to assure authority in entrances. The lead-boys by reason of their longer training and experience are presumed to have acquired technical reliability as well as tonal amplitude, and it is easy to understand the reluctance of choirmasters to disperse their resources, especially in difficult compositions.

However, the question of the ideal shows itself again, and tonal excellence being the ultimate criterion of choral efficacy, choirmasters should serve *tone* first, trying to train even the youngest boys so thoroughly in the repertoire, that they too become dependable leads.

Here is another *caveat:* guard against a tendency to make concessions to the many supposed exigencies, which menace the quality of vocal tone, for many of these are unreal.

A further application of the thought influencing the establishment of Precept No. XI is in the direction of programme-making.

Just as it is perilous for boy-sopranos to vocalize chiefly in the broader forms, and to sing together in formations fostering the more ample utterances, so is it hazardous to place several numbers, requiring sustained *fortes* and sturdy ascending progressions, *consecutively* on service-lists or concert programmes. Sometimes the requirements of the service itself make such programming necessary, and frequently the performance of an oratorio or cantata involves a succession of *maestosos, con grandezzas,* and *con bravuras.* Under these circumstances the conductor will be obliged to seek in the score itself every latent opportunity of applying the *protective* factors of vocalism. In Divine services, the frequently recurring Responses furnish excellent opportunity for invoking these factors.

But generally, it is practicable to arrange miscellaneous programmes so that the apposition of loud and soft, climactic and restrained is readily achieved. Some years ago the writer conducted a series of two hundred and forty concerts on a single tour of twenty-five thousand miles in six months. The programmes included many of the broadest choral compositions which can be artistically interpreted by boy-sopranos. The vocal condition of the boys through the entire tour, and at the completion of the tour, was unimpaired, because in addition to adequate attention to the protective elements of vocalism at rehearsals, each programme was so constructed that the boys had opportunity to *vocalize in public.* A juxta-position of motets in consonance with the conviction expressed in Precept No. XI was maintained, throughout the entire tour. To "make assurance double sure," and so that each programme would have "an anchor to windward," the writer composed a two-part descending number for the sopranos, in which the tenors and basses carried sufficient of a melodic *cantus* to distract the audience from what was really in progress. There are many considerations to be studied in the making of programmes, and the writer advances the foregoing as of importance.

The next step in our *Gradus ad Parnassum* is a psychological rather than a purely vocal process, for it concerns the instinct of copying. Imitation is a trait of the entire race, but the instinct reveals itself as most acute in boys. Whatever may be the validity of anthropological arguments in the matter of man's evolution from a Simian prototype, it is certain that boys share with monkeys a predisposition to ape. Sound pedagogy utilizes this tendency by proposing good examples to be copied, and in the cultivation of tonal beauty much and speedy progress can be made in this manner.

It is good psychology to have boys and adults set an example for themselves, observing the quality of their best notes. The simple fact of pointing out that there are already very good tones in the compass, increases interest and excites ambition not only to perfect those tones but to copy them throughout the whole range.

A skillful organ voicer, having voiced several pipes, naturally selects the one among these which most closely approximates the timbre he is seeking to develop, and makes this the standard for the entire set.

There are various ways of ascertaining the best notes of a voice. Sometimes the singing of a simple song, which is attractive to the singer, reveals them immediately. Even the intoning of the scale will show some notes to be better than others, but the writer has found a special type of vocalization, furnishing points of repose, to be the most expeditious and profitable procedure. Thus:—

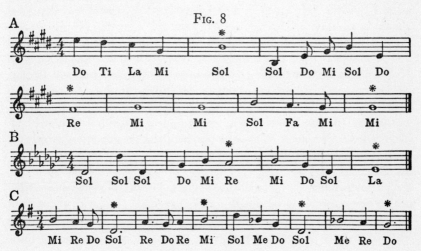

Fig. 8

A

Do Ti La Mi   Sol   Sol Do Mi Sol Do

Re   Mi   Mi   Sol Fa Mi   Mi

B

Sol   Sol Sol   Do Mi Re   Mi Do Sol   La

C

Mi Re Do Sol   Re Do Re Mi   Sol Me Do Sol   Me Re Do

At the points marked *, the best inherent qualities of a voice will probably reveal themselves, because, first, they are points of repose, where the voice, being prepared by the moderate movement of the preceding notes, finds time to show itself to advantage, pausing and posing, as it were, for inspection; secondly, they are the interesting strategic or focusing spots of each melody. The aesthetic satisfaction subconsciously felt upon arriving at these focal points is sure to influence the quality of tone. In the same manner as love, hatred, pleasure, displeasure, joy and sadness affect the quality of the speaking voice, so that even if the words be indistinguishable, the mood of the speaker can be instantly detected, the reactions of a singer to strategic notes are immediately evident.

Some experimenting is necessary to determine the pitch at which the above exercises will be used most profitably. When this has been established, and the singers have shown unmistakably that the focal points are pre-eminently their best notes in each exercise, they should be directed to copy in imagination this quality when the exercises are sung at different pitches. Frequent repetition of such exercises with sufficient comment as to the excellence of the tone-quality produced, are a most effective as well as a simple procedure.

The writer has valued in his own experience the cultural worth of this plan, having observed many individual singers and groups of singers respond gratifyingly, especially at the second focal points of exercises 1 and 2.

The harmonic accompaniment will be discussed later as a rich resource for enhancing the worth of such practice. In passing, the writer admits that the use of a dissonance at both of the above specified focal points has contributed much to their efficacy.[1]

The lighter stops of a pipe-organ, if judiciously chosen, furnish good examplars, and choristers profit greatly from occasional vocalization with organ accompaniment. The suitable stops for this purpose will be suggested presently as the development of specific timbres in the voices proceeds.

Another useful device for the promotion of warmth and breadth of tone is the employment of favorite phrases from the repertoire which the singers have been studying.

Until the completion of the Fifth Stage, the voices are not in a condition warranting the practicing of songs, for the obvious reason that upward progressions have not yet been introduced. But with the start of the broadening exercises, it is opportune to introduce the actual singing

[1] See Chapter XIV.

of compositions. The same precautions must be taken here as at the other onward steps of progress, and the practicing of hymns, motets, etc. must be set in careful apposition to protective vocalizations.

Much of the singing, while the intervals and time-values of an unfamiliar piece are being learned, should be done *pianissimo, with the hum and POO, MEE, MAW.* More of this anon; the foregoing is interpolated here as another caveat lest the student choirmaster be heedless of the tonal hazards encountered at the start of song practice.

The reader has doubtless noted that the choral technique favored in this treatise is a congeries of principles, precepts and caveats. It seems necessary, observing the failure of many talented musicians to bring their choruses to the perfection hoped for, to warn at every step of possible dangers and unsuspected contingencies, while principles are being unfolded and made applicable by precepts.

In this instance, however, the choristers are presumed to know some numbers, at least "by ear," and phrases of those that appeal strongly to the choristers serve well as vocal exercises for increasing consciousness of their best notes. If the singers like to sing them, it is probable that they will unconsciously impart their best tone-quality to the singing.

The more judicious exercise the best tones receive, the quicker will the poorer ones improve.

The cultivation of a natural reed tone is of great value in replacing the pallor of hooty and white tones. The reader will have already observed the frequent use of *MA* (pronounced Mah) in the productive exercises recommended. This sound is the natural vowel sound of reeds as will readily be concluded from an experiment by John Tyndall, physicist, concerning the utterance of a reed mounted on acoustic bellows; he writes: ("Sound," p. 227 seq.) "When upon the frame of the reed, a pyramidal pipe is fixed, you notice a change in the sound; and by pushing my flat hand over the open end of the pipe, the similarity between the sound produced and the human voice is unmistakable. Holding the palm of the hand over the end of the pipe so as to close it altogether, and then raising the hand twice in succession, the word "mamma" is heard as plainly as if uttered by an infant. Thus by associating with a vibrating reed a suitable pipe, we can impart to the sound the qualities of the human voice. In the organ of voice, the reed is formed by vocal cords, and associated with this reed is the resonant cavity of the mouth which can so alter its shape as to resound at will, either to the fundamental tone of the vocal chords or to any of their overtones."

The use of the *OO* sound in the Stages has tended to eliminate the

natural reed quality from the voices, because the production of *OO*
requires a formation of the oral cavity and a labial aperture, which
minimize overtones. But careful vocalization on *Ma* will help to restore
the reed-quality especially if the exercises involve the alternation of high
and low tessituras, as in the following example:—

Fig. 9

natural reed quality from the voices, because the production of *OO*

The apposition of the high and low tessituras effects an acoustical
reaction which promotes development of color and clarity, the high tessitura developing more piquant overtones which the lower will seek to
duplicate, while the lower will set forth more clearly the richer reed
quality and offer a bait to the higher.

The wide opening of the mouth for the utterance *AH* which is
simulated by the conical bell of the oboe (double reed) and the carrying
through of the vibrations of the vocal chords (double reed) to the resonant chambers by the consonant *M* must of necessity emphasize the reedy
character of the resulting tone.

As Tyndall showed the resemblance of a tone produced by reed
pipe and palm of the hand operating together, to the human voice, so the
judicious exercise of his synthetic "mamma" will tend inevitably to restore a reedy quality to voices and to rectify the subnormal ghastliness
of white lyrics.

Needless to say, the alternation recommended, if carefully practised,
will also aid in the acquisition of an evenly balanced voice, which can
carry its color without change throughout its complete compass.

A school of vocalism had certain vogue in England during the late
Nineteenth Century which candidly aimed at duplex timbre—one for the
lower voice, and the other for the higher. The effect was as distracting as
it was inartistic, for one was constantly awaiting the points at which a
clarinet tone would cede to a flute tone, and vice versa.

Homogeneity is essential if the various vocal registers are to serve as
a unit and give convincing expression of a definite musical thought. The
sudden employment of *falsetto* on the top note of the "Salut d'Amour"

(Faust) has always impressed the writer as a vaudeville banality frustrating the dramatic expression as well as the musical continuity.

Art does not permit caprice in coloring.

Random changing of organ stops frustrates the art of organ registration, and nomadic meanderings from flute to oboe to strings to brass have no kinship with the subtle art of orchestration. Similarly a patternless succession of *piano* and *forte, diminuendo* and *crescendo,* regardless of the curve-line of a composition or the undulation proper to a particular style, is a caricature of the art of dynamics.

Such examples of mere gadding about, indicative of no artistic goal, are paralleled by the aimless changes of color which frequently appear in the different vocal registers.

The writer recalls the futility of some operatic appearances of a much advertised visiting Diva. She was a contralto of rare natural endowment, but her voice revealed itself in three panels, as it were:

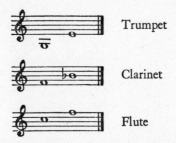

Trumpet

Clarinet

Flute

The quasi-antiphonal effects which her triplex voicings achieved, were at first amazing and amusing. But soon they became like a continuous performance of Orlando de Lasso's "Echo Song"; they interfered with the unity of impersonation required in opera, and became a grave menace to the box office.

Certainly, there is a difference in the tints of color which high, middle and low notes can produce. But this is a graduated difference. There is no difference of genre between the *E* and *G* strings of the violin; the differences in pitch and the consistency of the strings are responsible for the variation in timbre, but they are both essentially violin strings producing a homogeneous tonal effect which is not confused with the sounds of other instruments.

The clarinet in its upper register frequently likens itself to an overblown flute (especially on the radio) but there is sufficient distinctiveness even in these higher tones to keep the listener conscious of the clarinet.

Homogeneity is a quality of vocal excellence which the choirmaster must achieve and maintain, if the various choirs of his choral unit are to function with the same unity of artistic effect that distinguishes the orchestra.

The addition to the vocalization suggested at Fig. 9 of the following line, after the former has been sung in both registers, will aid in clarifying the reed quality in the middle register:—

Mah Mah etc.

The process of recreating the reed-color in boys' voices is attended, of course, by the danger that their intonations will lapse into the unqualified "chest-tones" of their first estate. Therefore, the choirmaster must use the protective *OO* frequently to minimize the danger. The correlation is the same as in the use of *pianissimo* to safeguard the voices while being broadened by the *fortes*. Note again the principle of apposition.

The string quality which can readily be associated with the flute timbre of the boy-soprano has already been initiated in the Stages.[1]

Colorless voices are useless in expressing the normal content of music. Color can be added to anaemic tones by amplifying the "Klang," i.e., the series of tones sounding above a fundamental. The use of vowel sounds which simulate the tonal-activities of orchestral instruments is a simple means of effecting this extension of partials. And, again considering the fact that singers must learn by imitation, it is recommended that vocal exercises be accompanied, whenever possible, by the instrument whose timbre is being sought.

Thus, in pursuit of more reed timbre for fluty voices, the aid of oboes and clarinets would be invaluable; likewise the accompaniment of strings would facilitate the acquisition of string-timbre.

The average choirmaster, of course, cannot avail himself of such aids, but many can use the organ for this purpose, and if the stops be carefully chosen, apply it successfully to the same end.

[1] See Chapter VII, "The Color Scheme."

CHAPTER V

Accurate Pitch

Pitch is one of the three primary elements of music. It is therefore a determining factor of music's validity. If the tessitura of a melodic line prevail long in the upper thin registers of voices or instruments, the aesthetic sensibility of listeners is vexed, either by the shrillness which the rapid vibrations of top-notes create, or merely because of the prolonged absence of the melodic line from the area in which the musical instinct finds its best satisfaction.[1] If, on the other hand, the tessitura tarries long among the low notes, the sluggishness of these and the resultant lack of clarity reduce the satisfaction of auditors.

If, finally, instrumentalists or singers perform "off pitch," if there be not a meticulous care in the accurate delivery of intervals, there can be neither content nor relish in the audience.

Players of string instruments, solo-vocalists, and choruses are heard more frequently "out-of-tune" than the other musical agencies. Inaccurate fingering and careless or defective tone-production are largely responsible for this most odious fault. Flattening or sharpening is the most repugnant slight offered to music. The fact that straying from pitch is always involuntary does not lessen objectively the indignity of the affront. Units that persist unconcernedly and smugly in offering the affront should be indicted for vandalism, and ostracized from the musical arena.

Confining discussion here to the erratic intonations and frequent aberrations from pitch which humiliate our modern choral estate, the subject is treated practically in the following divisions:—

1. (*a*) Flattening, general causes and remedies.
   (*b*) Flattening, occasional causes and remedies.
2. Sharpening, *a* and *b,* as in 1.
3. Both faults in accompanied singing
   (*a*) during rehearsals
   (*b*) during performances
4. In unaccompanied singing, *a* and *b,* as in 3.

[1] See Fig. "1," page 7.

71

It is not only with the vexatious uncontrol of pitch which permits excursions far afield that we are concerned; the slightest deviations from rectitude must be included, for these, although less offensive naturally than the former, constitute a definite handicap to choral virtuosity. These lesser deviations and inexactitudes may in the long run be more baneful, because less readily observed, diagnosed and corrected. Absolute accuracy of intonation must be the standard.

The subject of equal and unequal temperament is not debated in this Chapter, the value of the issues involved being academic rather than practical.

The phenomenon under observation here is the very widespread tendency of all types of singing units to sing "off pitch." Sometimes one or more single lines will go out-of-tune, the others remaining true to the pitch. Sometimes there are temporary lapses, sometimes frequently recurring lapses on single lines or in the complete ensemble, with returns to virtue at strategic points. On other occasions the whole unit is observed in a steady descent (less often in ascent) to a different key. This weakness is probably more general than the others and furnishes for choirmasters and concert choral directors the world over a most annoying problem.

In the course of many hundreds of lectures on the subject of choral technique, the writer has been questioned more insistently about the disconcerting inelegance of choral singing "off pitch" than any other item in the art. The tendency to sing "off pitch" (usually to sing "flat" except in trained choirs of boys) is a weakness not confined to amateur ensembles.

It is a chronic affliction of many prominent choral societies and celebrated choirs.

In spite of the anxiety expressed by the directors, nothing very practical has been done about the matter, and the units which years ago were wont to start an *a cappella* number in the key of *G* and proceed furtively to *F#*, *F* natural and mayhap conclude in *E* natural, seem to have handed on the unlovely tradition to their successors. The defect is less intolerable in *a cappella* singing than in accompanied numbers, since the deviation in the former can be accomplished furtively, while in the latter, the persistent insistence of the accompanying instruments proclaims the transgression of the chorus with mocking ruthlessness. But the uncertainty, decreasing vitality and increasing inertia associated with even the stealthy forsaking of the proper pitch is most obnoxious to the best canons of art as well as subversive of the composers' intentions.

Naturally, the first necessity is to identify the cause of deflections from pitch.

Probably there are several causes conspiring together to bring about the disfigurement. All the possible causes must be familiar to the director, and he must become skillful in recognizing which of these are responsible at a given time for the fault, and be prepared on the instant, whether in practice or in performance, to apply the necessary remedies.

The reasons of out-of-tune singing find their origin in: 1. (*a*) General causes: vocal defects; (*b*) Occasional causes: Unsuitable repertoire; unsuitable keys; unsuitable tempos; unsuitable dynamics; lack of application of compromise resources of interpretation.

The first inquiry should be directed to the vocal defects which in the majority of cases are chiefly responsible for the condition. Frequently the trouble is found to be due in some measure to the other specific causes, but, as a general rule, organizations which consistently tend to stray from the established pitch are found defective in the vocalism, of one or more of the choral lines, or more rarely, defective in blend or balance of parts.

1. (a) General Causes and Remedies of Flattening

The vocalism which is productive of such pernicious results is found at fault in one or more of these points: breath-control; posture; forward focus; thinking and singing up to notes.

The proper emission of tone is predicated first upon an adequate supply of air from the lungs. Without steady pressure of air against the vocal cords no intonation can be relied upon to be true, nor can a definite pitch be securely maintained. If the vocal training of the chorus has been conducted systematically according to precepts which apply the principles outlined in Chapters II, III and IV, and if the director consistently maintains the tone-production at a high level of artistry, it is unlikely that the tendency to sing flat is due chiefly to these general causes. But the average chorus, amateur and professional, is neither sustained in free vocalism nor trained at the outset in correct tone-placing.

The faults in this connection are evident at once to any specialist who listens to the average chorus in rehearsal or performance.

A fair and careful survey of the choral standards prevailing generally today proves this contention true. The lack of correct tone-production is the principal deficiency of singing ensembles; this accounts not only for inadequacy of tonal color and beauty, but for the tendency to sing "off pitch." It would be remarkable, indeed, if a chorus, wanting in the primary requirement of choral facility could sing "true to pitch" at all times and with precise accuracy. But let us consider the case of a well trained unit, which occasionally falls from the established pitch. Let the choirmaster first discover in which choral line the inclination to slip is manifesting itself. Next, he should immediately investigate the breath control of the offending line. He may discover that many of the singers on that line neglect to inhale as deeply as possible before attacking a phrase. Even trained singers, through carelessness, inadvertence, or fatigue may be negligent in this, especially if the opportunity for breathing be meagre as is often the case in a rapid continuity of notes and phrases. Perhaps, on the other hand, the flattening choristers may be found wasting breath by explosive impact with a note or a series of notes to be sung *sostenuto*. After the extravagant impact, there is perhaps not sufficient breath left to maintain the pitch accurately and steadily for the required duration.

Inadequacy of air supply as a general cause of flattening is well known to organists who in the not too distant past were called upon to play organs in which "robbing" was a troublesome defect. Many of the old type organs had a wind supply insufficient for the needs of the complete instrument, and as the organist drew additional stops each oncoming set would "rob" some wind from those already in use, and immediate and progressive flattening would ensue. The flat playing of wind instruments by elementary pupils is another illustration of the need of a steady and sufficient supply of air to keep notes in tune.

If the choirmaster detect notable carelessness in breath control, he may at once conclude that this neglect is at least a contributory if not the principal cause of the flattening. The necessity of improving the breath control immediately is paramount. At rehearsals he can, of course, call attention to the need directly; at performances, he should use a prearranged signal which makes the choristers aware of the need.

Sometimes the posture of the singers is responsible for the inadequate activity of the lungs. A slovenly position, the shoulders stooping or the body resting listlessly against a chair or choir-stall will interfere with proper breathing. If the Paulist Choristers show the first tendency to deviate from the heart-line of an established pitch, the writer investigates the posture of the singers, usually finding that owing to the fatigue of long liturgical services, both boys and men have begun to drape themselves over the chancel desks and stalls. In concerts the correct posture is usually assured by insistence on the placing of one foot slightly forward of the other.

Another general cause of flattening is poor focus of tone. If there be excessive rigidity at the base of the tongue, or undue activity in the adjacent muscles during the production of tones, the cords and resonators cannot function without restricting interference. The result of the tightening of the membranes, muscles and cartilages is a "swallowed" tone which by reason of its inertia is almost impossible to hold securely to a given pitch. The use of consonants in the vocal exercises should have eliminated this fault as a cause of flattening, but if it displays itself from time to time, the director must be more emphatically attentive to the value of the labials. Passages in which the temptation to flatten begins should be vocalized with *MOO, MAH, MEE, POO, PAH, PEE*, etc. according to the timbres of the voices.[1] The use of *legato* in such phrases should be temporarily abandoned, substituting a light *staccato*. After each vocalization of the measures involved, the words should be sung, the choristers intent on focusing the syllables as far forward as possible, trying to address these with the fluency acquired in the vocalization.

The singers must be trained thoroughly to project the tones mentally as far forward of the cords as possible. If the concept of forward placing has become the choristers' fixed idea of correct musical utterance, they will generally be found to apply this concept almost invariably and unconsciously. Even the difficult *Ah, EE* and *AY* sounds, which recur so frequently in many languages without prefixed consonants, submit in some degree to this control, for although it is impossible to produce these sounds, unarticulated by consonants, without a perceptible pressure of air below the cords, the singers are subconsciously impelled to minimize the throaty reaction and to poise the first possible ensuing emission directly upon the lips or the tip of the tongue.

If the flattening be actually due to the lack of free tone-placing, and if the alternation of vocalizing the passage with the singing of the text be of little avail, it is profitable to divide the singers into two groups, one vocalizing the notes staccato and the other at the same time delivering the words. The latter group is directed to copy the production of the former as far as possible. The troublesome phrases should be sung at higher pitches, and eventually in the key of the composition. The two groups should alternate in their respective assignments.

Approaching notes mentally from below and the actual singing up to them is an associated general cause of flat singing. Like the fault of

[1] See Chapter III, Part II.

"swallowing," it involves the thickening of the voice, since it predisposes the singer, in the mental preparation of the tone, to carry the weight of lower to upper notes. It must be borne in mind that initiative in the management of vocal sounds is vested in the faculties of the mind. The mechanism of the larynx and the adjacent muscles responds (unless the anatomical apparatus has been injured by habitual abuse) to the direction given by the picture of the tone observed in the imagination. Thus the physiological and mental factors in tone-production must co-operate. If the concept of the tone picture be a heavy, struggling-up species, it will be almost impossible for the larynx to produce a lighter and controllable species. Likewise, if the larynx has been committed to chronic misbehavior, the mental concept will be unable to reveal itself.

The lower the note the slower the vibrations; the slower the vibrations the less elastic the tone; the less elastic the tone the heavier it is; and the heavier it is the more weighty, slothful and unmanageable it becomes. For illustration, contrast the vitality of the open $É$ strings of the violin and Bass viol.

Therefore it is necessary to conceive the tone in relation to its overtones, that is, to think it as having its origin of quality above the pitch of its fundamental. All this is theoretically in accord with the physics of sound, and practically in accord with the psychology of tone-control. If the singer conceive the quality of tone as determined above, the mind will immediately transmit to the vocal mechanism an order to *descend* to the fundamental. Each note, high or low, in upward as well as in downward progressions should be approached mentally from above. This prescription effectively overcomes the temptation to carry up the consistency and acoustical gravity of lower notes to the upper planes where each higher note must necessarily become increasingly more mobile, buoyant and vibratile.

The general causes and remedies of flat-singing seem to the writer to be those outlined above, and the experience of many years with choristers of all types confirms his conviction that if the fundamental principles of good vocalism be applied consistently and faithfully, the intonations and sustained utterances of a chorus will be true to pitch, except when one or more of the occasional causes may be responsible for lapses.

1. (b) Occasional Causes of Flattening

The choice of repertoire sometimes affects the accuracy and steadiness of pitch, for the selection of numbers to be sung must be influenced by consideration of the color-scheme of the chorus, the balance of parts, the church or hall in which the singing is to be done, and the atmospheric conditions prevailing at the time of the performance.

The first of the seven principles of the tonal color scheme [1] is that "the color scheme of a chorus determines the propriety of its repertoire." The application of this principle in its broader aspects concerns the need of establishing an affinity of fitness and compatibility between vocal timbres and the specific species and moods of the compositions to be interpreted. But it may be invoked also in its relation to the problem of singing out of tune. For example, a chorus made up from various categories of timbres on the alto, tenor and bass lines, but having sopranos chiefly of the flute type, will have difficulty with selections in which the soprano tessitura is low. The lack of piquant overtones in the treble part is felt by the other parts and, especially in homophonic music, the melodic line is not sufficiently delineated to permit a continued awareness of the true pitch.

Similarly, when the alto line is delivered by a dominant contralto timbre with the tessitura high or low, the murkiness of this important interior part clouds the pitch-lucidity sometimes to the extent of unsettling the other lines.

With a majority of lyric tenors, unless they be of well defined reed-quality, the tessitura lying low, the director will have the same experience, as well as with a bass unit of notable profundo timbre, the tessitura lying high.

Of course, there are expedients which can be employed to offset the influence which unsuitable timbres exercise with subtlety over the pitch-sense of ensembles. The use of such expedients to overcome faults at the expense of interpretative symmetry will be debated fully in a second volume.

In *a cappella* music, it is important for the director to study the proposed program in relation to the balance of parts and the blend of the voices. If the balance is disturbed by an excess of basses, it is usually difficult to hold a chorus to precise pitch unless one of the expedients or compromises referred to be used. Likewise, an indifferent relationship between the tenor and alto-lines will tend to promote flattening especially in the minor mode. [2] Anent the consideration of the acoustics of the place in which the music is to be sung, it may be established with certainty that in small halls or in larger halls with flat and low-studded ceilings, the polyphony of the 15th, 16th and 17th centuries is difficult of performance,

[1] See Chapter VII, "The Color Scheme."
[2] Chapter XI, "Blend and Balance of Parts."

except by a small group of singers, proper attention being given to the selection of the pitch, the tempos, the decibels of quantity used, and the dynamic undulations.

After having toured the country for years the writer became convinced that the only sure way of keeping Palestrina on the key in small, flat-ceiled, or dead rooms, was to keep him off the programme. Polyphonic music needs head-room to assure the floating about of the partial tones of many involved and interlaced choral lines; if the head-room be inadequate it is practically impossible to secure the buoyancy of tone requisite for accurate pitch.

The barometer should be consulted as well. Numbers which are among the most satisfactory and convincing compositions in a repertoire on clear days, sometimes go miserably out of tune on rainy days. The change of keys and tempos to offset the depressing effect of heavy atmosphere of wet weather is frequently helpful, but generally, if the director be free to change the programme he is well advised to eliminate polyphonic music on such days and all *a cappella* music in the minor mode.

Another reason for occasional lapsing from pitch is the selection of a key for an *a cappella* number which is unsuitable to the acoustic features of a hall. A composition successfully pitched in *G* in Carnegie Hall, New York, may need the extra vibrations of the key of *A♭* to meet the tonal conditions of Symphony Hall, Boston.

It is sufficient here to call the attention of conductors to the influence which the choice of key exercises upon singers especially in the delivery of unaccompanied music. While this influence is less noticeable, and therefore less of a hazard in accompanied numbers, it is clear that transposition occasionally promotes an easy adherence to a unison of the vocal and instrumental contributions. But, as transposition of the accompaniment requires a special facility which is not the gift of the average accompanist, and since it is signally impracticable in the case of orchestral accompaniments, it is not insisted upon as a generally feasible practice. However, it is comparatively easy for the average accompanist to play in sharps the scores written in flats, and *vice-versa*. A choirmaster can safely avail himself of the advantage of raising or lowering the pitch by a semitone without taxing unfairly the resources of an accompanist. For example, in the Church of St. Paul, New York, it is the custom of the writer always to transpose numbers written in *E♭* to *E* natural, if the tessitura of the sopranos be low or medium, or the progression of their melodic line be upward. The key of *E♭* in these circumstances fails to develop sufficient vitality in overtones to impress the singers' musical consciousness with a precise image of degrees of acuteness or graveness. As has been already pointed out, a precise image of these degrees is essential to singing in tune. Likewise, in the same great church, the key of *D* natural tends to disturb the steadiness of pitch when tenors and basses are singing in unison, without alto or treble voices, and the key of *D♭* is habitually substituted.

In lieu of and in addition to the transposition of accompaniments, there are usually resources to be found in the material of the accompaniments themselves which may be utilized to prosper unison pitch between singers and instruments.

Very slow tempos, notably in sustained music, tend to influence the unisonance of singers with the established pitch. Excessively slow movements react disadvantageously on the musical instinct, for movement and readily discernible pulsations are of the very essence of rhythm. It is the periodicity of impulses that differentiates music from mere noise. Consequently, in the ratio of less frequently recurring time pulsations (the beats of a measure), the musical instinct is less sensibly stimulated and the consciousness of both quality and accurate pitch is correspondingly lowered.

The difference between flatness, non-resonance, and artistic uselessness on one hand, and rectitude of pitch, vitality, and aesthetic worth on the other, may lie in the one extra degree of slowness which denies to a dawdling tempo the activating principle of rhythmic pace.

Thus a slight acceleration from too pensive initial *largos* and *adagios* will frequently deter a group from flattening. Some directors are temperamentally slow, and convey the depressing effect of this idiosyncrasy to the singers, not only in the choice of under-speed tempos but in the languid or lumbering gestures by which they essay to beat the time. Under the baton of such conductors, unless they can be persuaded to study and follow nature's metronome of tempos, all sustained music becomes ponderous and elegiac, and even the livelier forms lose the spring and grace which are their chief charm.

Slow tempos and flattening are allies, and the stealthy encroachment of the former upon the breath control as well as upon the rhythmic instinct of singers invites the latter to make its appearance.

As a judge in choral competitions, the writer has several times observed the impossible tempo set for a chorus to send it off key within a few measures thus forfeiting the prize to an ensemble of fewer vocal excellences.

These occasional causes of flattening have their origin in the same generic fault as the general causes, i.e., lack of mobility and freedom in tone-production. The general causes are intrinsic to the act of singing, while the special causes are extrinsic. To prevent the former, the director places the responsibility directly upon the singers, but in avoiding the influence of the latter he is himself alone responsible and should therefore devote himself to a comprehensive study of the acoustical and psychological principles underlying the foregoing considerations.

The use of dynamic variations may affect the accuracy of choral pitch, even if these variations be in accord with interpretative principles. For example: a bass chorus, delivering a *crescendo* as indicated in the score from *pp* to *ff* through a progression of accidentals to a new key can easily unsettle the others' certainty of pitch. In this circumstance, either the *crescendo* must be modified or the notes in another part which may be en rapport with the harmonic evolution in progress, underlined, as it were, and brought out to establish an aural understanding of the change.

In one hall the temporary prominence of one part may be convincing and gratifying, while in another it may disturb the serenity of the other parts. This fact is frequently observed when the prominent part is called upon to emphasize the intervals which create the minor mode and mood. In polyphonic motets and madrigals written in the "hypo" modes (Hypo-Dorian, Hypo-Phrygian, etc.) the relationship of the altos and tenors must be observed, for if the choral axis which these voices comprise be always permitted the same degree of *crescendo,* without regard to the acoustics and other considerations, the resulting quasi-minor hypo-modality (except in the Hypo-Lydian, and Hypo-Mixo-Lydian modes) will have a depressing effect particularly on the soprano chorus.

Conversely, the bringing of one part out beyond the others may on occasions prevent the group from flattening. For example, an alert conductor never fails to emphasize the baritone *D* over the bass *G* in the "Ave Maris Stella" by Grieg, as well as in many Russian numbers, notably the motets of Rachmaninof. The influence of the double pedal point with the fifth underlined is most active in keeping the entire ensemble "on top of the notes." [1]

The underlining of certain notes at times to assure satisfactory pitch to one or more parts is highly recommended. The baritone singing correctly the fifth above the bass is always a source of strength in this connection, and there are other notes in chords and whole passages which may be brought out with good results to the ensemble. Here are a few examples:—

---

[1] See Chapter XI for special usefulness in "Blend and Balance."

D in the first tenor line gives a sense of security to the sopranos on high *B♭*.

C♯ in the first soprano line, underlined for two beats points up the minor interval and dissonant note of the alto line. Underlining is unnecessary as the dissonance resolves on the third beat.

D in the alto line, being the dominant, helping the bass line feel the leading tone close to the ensuing tonic.

The whole tenor phrase, since the part rotates around the dominant.

The advantage of emphasizing the mediant when lying under the fifth in two part numbers is indicated in a following chapter.[1]

Many of the exercises suggested in Chapter XI serve not only as agencies for promoting blend but for developing sensitiveness to accurate pitch. The two part vocalizations given at Fig. 2 of Chapter XI are especially conducive to that end. In these exercises, when employed specifically as convoys of pitch, the second line should be emphasized slightly, since it presents the key note or dominant in strategic positions.

The following exercises suggest a profitable practice, an excellent opportunity being offered the singers to test the precision of their utterance, by the merging of many voices on one note an octave above its fundamental.

[1] See Chapter XI "Blend and Balance."

Thus:—

For S.A.T.B.

FIG. 1

(1)

(2) For Sopranos and Altos, or Tenors and Basses

In exercise No. 1, the unison-octave established by trebles and altos over the tenors and basses presents important intervals of the scale without embellishment. The exercise should be sung unaccompanied, the lower part more prominent than the upper. These recommendations should be followed carefully if the full value of the exercise is to be gained. For without the interference of a tempered instrument (which is probably also out of tune with the standard equal temperament) the singers can readily sense the perfect octave which of course is the basis of all consonance. The tenors and basses deliver the fundamental tones here, generating the octave as the first harmonic. Therefore if the voices singing from the treble staff are used *pianissimo,* and the lower voices *mezzo-forte,* it is reasonable to hope that the actual singing of the higher notes will be influenced by the harmonics, and therefore lead to a perfect pitch. The measures in which the voices sing in harmony present an immediate opportunity of carrying the precision of the unison-octave to a more complex combination. It will be noted, that in conformity with the principle of apposition, the excursion into the more distracting harmonized measures is followed by a return to the unison-octave combination.

In exercise No. 2, the unison-octave, fundamental-harmonic arrangement is used again, plus the absolute unison in the second, sixth and eighth measures. As with all exercises, these should be practiced in various keys.

The following, final, suggestion for exercising the voices together in correct intonation combines several helpful factors from the science of sounds:—

Detailed analysis of these exercises is unnecessary since it is clear that each part is given opportunity to move on the important pattern of tonic and dominant, while the other parts are sustaining these sentinels of pitch. Alternation of the *fortes* between moving and sustaining parts is recommended. Each exercise should be sung several times at various pitches and tempos.

Such exercises are not a necessary feature of routine rehearsals for choirs which sing normally with correct vocalism, but it is profitable to apply them from time to time, particularly after a performance in which irresolution in intervallic skips has been noted,—and always during practice periods which precede a trying programme of *a cappella* music. The selection of the tonic-dominant pattern as signally efficacious for inculcating pitch consciousness will justify itself to a director after one or two experiments with it. Generally, one may depend upon correct vocalism, good balance and blend, studied choice of repertoire, keys, and tempos to guarantee accurate pitch. It has been the experience of the writer to escape the blight of out-of-tune singing for months on end without the necessity of applying special or emergency expedients. However, occasions are sure to arise, sometimes altogether without hint, when recourse must be had to unusual strategy in order to outwit the discordant imps which lurk on every space and line of the staff, and above and below, to tempt a chorus from rectitude. Some suggestions as to meeting the exigencies of such occasions are offered in the concluding divisions of this Chapter.

2. (a) *General Causes and Remedies of Sharpening*

The inclination to sing sharp, under certain conditions, is more generally characteristic of trained than of untrained singers. Untutored and slovenly vocalism usually predisposes persons to flatten but this cannot be alleged as invariably the case, for sometimes the faults or conditions which cause flattening in one instance will cause sharpening in another. It is valuable, in this connection, however, to point out that the very zeal itself by which a chorus has been freed from the tendency to flatten is sometimes responsible for the other defect. Over-training, over-anxiety, and excessive effort are frequently discovered to be the only causes for a chorus singing unpleasantly sharp. These defects of virtue, as it were, are sometimes less susceptible of treatment than graver faults, and it is therefore encumbent upon conductors of carefully trained choruses to watch for the first signs of a venial but obstinate defect. Easily curable if treated immediately, it becomes progressively worse if neglected, until it is chronic and practically incurable. Probably the aesthetic disaster wrought by sharpening or flattening is equally grave, but habitual sharp singing has always seemed less tolerable to the writer than a definite unblushing flattening. The former is altogether unnecessary, since the chorus has been carefully instructed and rehearsed, while the latter is practically a necessary concomitant of the many other faults of an untrained unit. There is a hint of arrogance in the sharp singing of an ensemble, while the lowly estate of the poor group which cannot hold its head up to the pitch is proclaimed by each succeeding note. The chief cause of sharpening is excessive tenseness. One explanation for the tendency of trained groups to sing sharp at times is that the singers are physically tired. Highly trained groups sing frequently and for long periods. They spend many hours each week in rehearsals. If they are called upon to sing difficult or sustained music, after having become thoroughly fatigued, they will probably sing sharp. If the fatigue be localized notably in the muscles of the larynx, extra physical exertion must be applied to overcome the languor; this involves overtaxing and strain. Under such circumstances, singers can carry their parts only by undue forcing of the vocal controls. This forcing tends to sharpen the notes very much as the lips of orchestral players, tired from many hours of playing, addressing the orifices of flutes and the embouchures of other wind instruments, cause a slight elevation of pitch.

Forcing and physical tenseness are inhibitive of the ease of delivery implied in true-to-pitch sounds. All tightening of the facial and thoracic muscles is communicated, in some degree, to the thyro-cricoid and the thyro-arytenoid muscles. The note produced in a constricted reed pipe takes on acuteness, except in the case of untrained singers who have "swallowed" the tone. The acuteness becomes progressively keener until all the notes of a passage are definitely above the pitch-line. There is something of "whistling in the throat" about the emission of tone in a constricted larynx. The tone seems to be struggling against the effort of the throat, not to muffle it, as in flattening, but to thin out its consistency and to lure it away from its true fundamental.

Undue tautness is commonly observed among singers in the excessive tightening of the lips and the rigid spreading of them in singing *EE* and *AY* sounds respectively, especially in the upper registers. Although a certain degree of exaggeration in the articulation of consonants seems to promote clarity of diction, an inordinate degree will induce an exorbitant tenseness. Even the labials and linguals, generally such helpful agents of free tone-production, if delivered with extravagant facial movement, will create a sharpening tautness.

The prolonged use of *forte* in a high tessitura disposes singers to exert themselves too energetically, thus intensifying the strain on muscles and ligaments.

The director must arrange programmes, rehearsals, and performances with these several considerations in mind. Otherwise, quite unexpectedly, his chorus will sing sharp to the pitch and fail without blame to execute the aesthetic intentions indicated. Obviously, the director has no control over the length or liturgical demands of ecclesiastical services, but when these are signally trying as in the offices of Holy Week in the Catholic Liturgy and in the Jewish Service on the Day of Atonement, he must employ all possible expedients and anodynes to minimize the laryngeal fatigue and consequent tautness of the choristers. Service-lists and choice of motets (there is usually a wide choice of available settings) should be made to provide frequently recurring opportunities for *leggiero* singing, in downward progressions, as already suggested in another connection.[1] Factors prospering accurate intonation are important assets.

In the writer's personal experience, there have been occasions when inadequate attention to service-lists was responsible for a considerable portion of the unit singing sharp at solemn moments when perfect intonation and strict adherence to pitch were of paramount importance. Proper arrangement of the Tenebrae Office on Good Friday night, for instance, requires that the boy-sopranos be assigned a minimum of chanting, for upon them rests the responsibility of effecting the great climax of the "Miserere," one of the most overwhelming moments in all sacred dramaturgy. If the boys be over-tired vocally (they are sure to be very weary physically), it is necessary to egg them on to extraordinary effort, which, in the case of sopranos notably, by excessive tensing of the laryngeal muscles, increases the tension of the vocal cords beyond the degree congenial to authentic pitch.

Mental tenseness readily communicates itself to the vocal mechanism and its effect on the tone-muscles is the same. Therefore, if singers be allowed to become unreasonably solicitous or apprehensive about a performance, the director may duly expect them to push some notes above the pitch-line. Similarly, too much rebuke and tart irascibility on the part of the conductor will predispose a chorus (particularly sopranos) to answer his acerbity of manner with an acerbity of tone. These foregoing considerations are in accord with Precept IV, which urges the director to "Keep the choristers in good humor."[2]

---

[1] See Chapter IV, "The Positive Development."
[2] See Chapter III, "The Five Stages" (The First Stage).

2. (b) Occasional Causes and Remedies of Sharpening

Among the occasional causes of sharpening which may be isolated from the general causes and treated specifically are: (a) breathiness and over-blowing; (b) expletive impact with first notes or phrases; (c) excessive vibrato and tremolo; (d) loud singing in over-resonant rooms; (e) too much underlining of accidentals; (f) too highly emphasized string timbre on the soprano and alto line; (g) too much reed quality on the tenor line; (h) carelessness in upward skips of sopranos and basses at *fortissimo*.

(A) Breathiness and overblowing tend to raise the pitch unpleasantly because the use of more breath than is required puts a pressure upon the cords which disturbs the required evenness of vibrations. The influence of overblowing on pitch is well illustrated by the experiences of "re-build" organ makers in applying the higher pressure of modern wind systems to the older types of organ pipes. Especial difficulty was found in adjusting the vibratory processes of old reed pipes to the high pressure, and frequently it was necessary to supply whole sets of new reed pipes. The forcing of an overabundant air supply against reeds, mechanical or human, superinduces vibrations in excess of those required to produce a given note. Franz Kneisel, founder of the Kneisel Quartet, to whom this writer owes much valuable information, related an incident which illustrates this fact: Nikisch the great virtuoso conductor of Leipzig was having difficulty in blending an oboe progression with the strings. The oboe part called for a crescendo from F natural to F#; the F# sounded out of tune and disrupted the tonal structure of the phrase. Nikisch wanted *both* the *crescendo* and the *F#*. He tried the phrase without the *crescendo;* it was in tune, but the lack of the dynamic increase in the oboe part made the phrase unconvincing. Finally, he directed the player to make the *crescendo* and overblow F natural instead of proceeding to F#. The overblowing of the F natural raised its pitch sufficiently to give aural impression of the sharp without in reality producing a note a full half-tone higher. Overblowing frequently is a concomitant of tenseness as has been pointed out, but sometimes it is due to carelessness. Unnecessarily quick exhalation, connoting waste of breath, involves the need of many short breaths to carry a phrase to its conclusion. The practice of gasping and panting, instead of inhaling and exhaling naturally, eventually brings about a change in the anatomical structure of the cords. For a notable excess of respirations causes the cords to assume an elliptical shape. With the cords out of proper alignment, the vibrations cannot be regular. The new anatomy imposes on the throat a new plan for vocal utterance, and this plan, being unnatural, is uncontrollable and insecure.

If the sharpening of the chorus be due to chronic breathiness, the director should investigate the vocal habits of the singers to ascertain the kind of vocalization practiced outside the choir-hall. He will probably discover that the vowel sound *O* is responsible for the condition and naturally recommend its discontinuance. An expeditious means of correcting the elliptical formation of the cords is to allow exercises for a time which involve the stroke of the glottis. The use of *AH* and *EE* without consonants causes a pronounced stroke and tends to make the cords convex at the point where the ellipse had made them concave. After a few weeks the elliptical formation should have disappeared, and it is important then to discontinue immediately the glottis exercises. Directors here may reasonably ask how the malformation of the cords can be detected, in view of the fact that stroboscopes and laryngoscopes are not available. The answer is the chronic waste of breath is itself a reliable indication of the condition. The noticeable escape of breath which conveys the impression of "the breath ahead of the tone" is due at least in some degree to the very aperture which the ellipse provides.

Careful attention to the fundamental principles of breath control and earnest practice in sustaining tones in connection with and after the discontinuance of the glottis exercises should remove this cause of sharpening.

(*B*) Expletive impact with the first notes of phrases is not only a grave impediment to the graceful continuity of musical movement but, obviously, a hindrance to pitch control. The addressing of first notices explosively leaves but little breath for the ensuing notes, which consequently must be forced with the likelihood of provoking the undesirable tension already discussed. Furthermore, habitual practice of the explosive attack brings about the elliptical condition because of the need it established for many respirations.

(*C*) The cultivation of an ultra-wide vibrato produces a heterogeneous tone-line, i.e. a combination of three definite pitches, the low, medial and high positions of the vibrato curve. The vocal richness accruing to tones from a moderate vibrato unquestionably enhances the quality of solo-voices. But the deliberate development of a wide vibrato in chorus singers, or the use of many high cycled vibrato-voices in a chorus is disastrous to unisonance of pitch. It is true that Caruso, Gili, Scotti, Frances Alda, Galli-Curci, Jeritza and many others showed wide vibrato range upon measurement, but it is also true that probably no living choral director could develop an artistic chorus from among them and their colleagues.

Vibrato is becoming quite the vogue among singers and students and considerable effort is made to acquire it, but this effort is conducive to chronic sharpness, except under skilled guidance, since the aim is to cause a tone to fluctuate between two tones which can be named, e.g. *C* natural and *C#*. In striving for the vibrato the student's thought, ambition and purpose are focused on the *C#* although the written note be *C* natural. Therefore a vibrato chorus could reasonably be expected to give more hint of the sharp than of the natural. It would be interesting to listen to a chorus of high-powered vibrato-ists tangling itself into the net of an eight-part motet by Palestrina, or even a simple *a cappella* fugue by Bach.

Much scientific research is being conducted in the field of vibrato and as the subject is unfolded more clearly, directors will be able to determine with greater conviction to what extent the fluctuation of sung notes may benefit an ensemble tone-quality.

Meantime high-cycle vibrato should be considered as a contributory cause of sharpening.

A distinguished orchestra conductor once asked my opinion of the performance of a certain violin-concerto. I replied that the performer impressed me with his technique and interpretative intentions but that he failed to play in tune. His comment was: "Oh! That's merely his well known vibrato!" In rebuttal: "Your gallantry disguises a criticism."

Personally I prefer to have accurate pitch as the substantial character of all tones, marking everything that may cause deviations from this as perilous to the aesthetic livelihood of chorophony.

The tremolo, while distinct from the vibrato, breaks the intonation into fragments causing such fluttering and fluctuation as to create the off-pitch atmosphere. It is due usually to the unsteadiness of the epiglottis and to the wobbling of a too soft membrane-lining of the nasal pharynx.

A pronounced tremolo is difficult to eliminate. Certain psychological explanations are sometimes alleged to account for it, but generally medication and even surgical treatment are required before the standard procedure of voice placing and control can be effective.

(*D*) Loud singing in over-resonant rooms creates a harshness of which the singers presently become conscious. The repercussion of sound waves against stone or terrazzo floors, hard walls and ceilings has the effect of putting too keen an edge on the tones. A certain ensemble excitation often ensues and the director can sense that presently a slight elevation of pitch will soon follow. This cause of sharpening is operative most often when the soprano tessitura is high and when the composition is in the bravura or fandango style. The remedy for this is of course immediate reduction of the dynamic level, and perhaps the future choice of a lower key.

(E) Too much underlining of accidentals is occasionally a cause of sharpening because of the preoccupation which it causes in the minds of the singers. An accidental, being alien to the prevailing key-tonality, must be delivered with great care to insure its authenticity. By habitual emphasis of these alien factors, singers readily develop a habit of forcing the accidentals, pushing them over the pitch line and conveying the sharp effect to the rest of the ensemble. The measures following a progression like the following will be in trouble if the alto G♯ be stressed:

It is very unwise to emphasize accidentals that lie above the staff in the soprano part. Even when the composer has indicated *ff* in this circumstance the director will be fortunate if he listen first to the effect the *ff* has on the general pitch of the organization. If it be injurious, then he must sacrifice the dramatic effect to a more fundamental need.

There are two opposite views prevailing among conductors in the matter of interpreting accidentals in music up to the appearance of the Polytonal School. One favors underlining them, the other prefers to keep them as unobtrusive as possible. It is an interesting question academically which will be debated fully in Volume II. But whatever the merits of underlining them may be interpretatively, the alert choirmaster will be always on the *qui vive* to protect the ensemble pitch against their subtle influence.

(F and G) Emphasis of partial tones, unless balanced with nice discrimination, is conducive to sharp singing. For example: the specifications of the organ in the Church of St. Paul the Apostle, New York City, include a brilliant five-rank mixture stop. The piquancy of the harmonics is sufficient to set the entire choir above the pitch after this stop has been used in accompaniment for a few measures, unless it is offset by a combination of dull timbres which counterbalance the brilliancy.

The vocal timbres which, by injudicious use, concur to have the same effect on a chorus, are a cutting string quality on the soprano, alto, or bass lines, and a piercing reed quality on the tenor line. The number, order, and intensity of the overtones of these timbres are such as to establish a quasi-harshness in the ensemble-tone, and if great care be not exercised to keep them well tempered by the simpler timbres such as the flute-tone of the soprano, the dark quality of the contralto, and the rounder type of baritone and bass, the chorus will almost inevitably sing sharp. A preponderance of string tone on the bass line in this range

will always affect the chordal superstructure unpleasantly, for an edgy, acute timbre works its way upwards communicating its keenness to the rest of the voices. Likewise a stressed piquancy on the alto line will immediately send the sopranos soaring above the pitch, while emphasis of such timbre on the soprano line is an irresistible invitation to all to follow it to a high aerie where the denizens of discord prey upon the symmetries of the art.

If adequate attention be given regularly to blend and balance, there is little probability that this cause of sharpening will be operative, but from time to time the many other needs of the moment distract a director, and the intense timbres of the chorus arrogate control to themselves. Personally, I have been so impressed with the necessity of correlating the piquant colors with the more tranquil choral tints, that I have come to sense the very moment when the more turbulent voices are preparing to assert themselves. String-basses have a strong urge to usurp the prerogatives of the conductor in the delivery of fast moving fugues; mezzo-sopranos accept opportunities of annoying the higher sopranos when their notes are a minor or major third apart, and the top *cantatrices* are inclined to assert themselves with amazing exclamations when, in homophonic forms, they carry the melody, *animando e crescendo* to a culminating apex.

The reedy quality of tenors requires mollification in the open leads of polyphonic music, and especially when together with the altos they are establishing the axis for elaborate contrapuntal movement.

(*H*) Carelessness in upward skips of a fifth or more, in the extreme parts always threatens the security of choral pitch. The inclination of sopranos and basses in a standard S.A.T.B. chorus, and of top-tenors and basses in a glee club, to increase volume in such skips is so general that the blending of these extremes is of utmost importance in the balancing and co-ordinating of the various choral lines.[1]

[1] See Chapter XI, "Blend and Balance."

If the melodic curve line of these parts be so capricious and nomadic as to be without a definite tessitura, the detrimental effect of careless skipping on the altos and tenors is less serious, but if the curve line be gentle, regular and fairly symmetrical, the occasional leap from a low or medium to a higher note surprises the tonal consciousness of the others, with the result of unsteadying the pitch.

In *a cappella* music, this disturbance is most baneful, for the saltation of sopranos and basses is more keenly felt than in accompanied forms where instrumental figures may help to minimize the surprise. If the unit has become accustomed for many measures to a certain degree of proximity among the several choral lines, the sudden noisy secession of the sopranos to a more remote position, or, a clamorous encroachment by basses upon the tenor area will necessarily challenge the tranquility of pitch-sense so necessary to the maintenance of accurate delivery. The elimination of this cause of sharpening devolves wholly upon the director who must give a warning signal as the sopranos or basses approach a phrase "out-of-tessitura."

3. The Treatment of Both Faults in Accompanied Singing

(a) During Rehearsals

In addition to the suggestions already offered for curing our modern choruses of the deplorable affliction of out-of-tune singing, some means for prospering accurate pitch are subjoined. During both rehearsals and performances, there are often opportunities to apply legitimate stratagem which will deter the unit from deviations at given moments, or if, *de facto*, already off the pitch, will rectify them or at least minimize the listeners' consciousness of inaccuracy.

During rehearsals, it is important to discontinue practice of the text immediately upon the first evidence of inaccurate pitch. A short vocalization, *downward*, beginning *pianissimo* with a gradual *crescendo, staccato,* on a vowel sound with the prefixed consonant *P*, should be given to the offending group. If the error be flattening, the vowel should be *EE* or *AY* to enlist the co-operation of the coaxing partial tones of these sounds. If the error be sharpening, obviously, the simpler *OO* and *AW* sounds should be employed. The vocalization should be simple and accompanied, for flattening, with open fifths as at Fig. 1, or for sharpening with double pedal-point and a treble figure as at Fig. 2:—

FIG. 1

FIG. 2

After a few repetitions of such an exercise, the offending group will probably have improved sufficiently to permit the vocalization of the notes of the composition itself. The offending group should still confine itself to *staccato* and *piano*, although the rest of the unit may sing the text with all the dynamic variations indicated in the score. Whereas it is recommended to practice all compositions generally *piano*[1] without *crescendos*, merely *thinking* the increase of tone, as a means of developing excellent blend and elasticity of ensemble movement, in this particular circumstance, it is profitable to call for *crescendos* and *fortes*, first from each associated part consecutively, and finally from all of these simultaneously in order that the out-of-tune singers may feel their notes accurately as related to other single parts and to the integral harmonic structure; the *fortes* should be sung *staccato*.

Pursuing this plan, I have frequently within a few minutes, loosened the constricted intonations of a group, fitting them easily and to a nicety into the pitch design of the composition. Sometimes the deviation from

[1] See Chapter XII, "The Control of Dynamics."

pitch will recur at the same point, in which case, the director must re-apply the treatment, and perhaps pause to investigate the general *status quo* of the singers' tone-production. Regularly, however, there is no recurrence of the error after the technique outlined has piloted the voices back to the correct acoustical trajectory.

If, however, there are several factors conspiring together to entice one or more groups from the true pitch, it is well to discontinue the accompaniment, temporarily, and to direct the unit to sing the phrase *a cappella*, first in a key above and then in the key chosen by the composer.

An excellent exercise to apply for a few moments, if the organization as a whole seems on the verge of serious flattening, is a progression (after a few *staccato* notes which are presumed to remove the over-tax from the laryngeal muscles), from tonic to supertonic, subdominant, leading-tone, and octave tonic, as at Fig. 3:—

FIG. 3

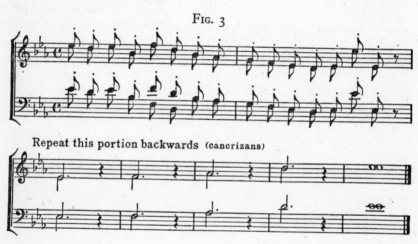

Repeat this portion backwards (cancrizans)

This figure should be sung first with sopranos and altos more in evidence than the lower voices, the latter functioning only as an accompaniment at the octave, and then with the tenors and basses dominating as fundamentals, the treble staff voices taking the role of harmonics. This alternation of acoustical relationships is a most effective means of inducing upper and lower voices to check the preciseness of their pitch against one another. In the first instance, the tenors and basses must listen carefully to the upper notes in order accurately to gauge the perfect octave below. It is easy to sense the perfect octave.

In the second instance, the tenors and basses, singing the notes as fundamentals, send up a pure-octave harmonic, which the higher voices must greet with most courteous vocal etiquette, or be indicted as acoustically rude.

The progression, *do, re, fa, ti, do* and its *per retro* answer, makes severe demands upon the tonal sense for correct intonation. The first hazard is the minor third *re—fa;* the ensuing tritone *fa—ti* must be conceived as extra-high and intoned without any effort, otherwise it will be either flat or sharp. The leading tone must be brought securely to the heart-line of the octave tonic at *ti—do.*

In the descending delivery of the figure, vigilance is necessary to avoid singing the *ti* too far below *do.* Usually, on the contrary, the next progression, *ti—fa* finds the *fa* not low enough, predisposing the minor third *fa—re* to uncertainty, some of the unit singing the *re* slightly sharp, and others according to its correct number of vibrations.

This exercise, to produce the immediate and gratifying results to which it is most apt, should be sung without accompaniment.

When the normal practice of the composition has been resumed by the whole unit, it is profitable, as a deterrent to relapse, to direct the accompanist to play very lightly, and if the harmonic structure permit to use the tonic-dominant pattern temporarily, as suggested elsewhere.

Usually this pattern can be employed at least for a few consecutive measures without interfering with the harmonic content.

The insistence of the tonic and dominant throughout serves well as a constant admonition to the singers, keeping well before their aural perception the pitch of the two most important notes of the scale.

The average conductor seems to rely upon the unfortunate and fatuous scheme of loudly hammering out notes on the piano, hoping to coerce singers to the correct pitch. This plan is not only ineffective but tends to make the singers dependent upon external help, for as soon as the written accompaniment is resumed, and the piano part placed in its proper relationship to the whole, the lack of the vigorous support which had been supplied is immediately felt and the last state of the singers is worse than the first.

During the rehearsals of accompanied music, the piano should be played very lightly, the right hand part being raised an octave. This latter strategy sets before the whole group, usually in an area in which no part is singing, a high, clear, easily discernible pitch-atmosphere, whereas, if the treble part of the accompaniment be vigorously projected in the area in which the choristers are singing the advantage of the upper octave clarity is forfeited.

(b) During Performances

The special aids to be invoked during the public performance of accompanied music to steady the pitch or correct it, if need be, have already been intimated in foregoing considerations.

If the piano is the accompanying instrument, in the case of flattening, the right hand part should be played an octave higher. Fifths and octaves should be emphasized, and if there be but little movement in the accompaniment, it should be supplied temporarily by breaking whole notes into a series of halves, quarters or eighths, etc. I have often restored a vacillating pitch by dividing a whole note chord into four beats of eighth note triplets. The sudden addition of greater animation to the accompaniment tends to lessen the mental slothfulness which often is a concomitant of flattening. The re-arrangement of solid chords into *arpeggios* is a cognate contrivance of value.

In the case of sharpening, the bass notes should be stressed in open octaves in quick pulsations, the right hand playing only the essential notes of the treble figure. Of course, it is presumed that the director will apply the necessary correctives discussed in the earlier divisions of this Chapter as far as may be possible in public. Such points as improvement in breath control, forward placing, etc., can readily be indicated by a code of signals which will not take the public into the secret.

If the accompanying instrument be the pipe-organ, the director can call to his assistance the various stop timbres which are known to be remedial.

Playing the organ loudly to overcome off-pitch singing is even more futile than the similar effort with the piano. There are few professional musicians who have not often observed the frustration of artistic purposes, as organists, becoming panicky when the chorus started to descend from pitch, drew on loud thundering diapasons and other stops resonant with a vast plenitude of sonorousness. A loud organ, instead of helping, increases the heaviness of the chorus, presently confirming it in a degree of inertia altogether inimical to correct intonation.

Quantity should be reduced both in the organ accompaniment and in the chorus. Light stops should be employed and a scheme of registration adopted which will promote animation, if flattening be in progress, or tranquility if the singers push over and above the pitch. Thus, for flattening, one should avail himself of the string, light reed and mixture stops, with a solid Violone 16′ or string Diapason 16′ in the pedal.

The string stops are especially effective, if chosen among the 4′ group, or played with super coupler if from among the 8′ group. For sharpening,

the 8′ Flute stops should be used in the middle register. This family includes of course such timbres as the Melodia, Clarabella, Gedecht, etc.
The simplicity of these qualities tends to lessen the atmosphere of
angularity and edginess which are associate features of sharpening. The
choice for pedal stops here is Bourdon 16′ and Gedecht 8′.

Even the electrotonic instruments which are now making their appearance may be operated so as to furnish definite assistance to a chorus which
needs tonal suggestions.

In the use of both piano and organ, I have found it advantageous to
play a minimum of notes during off-pitch episodes. Sometimes the very
thickness of the chordal structure has a depressing effect on the vocal
sensibilities of a group, when it is, therefore, better to present only the
contour of the chord.

On rainy or very humid days, it is my custom, not only to transpose
compositions to a higher key, but to play all introductions and interludes
with high string and reed timbres predominating. This practice is designed
to keep the choir aware of the necessity of forward placing and high conception of notes, to offset the heaviness of the atmosphere.

On bright cold days when there is plenty of ozone in the air, I use the
flute-family of stops for the introductions and interludes in order to avoid
the mistake of creating too much brilliancy which the singers will emulate.

Flattening is associated in my experience with humidity and small
rooms, sharpening with invigorating, dry air and large resonant halls.

4. Both Faults in Unaccompanied Singing

(a) During Rehearsals

There is little to be added to the recommendations made throughout
this Chapter as to aiding a chorus to remain true to pitch during the
practice of *a cappella* music. The application of the principles and precepts
already emphasized should produce a consistent accuracy of pitch.

It should be insisted, however, that once the single parts of an *a
cappella* number have been learned, the piano should not be used, except
as an unobtrusive encouragement to a single line, when for a few measures
it may be used without harm, *an octave or two higher*.

Directors will facilitate true intonation of *a cappella* music by selecting
the pitch best suited to the room. Frequently directors use the pitch in the
rehearsal-hall which has been selected for the church or concert auditorium.
This may be a mistake, for if this selection be not in accord with acoustic
properties of the practice room, much time will be wasted in trying to hold

the unit to pitch, and a feeling of uncertainty will be created in their minds, which may imperil the public renditions.

(b) During Performances

In the actual presentation of *a cappella* music, the director must be prepared to wrestle with the urgent emergency created by a single choral unit abandoning the established pitch, while the rest of the singers adhere to it.

The synchronous descent of all the component parts, while offensive to true artistry, does not cause the cacophonous ugliness which shocks the ears when a single part is permitted to wander, *ex tempore,* rudderless in an alien key, while the others proceed with persevering steadfastness in the charted channel.

There is no equally embarrassing moment for the conductor of a chorus from which an artistic product is expected. In the earlier years of my professional career, I would become so bewildered at such unfortunate moments as to be altogether helpless. And I have observed many other conductors face the same predicament without graceful escape.

But after much experimenting, I have found that certain tactics can be used to relieve the burden of such vexatious situations. If it seem unlikely that the straying part can be quickly enticed back to the fold, there are two courses open to him to prevent a disastrous denouement. He can either subdue the nomads by reducing them to a faint *pianissimo,* raising the other parts to *fortissimo* prominence, or give the recalcitrants "their heads," signalling the other participants to withdraw altogether for a few measures, until a new pitch has been definitely established by the erring part, to which presently the rest of the ensemble can accommodate itself. Of the two courses, I prefer the latter as surer of redeeming the situation. In the former, it is feasible sometimes to rely upon the concordant parts to re-establish the pitch atmosphere while the discrepant line is quietly becoming aware of its transgression but generally, once a single part has clearly isolated itself from the ensemble, it is reasonable and in accord with experience to conclude that this part is intent upon creating a new pitch and that nothing can deter it from its purpose. Therefore, the better plan is to urge the erratic group to proclaim the new pitch loudly, while the others are silently listening. In polyphonic styles, which require consecutive leads, all mutually interdependent upon one another, the conductor is forced to allow a few discordant entries in order to keep the piece going, but if these entries be made *pianissimo,* and the voices discontinue their lines immediately upon the completion of the entries, the new pitch will quickly establish itself. Only a few seasons ago, the soprano chorus of the Paulist Choir took an excursive ramble from the pitch in the midst of an involved five-part number of Palestrina. The motet was pitched in C natural, but the sopranos made it evident that C# was more to their liking. Disaster threatened at a Solemn Pontifical Service. I sent the altos, tenors and basses first into an "echo" *pianissimo,* and then signalled them out, the while urging the sopranos to an unaccustomed *fortissimo.* The violence with which the *fortissimo* established C# as the pitch to be used arrested the attention of all the others, who, when signalled in, easily delivered their parts in the new pitch.

If the basses be the transgressors, the first course is as useful as the second, for by emphasizing the higher voices, while the basses are either tacit or jogging along *pianissimo,* the clarity of the more acute upper tones immediately influences the lower, except in choirs where the leading basses sing with a markedly sluggish and dark tone-quality.

The altos and tenors comprising the choral axis, and being thus intimately related, must be "given their heads" if either part deviate seriously.

Another device for escaping from this unpleasant situation is to have a small group of notably reliable singers appointed to take over the number by themselves, as soon as the director becomes certain of the danger symptoms. This, however, is not a generally feasible course since the cessation of all but a few voices in numbers traditionally sung by a complete chorus would disclose the trick.

There are, of course, certain specific resources which a director can use in public to dissuade singers from the particular faults which will cause deviation from pitch. Some conductors have developed extraordinary facility in preventing serious difficulty, by signalling a warning when any phrase has been sung carelessly. Thus if a descending progression has been sung with the notes too far apart, the conductor should immediately call attention to the fact by a prearranged signal. In this particular case, it is my custom to snap open several times, in rapid succession, the thumb and middle finger of the left hand; this warns the singers that they have done something which may soon cause flattening, at the same time urging them in the next upward progression to sing the notes far apart in order to bring the pitch back to the heart line. Likewise a signal for *staccato* will frequently circumvent the ill effect of a few ascending notes delivered *portamento.* By a slight gesture towards his chest the conductor can successfully admonish of unsatisfactory breath control,—as by touching his chin he can indicate that greater relaxation is needed in upper notes.

A resourceful conductor will learn from his own experience many expedients which he can inconspicuously employ on the podium. To bring to the attention of the singers that something is amiss and in need of immediate correction is one of the outstanding duties of a conductor. For public performances, he must become a master of foresight, sensitive to all hints of oncoming trouble and quick to diagnose all symptoms.

But the ability to sing accurately and steadily on pitch, under any and all circumstances, cannot be inculcated from the conductor's platform. It must be acquired in the rehearsal room and it depends altogether upon the intelligent, consistent, and uncompromising application of the principles and precepts expounded in this and preceding chapters.

CHAPTER VI

Dramatic Voices

A thorough understanding of dramatic voices, their training and use, is as essential to the master of chorophony as skill in the development of lyric voices.

It is argued in Chapter X that "the color scheme of a chorus determines the propriety of its repertoire," and accepting this as an elementary principle, it is clear that choruses lacking dramatic voices must confine themselves to non-dramatic forms. Just as relatively light voices and a minimum of emotional expression are necessary for *a cappella* polyphony, so the broader voices, vitalized with all the resources of dramatic imagery, are needed for the convincing performance of most modern compositions. There is, of course, an extensive repertoire of modern choral music which is marked by the restraint and emotional simplicity of the classic polyphony: short pieces like the Cherubic Hymns of Russia, the many lyric settings of "Ave Maria," "Ave Verum," etc. There are, too, notable episodes in the great dramatic oratorios, in which lyric, unimpassioned vocalism is clearly indicated, for example: "How Lovely Is Thy Dwelling Place" (Requiem, Brahms), the "Introit" (Requiem, Mozart), but the overwhelming majority of modern compositions requires dramaturgy and emotional personification for appropriate presentation.

Generally, the curve-line which the voices follow indicates the category of a number, as dramatic or non-dramatic. The curve-line of the modal music is regular and restricted. Verify this by looking at any page of Gregorian Chant in the "Liber Usualis" or any voice-line of Fifteenth or Sixteenth Century Polyphony. It may be said to have an almost unvarying *tessitura* prevailing from the beginning to the end of a composition in each voice line. But the curve line of modern music is characteristically irregular, unrestricted, and changeable. It indicates that the composer hoped for an intense manifestation of emotional reactions.

A casual glance at the score of Palestrina's "Stabat Mater" reveals calmness, restraint and simplicity of expression, while the pages of Rossini's setting of the same Sequence show the need of the full complement of musical dramatics.

Parenthetically, here, the writer urges choral directors to make the curve line a subject of serious study, for, as will be set forth in Volume II of this series, it is a most important factor in interpretation. The ease with which distortion of effect is achieved when one does not accept the hints offered by the curve line is well illustrated in Richard Wagner's edition of the Palestrina "Stabat Mater." Into the simple curve line of these gentle polyphonies the great genius of operatic expression read elements of music-drama, theatrical declamation and personal agitation which do not belong there. Witness his dynamic indications: the *subito fortissimos* following *pianissimos* without logical connection in the text or the music: the operatic contrast of first and second choirs chanting their horizontal lines *vertically* and with unseemly amplitude; the choice of a dynamic panel for narrating the death of Christ (Dum Emisit Spiritum) much more appropriate psychologically and aesthetically to the "Ride of the Valkyrie."

The writer admits that the precise degrees of conceived tonal amplitude by the polyphonic writers is ultimately a matter for conjecture. There is little of authentic information available. But it is clear that lyric voices are the proper medium for the older music and that dramatic voices prove their usefulness in the broader styles of modern composition.

Dramatic voices have assumed a gradually increasing importance since the middle of the Seventeenth Century, and beginning with the Wagnerian epoch they have been signally favored by the composers of operas, oratorio, and song-cycles.

One explanation for the ascendancy of dramatic singing may be found in the development of orchestral accompaniment, for the sonorous, multicolored and many-octaved instrumentation scored by modern composers provides a background against which light lyric voices could struggle only in vain.

But the fuller explanation is disclosed in the fact that the richest and most distinctive repertoire of modern music is an impressionistic dramatization of personal and emotional experience.

Perhaps the development of the modern dramatic voice would have occurred earlier if the Church had not been the chief custodian of the art of music. In the monasteries, music grew from the amorphous uncouthness of its pre-Christian state into the symmetrical shapeliness of a definite art. Monks watched over it; Levites sang it; its exercise was guarded and guided by ecclesiastical legislation. Considering the fact, furthermore, that the Church consistently excluded the expression of intense emotion from the liturgy and limited the solo-performance of chanters to short phrases, it is clear that dramatic singing, as we know it, was not suited to Her purposes, and therefore not cultivated.

The function of the chorus in the era of the Greek tragedy would imply some degree of dramatic utterance. Certainly, upon such occasions as the Feast of Bacchus, the coryphaeus would elicit dramatic outbursts from the chorus, but generally, the *probasis* (recitation or commentary by the chorus) was probably given with the restraint which we associate, rightly or wrongly, with the lyricism of the Athenians.

There is good reason, too, for surmising that the "scrop" of Central Europe, and the minstrel of Western Europe, entertained the bourgeoisie of the Middle Ages with full-toned and theatric singing of their verses, but probably the average musician considered such singing mere ostentation vulgarly irrelevant to the serious and aesthetic aspects of the art.

It is reasonable therefore to associate the cultivation of dramatic singing and of solo voices with the growth of the operatic style. Good music, until the Seventeenth Century, avoided the expression of passion. But the new school of Galilei, Peri, Gagliano and Monteverdi, concerned itself mainly with the oratorical expression of words in full passionate declamation. The ideals of their new era seemed to be these: the inflections of the voice in dramatic singing should be regulated by the best principles of rhetoric; whatever the spoken word would reveal upon the lips of an orator, the sung word should reveal upon the lips of a singer.

Thus, rhetoric and music becoming intimately associated, a new style of vocalism began, of necessity, to grow. This association produced the modern school of dramatic music and the type of voices and instruments necessary to its performance.

Dramatic singers of distinction, therefore, are notable for the emotional breadth and timbre of their voices, at the same time excelling in all phases of the art of histrionic utterance.

The aim of the tutor is thus twofold: he must engender a fine sense of rhetorical delivery, and he must lead the singers to a free use of all the dramatic agencies of the vocal apparatus.

This twofold responsibility is obviously the obligation also of choral directors who undertake to interpret the great modern choral masterpieces. Many choral directors prefer to conduct the dramatic types of compositions. Perhaps they do not suspect the reason, which frequently is merely because it is easier to substitute a counterfeit (satisfactory to themselves) for dramatic effect than to disguise the tonal and interpretative inadequacies of mediocre polyphonic (lyric) singing.

This is noteworthy:—One of the outstanding causes for the general deterioration of choral singing is found in the unwitting substitutions which many directors make for the qualities of legitimate drama.

Their substitutions are, of course, vehemence, excitation, and melodrama. Drama, in speech and in song, is essentially the portrayal of a scene, the describing of an event, the stressing of hopes or ideals, the manifestation of emotional reactions. It appropriately invokes noise, agitation and frenzy only when these, in proper degree, are indispensable to the convincing depiction of the dramatic intention.

In the theatre, soi-disant actors who always over-declaim, strutting about and employing extravagant but inept histrionics, are known as "ham actors," but their cousins-german, the soi-disant dramatic singers whose only interpretative resource is excessive quantity of tone, have unfortunately escaped a by-word of reproach. If the ratio of pseudo-singers to orthodox artists were not higher than the ratio of "hams" to fine actors, there would be little justification for deriding them. But music is more sorely plagued than the theatre. The influence of sham Thespians upon the stage is negligible, but the influence of bombast upon music, and particularly upon vocal and choral music, is becoming critical.

Subtlety is required to convey the finer nuances of emotion in dramatic music, but there seems to be a minimum of this in contemporary exhibitions. Exhibitionism and subtlety are ill-mated partners. Throughout the musical arena the bacilli of *forte* and *fortissimo* wax epidemic, and the choral masterpieces of yesterday and today succumb to stertorous and lethal attacks.

The basic dogma for a conductor to accept here is that dramatic expression does not concern itself exclusively with loudness or vehemence. It concerns itself, first, and more frequently with *color, intensity, duration* (rubato), and then only with *quantity*. Without these primary qualities controlled and employed with deftness, *art* invites, for any performance, the old Latin sneer "Vox et praeterea nihil" (mere sound).

Therefore, the conductor-tutor must know how to assist his singers in the acquisition of these qualities.

Given a lyric voice, carefully nurtured to its full meed of lyric grace:— can such a voice be developed further—out and beyond the properties of lyric vocalism—to the broader requirements of dramatic singing?

Having in mind the prevailing misconception of the word "dramatic," I aver emphatically—NO!

One of the reiterations of this treatise has been that dramatic sopranos (in the sense of *loud* sopranos) may safely be lyricized (i.e. softened), but that naturally light voices can never essay to transmigrate into the quantitative character of "dramatics" without permanent sacrifice of quality.

Considering the almost universal misinterpretation of the essentials of dramatic singing, I have deemed it wise up to this point, to insist on this dictum, without qualification. But, having made clear that drama in singing is not synonymous with excessive quantity of tone, it is safe to modify this insistence and to admit that there are dramatic qualities which even typically lyric voices can acquire, although these are obviously fewer and more restricted than the full complement of theatrical singing which lies within the natural endowment of the greater voices.

I mean specifically that the effective resources of emotional consciousness, color-variation, and intensity can be added readily to the singing of even the lightest voices, although, as it is noted in another Chapter,[1] the voices of boys lose a certain praeternatural charm if they be exploited for dramatic effect.

The first step here is evidently to indicate how lyric voices may assume the fundamental virtues of more convincing expression, and later to discuss the technique by which the broader, properly designated dramatic voices may acquire vigor, high pressure, resolution and ardor without embracing the burlesques of Gargantuan mimicry.

How may one reasonably hope to re-create the floating, lucid tones of lyric sopranos, which compare favorably with the vocalism of trained boys, into sounds which convey at once the primary quality of dramatic singing, i.e., a sense of personal cognizance of emotional experience.

Obviously the first step does not concern itself with mere vocal exercise. It has to do, rather, with the training of the singers to incarnate the varying moods of the script, and by meditation upon the principal ideas revealed there, to learn to declaim the text with unmistakable evidence of having been moved by it. Thus the first task is to accustom singers to *think* and *speak* consistently with the thought of the composer. It is by no means impossible to increase the dramatic utterance of even the most placid stoics, if this be the starting point. "Nemo dat quod non habet"—"no one gives what he has not"—is a celebrated truism. But it is equally self-evident that one may acquire, by the insistence of habitual effort, what at a given moment is lacking.

Experience avers to all connoisseurs of art that many skilled executants are merely natural technicians, lacking the "It" which modern parlance has chosen as its ripest word for romantic, dynamic and "over the footlights" appeal. Others acquire technique by much effort—but tech-

[1] See Chapter VII, "The Color Scheme."

nique only. Many are without spontaneous resources of self-revelation. But this does not imply that if teachers knew and practised psychology as well as Czerny's Five Finger Exercises, they could not pilot their students to a reservoir where there is plenty of "It."

One of the oldest sophistries about the exercise of the musical art is that only those who have lived up and down the whole gamut of human experience, happily and unhappily, now recklessly intriguing, now repenting in tears, now elated and anon depressed, can give voice to the moods which composers will to be expressed. If such a tenet were psychologically true, the price of artistic performance would be disastrous. Certainly, if a soprano can sing the seductiveness of *Manon* only after trying personally to allure an ineligible *Des Grieux,* Massenet's lovely music should be eliminated from operatic repertoire. It cannot be true that the only baritones who are equipped to give a convincing portrayal of *Iago* in *Otello* must be themselves adepts in fraud and falsification. Does an authoritative reading of Straus' *Salome* or Charpentier's *Louise* require a conductor whose musical perspicacity and emotional understanding have been stimulated to virtuosity by aphrodisiacs? No, it is not necessary "to have lived" as the adage holds for successful interpretation. It is necessary only to have surveyed mentally the emotional wellsprings of each episode to be rendered, and being thus in tune with the state of mind or emotions indicated, to enact this, first in speech and later in song, as sincerely and intensively as possible.

A soloist or a group of singers must first be under the spell of the mood of a song before changes of vocal timbre, intensity or dynamics will prove effective. Singers must and can readily learn to put themselves literally in the control of the song-mood, thus relinquishing to the subconsciousness the task of selecting the appropriate vocal elements. The subconsciousness is man's treasury of aspirations, sympathies, impressions and aesthetic sensibilities, and in the ratio of its manifestation through a voice is there drama in its singing.

On several occasions I have converted loud singers into dramatic singers by just such coaching.

I remember a large festival chorus which I was rehearsing in Verdi's "Requiem": the "Dies Irae," "Sanctus" and "Libera" give singers unexcelled opportunities for what they conceive to be dramatic effects. At the first rehearsal, there was plenty of noise but no drama. The terror of human souls contemplating the dire possibilities of Judgment Day ("Dies Irae") and the shock of the great Trumpet of the Angel summoning all men to the Throne were not even suggested. I set about inculcating an appreciation of what the immortal poem expresses so graphically. Presently, I directed the group to *think the text intensively while singing it pianissimo.* The appearance of the dramatic elements was immediate, and when in later rehearsals and at the performance, I invoked the full quantitative resources of chorus and orchestra, the effect was overwhelming. I think that I shall always be moved by the recollection of the hysterical "Salva Me" (Save Me, O Lord) which came through those five hundred voices from five hundred hearts and minds.

I have heard innumerable performances of Antonio Lotti's eight-part "Crucifixus." Although this *a cappella* masterpiece belongs to the early era of impressionistic singing, there is a great need for dramatic expression in the *crescendo poco a poco* of the individual parts as they picture to listeners what is implied by the single word "Crucifixus" (He was Crucified). I have seldom heard more than an increase of quantity in this *crescendo;* this mere increase of noise is not only unconvincing, it is distressing, because the sequence of dissonances in progress sounds positively ugly, if the intensity and sincerity of the singing is not immediately manifest. With the word "Crucifixus" deeply felt and expressed with rising awe, the dissonances make a different effect—they establish an impression of horror that Jesus Christ could have been really crucified.

While seeking real drama in performances with mixed choruses, it has been my experience to learn that many alleged dramatic singers are not only reluctant but positively afraid to give intimation of dramatic effects. They find it difficult to forget themselves and take on the temper of mind appropriate to the portrayal. Self-consciousness is inhibitive of sincere and convincing performance of a role. Dramatic choral compositions require the ensemble to assume and vividly to depict emotional roles just as insistently as individual parts in the theatre demand proper delineation from the *dramatis personae.*

Therefore the singers must be taught to think, read and declaim dramatically, without self-consciousness; applying to their speaking intonations, all the undulations, varying intensities, and oratorical eloquence which the emotional and rhetorical content of the piece require.

If they cannot *speak* the text with telling effect, they will be unable to sing it dramatically. And so, in the preparation of great dramatic cantatas, or the rehearsing of motets and anthems which portray the agitation of human emotions, singers must be content for awhile to be students of theatrical elocution.

Having acquired an adequate concept of the dramatic elements involved, the singers are prepared to study the musical elements and to correlate both. If the histrionic needs of the text be appreciated thoroughly and with artistic sympathy, the singers will instinctively use the colors which in their individual voices are best suited to serve these.

The "Color-Scheme" dictates [1] that the conductor stress the proper timbres in the interpretation of all types of music, but in the candidly dramatic forms, in which impersonation, emotional reaction, and delineation of impulse are the paramount features, there is nothing gained by insisting that the individual singers try to emphasize any one timbre. Probably in such compositions, all the timbres of the choral spectrum are needed to carry across to listeners the full reaction of the ensemble to the moods which are being unfolded.

In dramatic portrayals, the absorption of the singers in the preoccupation of recreating a scene or a mood makes it impossible for them to invoke any but the primary timbres of their voices. To super-impose the effort of copying other timbres would distract them from the contemplation of the picture which they are painting. If it be opportune to emphasize a certain timbre, the conductor has merely to stress the contribution of the proper voices.

However, an important item to be noted here is the homogeneity of tone-quality which must be developed and maintained throughout the compass of the various voices if dramatic expression is to conform to the primary principles of art. Evenness and affinity of colors must prevail between the upper and lower registers of all the singers, especially the dramatic sopranos and basso-cantantes. Germaneness and consistency between higher and lower timbres must be conserved at all times in superior solo or ensemble singing, but conductors are often tempted to allow singers to abandon this principle when the elan of climactic moments seizes upon their histrionic instincts, and high notes of one category are immediately followed by low notes of another. Piercing high trumpet tones give way suddenly to widespread sounds or guttural convulsions when the soprano part plummets to the depths as in the title role of "Carmen," and Escamillo's boisterous straining at the high braggadocio of the Toreador ridicules itself in the husky *stroh* of the nadir or the disappointing adynamy of the low focal points of the main tune.

The continuity of color which art requires to be maintained between the various registrations of voices cannot be sacrificed without loss. Even in the distraction which the excitement of arresting drama engenders, a cultured audience does not overlook or condone gross neglect of this matter.

[1] See Chapter VII, "The Color Scheme."

The unrestrained pursuit of theatrical authority in the performance of cantatas and oratorios with almost total disregard of the prerogatives of the purely vocal factors, has neutralized the efforts of many choral societies. Therefore, the conductor must at all times be in control as a modifying and moderating influence.

In the use of their natural vocal tints, except as indicated above, trained singers will probably not project tonal qualities at variance with the dramatic presentation in progress, while, on the contrary, the animation and resolution which are impelling them will readily excite them to an excess of quantity.

The principles underlying the degrees of quantity to be used under various circumstances furnish an important and interesting detail for study in Volume II, in connection with the general resources of interpretation. It is relevant here merely to refer to them as a restraining influence, considering the ease with which singers, and particularly dramatic singers slip into an unwitting use of redundant amplitude. Frequently the dramatic effect of solo and ensemble numbers is thwarted by the application of decibels of quantity which are not only superfluous but destructive of the aesthetic propriety which must always prevail. In bold and striking passages, whether they be climaxes, processions to or recessions from climaxes, both singers and instrumental players are wont to deliver their parts in the loud tones of their most intense dynamic panels. Frequently, therefore, the quantitative growth which should mark the gradual rise to a climax is prevented, preliminary movements and sentences having been set forth with the totality of sonorousness without a decibel withheld. Obviously, the high degrees of intensity and amplitude must be reserved for the high points of the context, otherwise an idiomatic constitution of drama, i.e. progressive movement towards a point of maximum importance, is infringed.

An important obligation of the director is, therefore, to establish a policy of strict economy in the expenditure of dynamic energy. The idiom of each dramatic concept will be preserved and prospered and the proper vocalization of the singers well served, if the director err by niggardliness rather than by extravagance in this connection.

A fine feeling for *rubato* should be cultivated among dramatic singers. A slight *accelerando* or *rallentando,* the shortening or prolonging of a particular note—and a graceful counterbalance between these factors of interpretation—will often determine the subtlety of dramatic effect. The study of *rubato* as an interpretative resource will be undertaken in Volume II, but it is well to advert to the point here, for in the preparation of a chorus for the broader forms of ensemble singing, an understanding and appreciation of this grace should be early inculcated.

The foregoing considerations may succinctly be epitomized as emphasizing the need of teaching dramatic singers the art of preoccupying themselves with texts, pictures, and moods; the maintenance at all levels of dramatic utterance and at all pitches in accordance and affinity between upper, medium, and lower registers; and, of paramount consequence, the tempering and control of the appetite for loudness and stridor which convert drama into melodrama, tragedy into burlesque and comedy into farce.

CHAPTER VII

The Color Scheme

There are evidently many possible groupings of voices for ensemble singing. These constitute as many different species of choruses. It is clear then that in addition to the general principles and precepts of chorophony which must be applied to all singing groups, a certain special technique must be introduced for each species.

Thus a small chorus of female voices presenting different features, requires different direction from a large chorus of male voices.

But the particular precepts which are addressed to particular types of choruses are fixed-upon as guiding corollaries to major and general conclusions. Thus, in the presentation of the point of view and subject matter of this Chapter, which are doubtless novel and even naive to many a *laudator temporis acti* who has guided choruses for decades through *mezzo-forte* fogs, *forte* sleets, and *fortissimo* gales (without ever suspecting the mystical tenuities of music or its habit of recreating in the rainbow), it is practicable to consider the color scheme principally in its relations to a standard S.A.T.B. chorus and the idiosyncrasies of sung polyphony. Probably the inspection of the subject in broader aspects will be adequate, for conclusions deduced can readily be modified and adapted to the particular composition of non-standard units.

The reader is invited to investigate the potential color scheme of an S.A.T.B. chorus; first, the standard "mixed" group employing women in the soprano and alto lines and secondly the liturgical choir comprising boys and men only.

Contrary to the procedure in harmonic analyses, in which attention is first directed to the bass, the examination of the elements which contribute to choral color should begin at the top, i.e. with the soprano lines. Generally, the first feature of ensemble singing to which a listener adverts is the high line, frequently because it is also the melodic line, but chiefly because the trebles maintain the highest tessitura of the chorus, and the higher the tessitura, the more there is, according to the physics of sound, to arrest the attention. A note impinging upon the ear drum with 880 vibrations to the second is a more aggressive candidate for immediate attention than a note with 440, granted that both are sounded with equal force.

In the matter of quality and color, one must therefore begin with the *high sopranos,* for they more than the others determine the grade to which a chorus is entitled, good, bad, or merely and intolerably mediocre. A choir can get on if it have good sopranos (and an imaginative director who knows how to dress them up with the tinsel of interpretative subterfuge), even if the other voices be inadequate. But the converse, however, is not true. The utterance of the sopranos is the first separable element of a choral ensemble to be discerned, just as a spire or roof line is the first separable detail to register with the eye upon beholding an architectural ensemble.

Therefore, the chromatics of soprano timbres are now set up for spectrum analysis and their aptness for polyphonic portraiture.

The average choral director seems to find meagre resources of color in a soprano chorus. Indifference and inattention to the many timbres available to the average chorus may have created a state of choral color-blindness, for it is difficult to explain the monotony of lackluster neutrality which characterizes modern chorophony, if the conductors were mentally or aurally aware of the variety of quality-tints assembled under their metronomic batons. As the magician's wand is a symbol for the quasi-miraculous, so the conductor's baton should be the token of super-musicianship, but, unfortunately, it does not honestly symbolize a notable degree of aesthetic perspicacity or artistic understanding; it is nothing of a token; it is only a stick of wood, a slender sliver marking time beats with the virtuosity and romanticism of a pendulum.

The baton poised over the average mixed chorus today should command, control and co-ordinate almost as many treble tone-colors as the baton of the symphonic conductor. If a conductor be a *bona fide* monochromist, executing his representations in one color, he has a natural restriction in this matter, and should therefore (if, having accidentally arrived, it be necessary to remain in the musical arena) confine himself consistently to the silhouette type of depiction. Gregorian Chant, many modern anthems, as well as American and British settings of textual platitudes or fustian jargon which need no color to set them forth should comprise his repertoire.

There are many timbres in the average soprano chorus. Sometimes special circumstances account for a notable lack of treble colors. Thus a choir of nuns who have sung for a number of years together, in the impersonal manner of the convent, will be found less richly endowed than the average chorus of externs.

The great composers of choral music recognized that many soprano timbres are available, as may be readily concluded from a study of their vocal scores. Any chorus director can discover this for himself by listening intently to the individual voices of his group.

The traditional classification of sopranos into the dramatic, lyric and coloratura, is inadequate for the complete needs of choral direction, for in each of these species, there are various timbres and modifications of tone-color. The threefold classification, therefore, should be considered as preliminary to a wider diversification. In the two lighter types, the lyric and coloratura, there are voices which are analogous to the sounds of flutes. Others show resemblance to string-tones; some intimate a combination of string and flute, and a smaller number suggests very light reed tones. The lyric species will usually include still further resemblances, notably in the middle-register, to the clarinet. In the group of dramatic sopranos, the sturdier and bolder colors reveal themselves, a broader string-tone throughout the entire range than was found among the lighter voices, an increase of analogy to the reeds, the French horn color, and finally a timbre not dissimilar to the lighter tones of the trumpet.

In an average group of thirty female sopranos, almost all of the tone-colors enumerated above will be found. Sometimes there seems to be a larger percentage of voices of the dramatic type than of the lyric and coloratura, but careful testing of the individual singers often reveals that many are forcing their voices, trying to sing out of their proper category. The greater *quantity* of tone which is thus achieved frequently deceives the listener as to the *natural* quality of a voice. Therefore the chorus master should conduct his survey of the soprano chorus quietly, not permitting any singer, in the first examination, to extend herself beyond *mezzo-forte*.

The purpose of the chorus master in this examination, is of course to ascertain the *status-quo* of his soprano color-scheme. If it be more limited than is usual, he faces at the outset the necessity of extending it, by inviting additional singers or by developing the missing timbres by specially devised vocal exercises. If the personnel of the soprano choir be a fixed group, permitting few changes or additions, and if it seems impossible to cultivate the missing timbres, he must study the problem of repertoire for elimination because it is obvious that such a soprano section is not adequate to the demands of all schools of choral composition. For instance, if eighty percent of the sopranos have the broad, dramatic, horn and quasi-trumpet tone, and the choirmaster cannot bring them under such control as to lyricize their intonations at will, he is not justified in attempting most of the polyphonic music of the fifteenth, sixteenth and early seventeenth centuries. De Lasso, Palestrina, Soriano, Vittoria, Lotti and their contemporaries are affronted, frustrated and gratuitously misrepresented by sopranos who cannot employ the light flute-string-oboe-combinations.

The broader timbres rob the soprano lines in this style of music of the mysticism which is its outstanding characteristic. The *a cappella* polyphony must *float*. There must be nothing of the "earth, earthy" about it, and in much of it a soprano tone-quality approximating the diaphanous is essential. The writer insists on this, being well aware that in continental Europe, where the Palestrinesque music is sung more often than elsewhere, the soprano timbre generally employed is robust, brawny, consciously self-assertive and athletic! Perhaps this is the primary reason why continued performance of the polyphonic style has failed to impress the modern world generally with its intrinsic beauty. That Palestrina conceived the current continental timbre as the proper soprano-tone quality for disclosing the disembodied spirituality of most of his music is incredible. If one "looks and listens" while almost any European choir is at work on the polyphonies of the great master, the disparity between what the eye can see in the score and what the ear experiences is distressingly convincing. The acoustics of the great cathedrals have helped to make the utterance of these choirs less annoying than they would be if singing in a parish church or a concert hall of average dimensions. There is no doubt that as the seventeenth century progressed, after Vecchi, Peri and Monteverdi—the rise of opera affected the style of vocalism. Dramatic expression was the aim of every singer. Vocalists were no longer interested in creating "a certain atmosphere on which the spirit floats" (Pyne on "Palestrina"); their enthusiasm was directed to the expression of personal and romantic emotion as *intensely* as their vocal aptitude would permit. Thus the timbres of voices which prevailed in the ecclesiastical era were superseded by the qualities suited for operatic expression. The former choral art—at least, as far as it is concerned with vocal timbres—was forgotten. For several generations there was little attention given to the polyphonic style, even in the choir of the Sistine Chapel. It remained for Abbe Baini to reintroduce the great Masses and motets of Palestrina in the early nineteenth century. By that time it is probable that the operatic vocalism had become a fixed consciousness

and that there was little likelihood of restoring the vocalism of the polyphonic period. Secular music had robbed the choral singing of its purer
forms, both in the structure of compositions and in the manner of singing.
According to Zoe Pyne in his "Palestrina, His Life and Times," p. 175
"—it is a matter for regret that musicians have so often failed to perceive the innate divergence of religious and secular ideals. The Latin
races, particularly, have sinned in this respect and even today, in spite of
a determined effort towards purification, it is possible to visit churches
celebrated for the beauty of their music, and to hear "O Salutaris Hostia"
sung with exactly the same sentiment and colouring as would be suitable
in a performance of the Preislied."

It is unlikely that Pope Pius IV would have made the following comment upon hearing the Mass in honor of Pope Marcellus (June 29,
1565), if the modern tone quality had been used by the singers: "These
must have been the strains which John the Apostle heard in the heavenly
Jerusalem, and which another John (Giovanni Pierluigi da Palestrina)
has renewed in that of earth." [1]

Futility damns the enterprise of any conductor who essays to perform
Palestrina with robust soprano-tone. The lovely intricacies, independences
and horizontal processes become "like sweet bells jangled, out of tune and
harsh."

Nor is such futility confined to compositions of strictly spiritual character. Until a very recent date, the art of madrigal singing was allowed
to lapse. The naive attractiveness of the texts and music of the madrigals,
ballets and "ayres" of the Tudor period have probably interested conductors ever since they were composed. But I personally never heard a
convincing, graceful, consistently artistic performance of this style of
music (although I had listened to many efforts both in America and in
Europe) until Dr. Edward H. Fellowes and Mr. Cuthbert Kelly combined forces to produce the enchanting singing of the "English Singers."
Among the outstanding qualities of this admirable sextet, is the lyric
quality of its vocalism. The structure of the Tudor madrigal being polyphonic, and the texts, although frequently romantic, being passionless
and ingenuous, the high colouring of broad dramatic tone-quality is necessarily intrusive. "Madrigals are generally," writes Charles Kennedy Scott
in "Madrigal Singing," "of a light type of fancy, and so weighty tone is
not appropriate to their expression . . . the settled pompousness of a
heavy voice has little in common with the airy freedom of a madrigal, nor
will it delineate a madrigal on the purely musical side."

[1] Cf. Graf's edition of Missa Papae Marcelli.

On the other hand, a choirmaster cannot successfully address himself to the dramatic repertoire, if his soprano chorus comprise only lyric voices. A breadth of tone which can carry over to the listener the sense of strong personal feeling and of intimate emotional experience is necessary for a convincing performance of a large and effective part of the choral repertoire. In the field of sacred music, especially of non-liturgical music, i.e. compositions not conceived primarily as part of the liturgical ritual, there is a wealth of material which a chorus deficient in the heavier timbres must let alone by every criterion of artistry. The greater part of the "German Requiem" by Brahms, in spite of its content of majestic music, would be inane, sterile, and namby-pamby if sung by sopranos possessed only of flute-like voices. Frequently, too, the tonal requirements of one work vary, just as the moods of the text and music vary. In the great composition just cited, the need of multiple timbres is apparent.

The elucidation of this point of view could be made most convincing by the submission to the reader of a survey of the many tone-qualities required for the proper presentation of standard oratorio choruses. But it seems sufficient merely to direct the choirmaster's attention to this primary approach to choral virtuosity, leaving a survey of the field to his own enterprise. Even a casual perusing of the choruses in the "German Requiem" should reveal that the qualities admirably suited to the text and musical structure of the second chorus "All flesh is as the grass" are equally unsuited to the fourth chorus "How lovely is Thy dwelling place, O Lord!" Nor is much study required to convince that the fugal chorus "All We Like Sheep" and the other fugues of the "Messiah" must be set forth with almost pure string-tone while the "Hallelujah Chorus" depends for the majesty of its potential effect upon the complete diapason of vocal elements.

The necessary tone-color is determined by the nature of the text and its musical setting, and to some extent by the technical requirements of a particular musical form. A fundamental need in the presentation of fugues is elasticity. In the orchestra this is achieved most fluently by the string choirs, and the application of the string-tone to the soprano lines in all such numbers as the choral fugues of Handel and the "Singet den Herrn" of Bach, gives a *mechanical* ease to their performance which cannot be achieved with the heavier timbres. A new school of fugal playing began to flourish among organists when a distinguished artist of Philadelphia startled a convention of organists by departing from the tradition of playing complete fugues with a heavy diapason registration. He presented the various contrapuntal lines each with its own color, each color being relatively light, and all tending to create clarity and elasticity in the ensemble effect. A few conservatives murmured that Bach himself used the diapasons. The obvious answer to that objection is that the organ in Bach's day was a limited instrument, the art of pipe-organ voicing not having advanced to its present state. In further rebuttal to such a reactionary challenge, it must be pointed out that the choir at St. Thomas Schule in Leipzig which Bach directed and for which he composed so many cantatas and motets, most likely employed a string-like tone in the soprano-section, for even in the writer's memory the choristers there have given evidence of a tradition in this regard. A quarter of a century ago, the St. Thomas sopranos had still a dominantly string-timbre and were thus clearly differentiated from the soprano boys of other continental choirs, in which an unmodified raucous "chest-tone" was the prevailing and unwieldy quality.

The comments of musicians who have failed to place the choral art in its proper perspective and have thus remained unaware of its great resources, upon being asked to make the color-scheme the basis for their training and conducting, can readily be imagined: "the chorus is not a symphony orchestra," "sopranos are not reasonably to be paralleled with flutes, oboes, strings and horns," "such similitudes are profitless," "is a choirmaster to have several groups of sopranos, each group singing only when its particular effect is desired?" etc., etc. If it were not the writer's conviction, predicated upon many years' close study of choral conditions, that the average choral conductor *honestly* misjudges the actual mediocrity of his work, he would be obliged to designate such likely comments as captious and sententious. But a great many phases of the choral art have failed to arrest the attention of the average master of choristers, for musicians generally have not felt the need of developing their aesthetic perspicacity in the direction of choral understanding. Therefore we should not be chagrined at the reluctance of choirmasters to accept what is to them a new viewpoint—at its initial presentation. With persevering study of all the objective elements of chorophony, the majority will inevitably adopt the color-scheme as a fundamental dogma of choral musicianship, and address themselves to the technical processes by which it is developed, as well as to the principles of interpretation which regulate its use. Here is an important premise which should guide every choirmaster: Voices of the lighter colors *cannot* be safely broadened to include *all* the dramatic elements, on one hand, but, on the other, the dramatic voices can be so exercised as to function as lyrics when necessary. The lyricizing of the broader voices does *not* involve the destruction of the dramatic elements.

The principle to be deduced from the foregoing discussion will be designated in this monograph as:—

Principle No. 1. "The color-scheme of a chorus determines the propriety of its repertoire."

We proceed next to bring under examination the sopranos of a liturgical choir, i.e. a choir of boys and men. The procedure here is not so simple as in the examination of female voices, because the *status quo* in which almost any group of boys will be found is not their natural vocal condition, but a condition consequent to serious abuses both in speaking and singing. Only after the successful application of the Five Stages of vocal training which are set forth in an important chapter in these pages,[1] will the choirmaster who had not previously specialized in boy-choirs discern for himself the tone-qualities natural to *boy-sopranos.* The average American boy sings badly. Therefore he is asked to take on faith, at this point, the few considerations here presented.

But boy-sopranos can give forth more beautiful sounds than any other singers.

For intrinsic loveliness, mystical intimation and ethereal grace, there is no other voice equally endowed. *A priori,* as the philosophers have it, i.e. considering the nature of a boy, one would be led to suspect that his vocalism would be ideal. His biology and psychology concur to offer him a singing voice free from the suggestions of personal consciousness, unhampered by the indications of strong emotional experience, and fresh with the buoyancy of childhood. The qualities admirable and desirable in certain types of music indicate the limits to which his vocal efficacy can be properly extended. The boy's vocal usefulness is largely if not altogether in one direction, and the proper conduct of a boys' choir depends upon clear perception of this.

Here is a primary *caveat!* Musicians must not approach the task of training a choir of boy-trebles, as if the boys were substitutes for female sopranos, required by liturgical tradition or ecclesiastical legislation. The boy must be analyzed as a specific musical instrument possessed of inherent and distinctive qualities. Boys ante-date women in the functions of soprano choristers. The history of music attests that boys were principals, not make-shifts, in all the stricter forms of public worship. Their selection is approved by sound reasons of aesthetic propriety. Doubtless, other reasons contributed to the establishment of this tradition, notably, the fact that women were considered ineligible for ecclesiastical service in

---

[1] See Chapter III, "The Five Stages."

the liturgy of Israel as well as in the liturgy of the Christian Church which
raised the office of the ecclesiastical singer to the rank of a Levite, this
office being attainable only by the male sex. Perhaps, too, as Edward
Dickinson has written in his "Music in the History of the Western
Church,"—the association of men and women in so emotional an office
as that of song was not considered desirable.

But, conceding that there were reasons other than musical which
argued for the establishment of boy-choirs as the ecclesiastical norm, it
is abundantly evident that the greatest musicians of the pre-operatic era
sensed important qualities in the voices of boys which are not idiocratic to
the voices of women. All the composers up to the conclusion of the polyphonic era assigned soprano parts from one point of view; those who followed, except in Russia and Greece, and excepting, too, the small minority
still concerned with the church style, considered the soprano line from
another point of view, and consistently wrote in congruous idioms. The
concepts of the two eras, the aesthetic purposes, the instrumentalities
were different. Boys were the sopranos (aided sometimes, in the Avigon
and post-Avignon periods of the Papal Choir, by adult male sopranos)
of the earlier era, women of the later. Palestrina's music bespeaks the
boy's voice, while the woman's voice is immeasurably more effective in
the music of Brahms.

The essential difference of quality in the soprano voices of boys and
women is emphasized by female dramatic singers. Acoustically, there is
little difference between the genres of tones of boys and female lyrics. The
emotional modifications which the dramatic soprano brings to her singing render her less suitable to *a cappella* music than to the colorful im-
pressionism of the Brahms School.

A choirmaster, therefore, who remains unaware of this essential difference will probably never bring a chorus of boys to a state of artistic
efficacy.

The writer is not concerned here with the debate that has waxed
vigorously for many decades as to the greater or lesser desirability of boys'
or women's choirs from considerations of expediency and the like. The
arguments *pro* and *con* on this mooted point are inconsequential at the
moment, for respective degrees of interest, enthusiasm, and concentration,
and therefore dependability, are not under consideration. Nor is it
opportune to discuss their relative reliability as to laryngeal conditions.
Certain facts in these connections present themselves from time to time
in this treatise, such as the readiness with which boys can acquire tonal
control, correct intonation in both equal and unequal temperaments,—

technical security, ease, and dexterity—interpretative elasticity—linear clarity and linear independence in the polyphonic forms—spontaneity in sensing the propriety and need of dynamic variations, and easy blend with the other choral lines.

The potential color-scheme of boy-sopranos is the point in discussion, and the premise is that there is a radical difference between boy-sopranos and dramatic women-sopranos. Therefore, the color-schemes will not be identical. But the singing of young lyric female sopranos can be made surprisingly similar to that of trained boys.

The definition of both the artistic potentialities and limitations is set by nature herself, as well for the boys as for the dramatics. Of course there are some elements of tonal utterance common to all sopranos, and thus the fundamental principles of vocal training must be applied to all without much modification. These common elements are paralleled by the identity in the "speaking" processes of different organ pipes; e.g. all flue pipes of eight foot pitch share certain structural features. These are dictated by the scientific formulae of the physics of sound. But in spite of these shared features, it is perfectly obvious that each different family of eight foot flues—diapason, string, flute—speaks with altogether different effect on the aesthetic sensibilities of the listeners. Sounds of a string quality, by reason of more active partials, make a more poignant impression than the lazy roundness of flute tones. No organist would escape impeachment for the indiscriminate use of organ registers merely because many of these are of identical pitch and approximate quantitative equality. Culture demands that he select his registration according to the compatibility of a timbre with the contour of a composition and the acoustics of the place where he performs.

The mystical characteristics of boys' voices which render them most suitable for unaccompanied polyphonic singing, must be approximated by the lyric sopranos of any mixed chorus attempting the Palestrinesque style.

Boy-sopranos and women-sopranos are flute-reed instruments of eight foot pitch. One group can be made to approximate the other in such matters as breath-control (with advantage frequently on the boys' side), range (although women-sopranos have better low notes), flexibility and correctness of intonation.

In the matter of color, the emotional difference manifests itself. Continuing to use the illustration of instruments and organ pipes, it may be said that the boy must be considered as properly effective only as flute, light string, light reed, and soft horn, whereas the spectrum of women-sopranos includes properly all colors and modifications of color possible to mechanical instruments except, of course, the instruments of percussion, plectrum, and frets.

Boys are restricted to the much more limited modifications of color for psycho-physiological reasons.

The physical estates of the two genera of sopranos are totally different. The glandular activities are not the same.

The whole being—body, conscious mind, sub-conscious mind, emotional fabric and nervous system reveals itself through the sensitive vibrating cords of the larynx. If the psychology of the boy were the same, generally, as the psychology of the woman, one would expect, generally, the boy's throat to give utterance to tones like the woman's, but if his psychology be different, naturally, one must look for different utterances.

The boy is in the psychological state proper to a child. In one sense, before puberty, he is much farther removed from the maturity of the man than the girl from the maturity of the woman. Even in infancy the boy is less self-conscious than the girl. His nature is to undergo major modifications at adolescence, and his throat will mark these changes by a physiological transformation. The girl's nature will rather develop than undergo change, and her throat will attest this fact by merely growing, escaping the anatomical readjustments of her brother.

All this, precisely, means that nature fits boys to express something of a different order than women, something less personal—something correspondingly less physical—something approaching the metaphysical—something, in the subtle intimations of beautiful singing, approaching disembodied spirituality.

The fullness of life seems to strive for expression in women's singing.

The high nobility of the maternal instinct is there to enrich every note with a personal, warm, thoroughly human character which is impossible to the boy—and which would be monstrous if discovered in him. Here you have it in a nutshell: the child and his mother, the small boy and the woman—the unawareness, the eyes, the smiles, the other-worldly sounds of the one, and the alert awareness, the conscious intensities, hopes, fears, and aspirations of the other.

The boy, therefore, as a musical instrument of real, artistic endowment, is suitable chiefly for the expression of impersonal thoughts, of concepts that have lived only in his brain as transcendental images. Music that calls for full, personal, conscious, emotional experience cannot be sung adequately by boy-sopranos, and if only inadequately, then without conviction, and therefore without the quality that gives life to all art.

Perhaps the best way of summarizing the foregoing considerations is to repeat that boys classify as the sopranos for Palestrina and the women for Brahms.

Accordingly, therefore, a choir of boy-trebles, if it is to be an effective vehicle of music, must be understood to be possessed of definite qualities which are proper to itself. If so understood and if guided and cultivated consistently, such a choir can be developed into one of the greatest and most convincing of all artistic mediums.

The obvious necessities of special repertoire and special technique are so inseparable as to constitute one outstanding necessity for choirmasters of boy-choirs, namely, that of considering these choirs as musical entities altogether apart and different from all other musical ensembles, in inherent character and aesthetic purpose.

In repertoire, the boys' metier will always be in music whose melodic curve-line is nicely balanced with upward and downward progressions symmetrically set off against one another; in music where tension between the melodic and harmonic elements is not such as to require personal consciousness of dramatic effect; in music whose dynamic contrasts are not so unprepared as to intimate the sudden surging—*sforzando*—of great emotion or the melo-dramatic *subito pianissimo* of spent emotion.

The melodic lines of the Gregorian Chant are dispassionate; so, too, in the compositions of the great polyphonists of both the Continental and the English schools, the vocal curve is simple. The official version of Gregorian Chant contains only one number in which a descending major sixth is employed. In Palestrina, one rarely, if ever, finds two long leaps in the same direction used consecutively. The tension between the melodic progressions and the harmonic elements effected by the mediaeval counterpoint is so slight, generally, as to give the impression that even dissonances take effect without perturbation, shock, or even the consciousness of the ensemble that one voice-part is momentarily altering the modal or harmonic atmosphere. Even the false relations so frequently encountered in the music of the Tudor composers fail to make singers aware of dramatic effect. In the music of Byrd, the alteration of the sopranos' $B\flat$ by the altos' ensuing $B\natural$, does not effect the tension that false relations stimulate in modern music. The dynamic variations of the polyphonic period are generally *poco a poco,* well prepared, and quite obviously in accord with the sense of the text. The principles of rhythm, accentuation, and stress, although complex to the modern eye at first glance, are simple. They grow chiefly out of the language being sung, and the undulations are serene, natural, and seldom, if ever, dramatic.

Therefore, the proper music for choirs of boy-sopranos is the music of the polyphonic period and such later compositions as are found to be similarly conceived.

It was indicated previously that a soft horn quality is discernible among the natural timbres of boys' voices, but for reasons of expediency, this quality is not recommended for general development. The findings, then, in this study of the color-scheme of boy-sopranos may be epitomized as:—

Principle No. II. "The timbres of boy-sopranos are limited to the flute, light string, and light reed colors, and the artistic usefulness of boys is chiefly in music that floats."

———————

Having ascertained the qualitative character of his soprano chorus, the choirmaster must seek next to gather corresponding information about his alto section.

The terminology applied to this section is somewhat confusing and accounts to a degree for the vagueness which prevails concerning the tonal functions of an important group.

Let us examine the nomenclature in general use.

One hears the following terms in connection with the voices which sing on the line lying between the sopranos and the tenors:—*altos, mezzo-sopranos, contraltos, male-altos, acute-tenors,* and *counter-tenors.* It would be difficult, probably, to bring the musicians of the world to unanimity in the precise definition of these terms. However, the etymology, original meaning, and most generally accepted definition of each should net a concept which will serve our practical purpose.

Thus the word *alto* comes directly from the Latin *altus* meaning *high.*

Therefore it cannot be properly used to designate a female voice, for the high female voice is of course soprano. Therefore it must designate a type of male voice. The history of music finds it in exactly that connotation. The alto was the voice higher than the tenor, frequently a falsetto production, although the Spanish vocal technique apparently included processes by which a natural tone production might be used in the alto range. Its

easy compass appears to have been and many altos could

add a fifth above without strain.

The word *alto* today is used generally to denote the part lying between the soprano and the tenor lines, and while purists would not applaud its use in the designation of women singers, it seems correct enough to refer to women as *singing the alto part.*

The words *mezzo-soprano* and *contralto* are the proper terms to be applied to women singing in the alto range. *Mezzo-soprano,* etymologically, signifies a *half-soprano,* therefore a voice which partakes of the timbre of the real soprano and the timbre of the *contralto.* It has rarely been used otherwise, although there are some (the singers themselves) who prefer to claim no kinship with the contraltos, considering themselves full-toned dramatic sopranos with somewhat limited upward range.

The easy compass for the *mezzo-soprano* is . The *con-*

tralto is the voice singing *contra,* against the alto or lower than the highest male voice. It is a voice weighty in character and was not recognized as an artistic medium until the nineteenth century. Its normal range is

although it is not uncommon for contraltos to sound

well in a more extensive compass.

The term *male-alto* carries the adjective unnecessarily as is evident from the preceding remarks about the *alto.* No doubt, when the latter word came to denote popularly all voices suitable to sing an *alto-part,* it seemed desirable to the English choirmasters to designate the sex of those actually singing it. Therefore the tautology.

The terms *acute-tenor* and *counter-tenor* are usually given as synonyms for alto by most musical lexicographers, and, observing the general use of the terms among musicians of the nineteenth century, one would reasonably conclude that these define the same voice. However, considering the three widely divergent types of tone-quality possible to altos, the writer for purposes of identifying these diversities will consider *male-altos, counter-tenors,* and *acute-tenors,* in this treatise, each as having specific qualities. That the nomenclature in this differentiation is gratuitous is conceded, but if there be actually three substantially different timbres of alto among men singers, and these be produced by a vocal technique proper each to itself, it seems reasonable to give each species a name.

With this preamble, we address ourselves to the two major species of female voices commonly grouped as altos in a mixed chorus, namely, the *mezzo-sopranos* and the *contraltos.*

Both of these voices belong rather to the dramatic than to the lyric species, although each has its distinctive texture. The mezzo-soprano can be lyricized to meet the needs of certain styles of composition throughout a large portion of its compass, but the contralto can successfully undergo this process usually only in a more limited compass.

While the mezzo-soprano is in reality a composition of the tonal features of both the soprano and contralto, it tends more towards the flexibility and clarity of the former than to the weight of the latter, and should properly function, therefore, on the alto line, to a different choral purpose. The tonal element which this voice borrows from the contralto

is the full-bodiedness of its lower register 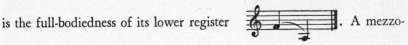. A mezzo-

soprano, then, can supply the sonority in this range requisite to the demands of most styles, at the same time, being free to rid itself of ponderousness in the high tessitura frequently assigned to the alto part.

The mezzo-soprano is a brighter voice than the contralto and is consequently more useful in defining the horizontal line in polyphonic music.

The contralto is in its natural texture, dark, sluggish, heavily laden. It would seem more apt for solo than for choral expression. Certainly the polyphonic lines of the Modal, Bach and Handelian schools are not enhanced by such tone-quality. There are mass effects, especially in the homophonic style, where the true contralto tone is admirably effective, but for general choral purposes the mezzo-soprano is more useful. Probably a notable percentage of women who call themselves contraltos are really mezzo-sopranos, for the anatomical structure of pharynx, larynx, false vocal cords, aretynoid cartilages, etc., as well as certain glandular features, are observed to be of greater dimensions in true contraltos, than is the mean average among women. Mezzo-sopranos, by forcing *quantity* of tone in the low register, imitating a quasi-guttural effect characteristic of the true contraltos, frequently deceive themselves into the belief that they belong to the latter class. There have been few singers like Sofia Scalchi, who electrified audiences in the latter half of the nineteenth century by an extraordinarily low natural voice, which she could at will, without

noticeable break in continuity of timbre extend to ♮.

It has been the writer's conviction for many years that the majority of singers classified as contraltos are true mezzo-sopranos misled by vocal teachers, who in their turn consciously or unconsciously placed *quantity* above *quality*.

From the foregoing it should be concluded that in the average chorus, the women presenting themselves for the alto line are in outstanding majority mezzo-sopranos. If the rare circumstance of the majority being true contraltos reveal itself, and the choirmaster cannot add sufficient mezzos to offset their weight, he must eliminate polyphonic *a cappella* music, and much that is accompanied, from his programme material.

There are, of course, many compositions, especially in the *a cappella* style, which cannot be adequately presented with females interpreting the alto lines, and this for the obvious reason that much music was written with the alto line conceived as "topping" the tenor rather than as lying under the soprano. I remember confronting this difficulty at a great festival of which I was the guest conductor. The mezzos and contraltos had given a remarkably satisfactory account of the alto line during rehearsals, but I found it practically impossible to blend their "et tibi dabo" of Palestrina's "Tu Es Petrus" motet with the tenors. Finally I was obliged to eliminate all female voices from the second alto part. The peculiar characteristics of the alto voice make approximation by women under certain circumstances almost impossible.

Among the mezzo-sopranos, three cardinal analogous timbres will be discovered: string, reed, and brass. There are episodes in which a compound of all three is desirable, while frequently the ensemble effect is more convincingly set forth if one of the three be accentuated. To assure himself accurately of the extent of his resources and to be in position to invoke these resources quickly, the choirmaster should know the singers upon which he can successfully place the responsibility of such emphasis, and their positions in the chorus bank.

In the early examination of candidates for the alto section of a liturgical choir, the choirmaster faces the same situation that confronted him with the sopranos: the voices are not sufficiently developed to reveal their true qualities. Only after having guided the changing voice of a soprano-boy "through the break," will he perceive the quality of alto-tone which is recommended by the writer as pre-eminently the best for male choirs. There is no such voice as a true boy-alto. The low, loud "chest tones" with which so many boys sing is frequently judged as adequate for the alto part, and choirmasters are wont to refer to such singing as of boy-altos.

Under the term *counter-tenor* the writer presents the special qualities most requisite for liturgical ends. The technique for developing this voice is discussed elsewhere.[1]

It would be unprofitable to debate here about the peculiar qualities of the male-alto and the acute-tenor, since these are placed logically for study in apposition to the counter-tenor. Neither the male-alto nor the counter-tenor is a natural voice: both are made, the former by introducing elements

[1] See Chapter VIII, "The Alto Line."

foreign to the natural estate of a man's settled voice, the latter by the preservation of certain soprano facilities during the changing period.

Although perhaps unable to place the alto part in its proper perspective regarding timbres, from principles advanced so far, the master of a boys' choir must convince himself at the outset that this part is of great importance. Many musicians advert to the alto-line as relatively unimportant, being more of a "fill-in" part than a principal, and their performances, especially of polyphonic music, attest their casualness. Among the many sub-divisions of chorophony which must engage a choirmaster's study, none must be more thoroughly explored than the proper direction and training of the alto part. Inadequacy or positive ugliness are the unavoidable results of superficial knowledge in this direction. Perhaps the alto part is less sympathetically understood today than any other phase of music, as well in composition as in both choral and orchestral conducting.

As a general rule the writing of the part is awkward, lacking in fluency, and gives evidence of serving to take up loose threads in the harmonic weave. This is almost invariably true in choral compositions—except in polyphony—and is frequently the case in orchestration.

In the latter, the secondary importance attached to the part is witnessed by the type of instruments designed for its utterance. Among the strings and reeds, certainly, the altos are the least consequential of the choir, having a minimum of assertiveness, vitality and resonance. The viola, the alto string, has a mild, lovely quality as a solo instrument, and a murkiness which serves in ensemble to darken the gaps between treble and tenor strings, but it has neither the piquancy of the violin nor the vigor of the violoncello; it is timid, lowly, reticent; as it were, fenced off from hearty companionship by its lonely looking C clef. Nor does the alto reed rise to sonorities or to any degree of tonal conviction, for the English horn playing only a fifth lower than the soprano oboe, with its diffident bell-shaped opening, is almost apologetic, inaudible when the orchestration is moderately full. The synthetic effect sometimes achieved by combining the upper notes of the bassoon and the lower notes of the clarinet with the pusillanimity of the English horn is chiefly quantitative, and lacks the power to solicit the attention readily engaged in the other orchestral lines. The English horn may be taken as a symbol of alto futility; it is even cheated of a correct name, for the instrument is neither English nor a horn.

The brass choirs fail to take much more serious cognizance of a distinctive alto timbre. Among the French horns, treble, alto, tenor and bass deliver the same uniform quality, and since, in contrapuntal music at least, variety of coloring seems intrinsic to its nature, the sounds contributed by the player to whom the alto part is assigned are inconsequential. They fail to establish an atmosphere distinct from the feeling created by the treble horn. Similarly the second trumpet, presumably essaying an alto line, is merely another trumpet sounding the same qualities as the first trumpet in a lower tessitura. There is no diversity of tone in the horn quartet, while the open brass provides one for soprano (trumpet), and another for tenor and bass (trombone). The first notable advance in symphonic expression will probably be in the improvement of the *alto* instruments; at present the orchestral choirs are all lacking in worthy mediums for the alto lines. In polyphony, all parts are structurally of equal importance; in homophony have not the altos and tenors at least a parity of value?

In the chapter devoted to blending the component choral lines into an ensemble of co-ordinated factors, the necessity of establishing a nicely balanced relationship of altos and tenors will be presented. With many points left to be amplified, the choirmaster is asked to accept these dogmas:—

Principle No. III. "The ideal alto tone-quality is not merely an extension downwards of treble quality, but a distinctive, vital coloring, sufficiently self-assertive to arrest attention to itself, and possessed of elements not common to other voices."

Principle No. IV. "Mezzo Sopranos are preferable to contraltos for the *alto line* in polyphonic singing."

Examination of the tonal resources of the tenor group may be conducted expeditiously, for there are only two major species, and candidates indicate their affiliation immediately. *Lyric* and *robust* are the accepted designations of the two species. The word *tenor* coming from the Latin *teneo* (I hold) originally designated the voice *holding* the plain song *cantus firmus* in descant and polyphony. Since the tessitura of some modes permitted the *cantus firmus* to lie in the middle register, extending not far into the upper register, it was easy frequently for the *robust* tenor to proclaim it, and only because of its etymology and its original use, does the present writer justify the designation of two such different types of voice by the one term, *tenor*. The *lyric* type is essentially different in color and usefulness from the *robust,* the former tending to a vibrating, volatile string or reed tonality and the latter identifying itself unmistakably with the sonorous amplitude of the *baritone*.

Range is not the criterion by which properly to designate voices.

Mme. Scalchi and other contraltos were able to sing freely in passages as high as those written for lyric sopranos, but were not therefore confounded with these. The mezzo-soprano frequently can sing as low as a contralto, but not having her dark timbre, is named properly a mezzo-soprano. There is much evidence to support the view that the average so-called robust tenor is really a baritone with higher than the average baritone range. Try a baritone (not a basso-cantante) and a robust tenor, for experiment, each in the same passage of a song in this tessitura

. A close kinship will be immediately evident, while the

lyric tenor, essaying the same comparison, manifests no affinity of timbre with either.

The tenor and alto lines form together a sort of contrapuntal axis around which tonally, if not always structurally, the outer parts seem to revolve. An axis must be adjusted with delicate nicety to the rotating parts if symmetry and freedom of motion are to result; in the ratio of its lack of adjustment is satisfactory rotation impeded. The contrapuntal axis is swelled to a preventive thickness when the dense consistence of the contralto tone and the fullness of the robust tenor are its material and dimensions. No facility in ensemble blending will succeed in achieving the readiness of motion essential to good polyphonic singing, if the alto-tenor axis be of the wrong proportions. The robust tenor, in higher modal areas, with his open-baritone timbre, and the contralto, when the part lies low, with her characteristic bulkiness of tone, contrive an axle of such size as to make any polyphonic rotation decisively impossible.

In vertical music and in some of the modern accompanied polyphonic music, the baritone-tenor is effective, but it is obvious that if the soprano and alto are to be like reeds and strings, in the sixteenth century style, a robust trombone-tenor is altogether disqualified from association. And yet choirmasters, the world over, assign these high baritones to the tenor polyphonies, seemingly unconscious of grave contravention of artistic principles. The baritone-tenor serves the opera well in a long list of roles, but no impresario with good judgment is discovered in the incredible blunder of assigning such a singer to the music of *Des Grieux* in Massenet's "Manon."

This preview of resources may be epitomized in:—

Principle No. V. "The horizontal demands of *a cappella* polyphony require *lyric tenors* in the high ranges, and *robust tenors* must not be employed."

The proportion of lyric and robust tenors likely to be found in any average chorus assembled without careful selection, varies so considerably, that no uniformity of experience can be alleged reasonably. It is true that there is a larger number of baritone voices among men than of lyric tenors and basses, as one may readily conclude from the general prevalence of the baritone quality in men's speaking voices. Therefore, the chances are in favor of a larger group of robust than of lyric tenors. It has, however, been the experience of the writer, frequently to discover more of the latter than the former. During some seasons lyrics seem to abound; at other times there is an inexplicable dearth. Perhaps the results of vocal teachers' efforts to *broaden out* lyric tenors into counterfeit robustos, are more far reaching at one time than at another. Not infrequently the alert choirmaster may identify a would-be stentor as a "good lyric gone wrong." The *nap* is off his voice, the *melos* has bade farewell to his larynx, and one of the essential elements of music has disappeared, i.e. *quality*. It is not an uncommon experience for lyric tenors to be told in the vocal studios that their voices are of far greater natural potentiality than they suspect, further, that it is lamentably unwise to restrict themselves to the diminutive and trickling purring to which they have been unnecessarily accustomed, and finally that under the expert direction of the adviser of the moment, their puny utterances will take on length and breadth and depth and— resonance enough for the Metropolitan! Keats' "little noiseless noise among the leaves" soon will become Milton's "sound of blustering winds." False diagnosis, dangerous therapy, dribble! The luckless lyric who submits himself to such unnatural re-making, eventually discovers himself in a state of vocal disrepair, fondly carrying the traditional "gold-brick" until over-fatigued by failure he recognizes the pedagogic chicanery. A lyric tenor in the unfortunate process of being metamorphosed into a Caruso, suggests to the writer Robert Browning's man, who "blows out his brains upon the flute."

The process of lyricizing robust voices of either men or women entails no aggression on natural qualities, no sacrifice of vocal orientation, no remote possibility of injury. The cases of lyricizing dramatics and dramatizing lyrics are not parallel in any sense. While the studio attack on lyrics is violent, the lyricizing of heavy voices is a delicate, refining process by which at suitable moments, the less dramatic qualities already inherent in voices may be allowed to function alone in short-lived episodes.

The analysis of choral structure shows two accepted species of tenor voice, and it is incumbent upon the choirmaster to determine immediately the likely character of his particular tenor chorus.[1] According to principles already announced as the basis for this approach to choral technique, the

[1] See Chapter X, "Tenors & Basses" for discussion of various types of lyric tenors.

conductor who feels he must work within a restricted color-scheme, is coerced by canons of musical efficacy to limit his repertoire. In consonance with Principle No. V, a predominance of robust tenors whom he cannot lyricize, renders the chorus unsuitable for polyphonic singing, except in such compositions as may have the modal *cantus firmus* lying low. Transposed modes, i.e. with the B♭ in the signature, usually prescribe a tessitura too high for the baritone-tenor. Considering the fact that the greater number of interesting polyphonic works were written by the poly-phonist himself either in a transposed mode or in modes naturally lying high, it is evident that a chorus lacking lyric tenors is effectively barred from polyphonic exercise.

The examination of the basses follows the same general lines as that of the other voices. An average group of fifteen or twenty basses will divide itself into three major classes, the *basso-cantante,* the *string-staccato basso* and the dark *basso-profundo.* Octavists are too rare and suitable only for too highly specialized needs, to be included among the normal categories. Nor is the baritone to be understood or treated as a species of bass voice, although its Greek derivation—*barutonos* meaning *heavy tone* —might lead one so to conclude. There is no doubt that when the bass line

lies in this area 𝄢 baritones can and do regularly furnish

adequate fulcrum for balanced choral movement, but only *quantitatively.* They lack the qualitative solidity so desirable in a plinth architecturally proportioned to the super-structure. At the risk of superfluous reiteration, attention is again directed to the canon of art which refuses the substitu-tion of quantity for quality. The baritone consistence of tone has not the tonal constitution of the true bass voice. The intertexture of elements in the true bass is c   nd more finely woven than is the lighter fabric of the baritone. T   so admirably paralleled in its two-fold type by the old v   rrent baritone instrument of the brass band, is   e choral ensemble, and will be seen in the ne   al voice around which the most satis-factor   ponent sections of a chorus will be ac-com   this voice sponsors and pledges ensemble cor   variously tempered tonalities, and, if cor-re   end a benign influence throughout the unit, f   ghest soprano. The *viola da gamba* or broad

ssertive and resonant in this range 𝄢

and contributes much to establish a consciousness of precise pitch throughout the ensemble, but generally it cannot be *covered* with the same effect as the other type, and is therefore not as flexible in the higher polyphonies. The roundness and pliability of the latter type qualify it for ready fluency in the upper areas, making it thus serviceable as a re-enforcement in *second* tenor lines. Its very roundness is, however, the defect of its virtue, for in the tessitura in which the baritone is to exert its best influence upon the ensemble blend, it is too murky to be efficacious. Therefore, a combination of the two baritone types should be sought by the choirmaster in the ratio of one of the string type to two of the baritone-horn type, the former contributing to one need, the latter to another.

The *basso-cantante*—singing bass—is presumed by his designation to be sufficiently free of the more ponderous components of the deep bass to sing fluently in any part of his range. He is differentiated from the deep bass in that facility, and from both types of baritone by greater sonority as well as lower range and a more ample resonance, the latter making his voice unwieldy in the upper parts of his range. Frequently, within the compass in which the voice remains elastic, the *basso-cantante* can reinforce the baritone line with excellent effect, but generally, the safe procedure is to assign the voice to the lowest choral line.

The *basso-profundo* is not precisely a rare voice, but it is by no means a common voice among men, as many choirmasters will attest. In thirty years of very active experience, the writer has had but few of these great voices under his baton. The explanation of the abundance of bass voices among the Russians and the relative scarcity among other races, is a matter for conjecture. Climate, racial characteristics, biology, dietetics, etc. being probable factors in the situation. However, it may be the experience of a choirmaster to have a number of these low voices in his chorus, and this being the case, he is in good estate for vertical music, but at hazard for polyphony. The *basso-profundo* is thus both an asset and a liability. In the homophonic style of *a cappella* music, this voice is usually superb; also it is frequently incomparably effective on the bottom line in modern polyphony where orchestra and chorus are deftly merged into a combined unit. But the music of the sixteenth century seems cemented down into the earth or chained like Perseus to the rock when a deep basso throws his weight against the Palestrinesque buoyancy. A casual glance at the voice-writing of the mediaeval polyphonists will demonstrate that the bottom line is frequently too high for flexible and well shaded performance by deep basses, and, further, that this is in the effective and elastic area of the basso-cantante. Of course, as with other heavy voices, if the lighter elements can be made to prevail in upper tessituras, the deep bass may serve usefully in the polyphonic music, but the writer recommends skeptical conservatism. In this connection, his memory of a performance under his own baton of Palestrina's works with an octavist struggling heroically, although unbidden, to lift his vocal tonnage on to the lightly constructed platform reserved for basses by Giovanni Pierluigi, and the resultant detonating crash of the whole contrapuntal structure, is so vivid that he would be as likely to allow a repetition as to assign the first violin part of Debussy's "L'Après Midi d'un Faun" to a contra-tuba. The congregation, startled by the cataclysm, must have felt that the great master's mystical wanderings had been arrested by Shakespeare's "deep dread-bolted thunder."

The *string-staccato bass,* perhaps more frequently encountered among Englishmen than elsewhere, while not unusually sharing the lower sonorities with the basso-profundo, is freed from excessive ponderousness by the string-timbre of his voice. His tones are thus more incisive, and dissociated more clearly, one from the other. In usefulness, he serves chiefly as a corrective to the basso-profundo, helping to throw some light into the vocal depths, and adding a sense of accurate pitch to the line. This voice, however, is generally obtrusive in polyphonic music, unless its quantity is attenuated.

These reflections may properly and succinctly be condensed as:—

Principle No. VI. "The choral line lying between the tenor and bass lines, is the richest vocal area for purposes of ensemble blend; therefore baritone voices, being of two kinds, must be co-ordinated and together related to this primary purpose."

Principle No. VII. "Although qualitative solidity is requisite as the substratum of a balanced chorus, and conceding that baritones cannot therefore substitute for true basses, the basso-profundo is artistically serviceable in vertical music chiefly, rarely in the sixteenth century style. The basso-cantante is the polyphonic bass."

It is incumbent therefore upon a choirmaster to classify properly all the lower male voices, his ear primed chiefly to detect the various qualities of voice rather than the dynamic energy employed and the mere *range* of voice.

The seven principles announced in this chapter constitute the writer's philosophy of choral understanding and choral training in the tonal implications of polyphonic singing. The use of the colors most appropriate to the dramatic and picturesque schools of choral composition is more properly a subject for examination in another volume.

If a choral conductor be resolved to draw upon the full color scheme of his component choirs he will find himself developing ready facility in choosing and emphasizing the vocal contributions of those whose timbres are best fitted to the aesthetic opportunity of the moment.

These principles will, of course, be examined thoroughly in their appropriate connections in Volume II, and the technique which this treatise is designed to set forth will be seen to follow as natural corollaries and amplifications.

Technique is of no value in any phase of any art unless it be a logical and practical method of executing the effects which the art itself is endowed to reveal. These effects may be deduced from a study of the resources of the art. The tonal resources of the choral art reveal themselves to the writer in the facts summarized in the seven principles. These seven principles are radii of a primary concept of choral possibilities and purposes. This concept is that the structure of a standard chorus is analagous to that of a symphony orchestra, that it is many-colored, sensitive beyond the mechanical limits of the orchestra, and more replete with resources of intimation and overwhelming artistry than any or all other instrumentalities of musical eloquence.

The philosophy and principles of choral composition and interpretation will be expounded in Volume II.

A chorus master who essays to build up a choral technique commensurate with the great endowment of the choral art, without this or some other equally sound philosophy of ensemble music as a basis, is making light of his undertaking, whether or not he be conscious of a slight to sincerity.

A definite, congruous technique is required for the proper training and conducting of a chorus, and this technique must evolve in due sequence from principles which are academically sound. This is the only cornerstone on which a fine product can be securely based, but if on another, then smugness will continue to sponsor mediocrity, and futility to pursue effort.

CHAPTER VIII

The Alto Line

The Changing Voice and Counter-Tenors

In polyphonic singing, each part being of equal importance, it follows that each voice-line should be equally effective. Defects in any of the constituent choral groups are emphasized by contrast with the excellence of the others. A beautiful soprano tone-quality, fluent, elastic, and colorful is set at naught by a throaty alto chorus, a group of robust tenors or a too predominant string-tone in the bass section.

Effective polyphonic singing depends primarily upon uniform excellence of all the parts.

Conductors must be convinced of this fundamental dogma, if they are to succeed in revealing the loveliness of the mosaics fabricated by the great contrapuntal masters.

In homophonic singing, the necessity of uniform excellence is not so insistent, for usually the lower parts are supporting the melodies of the upper. But merely because, in this style of singing, the tune seems to be the most discernible element, one should not be satisfied with an inferior support by the lower voices. The richness of these latter voices adds to the *melos* of the tune and good tones add beauty to the harmony just as bad tones subtract from its effect.

Furthermore, the majority of choral directors do not limit themselves to the homophonic style. Even this style itself is frequently diversified by contrapuntal passages, requiring from all the groups the same independent excellence needed for authentic polyphony.

Naturally, a perfect blend of voices can never be achieved if the director be content to develop only a good soprano line, leaving the other lines to the uncertain custody of indifferent voices.

It is therefore amazing to encounter instances of complaisance on the part of good musicians, who, having conscientiously toiled to achieve a fine soprano tone, take little cognizance of the defects of the alto, tenor and bass sections. One finds this complaisance chiefly among the directors of boys' and men's choirs. Perhaps these directors focus their attention so steadfastly upon the great need of training the soprano-boys that they come finally to concentrate all their attention upon them. I have listened to many choirs, in which the boys gave an admirable account of themselves—to the great satisfaction of the conductors—but in which the ensemble effect of the choirs was robbed of artistry by the defects or inadequacies of the other voices. If one fails to keep the concept of an ensemble composed of other voices as well as of sopranos clearly in mind, the probability is that only the sopranos will remain in perspective.

Considering the fact that sopranos and basses must be blended in the ensemble, before being adjusted in balance to the altos and tenors,[1] it might be more logical to study the properties of bass voices next, but the relationship of the counter-tenor alto to the changing voice of the boy-soprano suggests the immediate investigation of all facts pertinent to the changing voice and to the various types of quality which may serviceably be developed for the alto line.

First, we shall consider the changing voice of the boy-soprano and his gradual growth into a falsetto alto.[2] This will involve further examination of the different type of falsetto alto which is produced *after the soprano voice has changed into a baritone*. These examinations will be of vital interest to directors who preside over boys' and men's choirs and to supervisors of school music who are confronted with the problem of the best course to follow with boys during the period of voice mutation. Finally, of course, the mezzo-soprano and contralto voices of mixed choirs will be considered.

The well trained soprano-boy has not only an easy compass of two

full octaves: 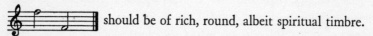 he has also an effective middle register.

If the principle of apposition has been carefully applied in his vocalizations after the purifying processes of the Five Stages, his voice in this range

should be of rich, round, albeit spiritual timbre.

This part of his soprano voice can be retained during the months when adolescence first attacks his childhood and begins stealthily to purloin his boyish attributes. Later, when the change into man's estate has been

[1] See Chapter XI, "Blend and Balance."
[2] See Chapter VII, "The Color Scheme" (Principles III and IV).

completed and his natural voice will have become fixed in the lower octave, the former voice, with modifications of the original color, may still function

as high as ♯ and in many cases, higher.

If the middle register was not restored and developed by exercises similar and equivalent to those suggested in Chapter IV, there is practically nothing to retain when the boy approaches puberty. Choirmasters who are content to let the training of the boys rest with the application of the principles of the Five Stages will not succeed in developing the quality of tone the author has in mind as proper to the counter or alto-tenor. Therefore, the success of the scheme to be suggested for retaining the superimposition of an analogous mezzo-soprano quality over the oncoming adult voice is determined by the success with which the precepts of Chapters III and IV have been applied. Occasionally, of course, one discovers a good counter-tenor voice which grew out of an inadequately trained soprano, but generally, the character of the latter pre-establishes that of the former.

If boys be allowed to sing notes above the staff beyond a certain time, i.e. when the first signs of approaching adolescence are manifest, it will be difficult if not impossible to guide them through the change period with success.

Choirmasters are loath to part with the senior choristers of a soprano section, for these are the dependable, well routined and full-throated lads who can carry the section through in the complete repertoire. Probably most of us have yielded to the temptation to keep boys too long in the upper reaches.

One strange phenomenon of the nearing change of voice is a notable increase of brilliancy on the high notes, and after a long experience, I know that it requires much courage and fortitude deliberately to take lead-boys out of the first soprano choir at the moment when they seem to be most valuable. Choirmasters who feel that the counter-tenor voice is of conjecturable value only, and that the sacrifice of four or five months of brilliant service on the soprano line is thus too meagrely compensated, usually let the boys sing on to the end, which, of course, is the moment when their voices crack and crackle, skyrocketing and plunging, chirping and grunting, the arytenoid and cricoid cartilages waging an undisciplined conflict for control of their vocal cords.

Voices exhibiting such a condition of collapse must be allowed to rest for two or three years until they have settled definitely into the lower octave. Sometimes at the end of the summer holidays, a boy is discovered to have developed to the breaking point, although at the finish of the preceding season there were no indications of the approaching change. But, generally, the approaching change is heralded in advance, and if a choirmaster be eager to save his trained boys to the choir, valuing the counter-tenor alto quality at its right appraisal, he will be on the alert to detect the earliest indications that adolescence is nigh, and apply a definite technique to their vocalism.

This technique must accomplish the two-fold purpose of allowing their adult voices to grow and mature naturally, without detriment, and of conserving facility in singing in the complete range of the treble clef. The fear is sometimes expressed that irreparable damage may be done to the larynx if an adolescent boy be allowed to sing while his throat is conforming and reforming itself to the acoustic physiology of adult in-tonation. But experience proves abundantly that if a proper system be followed, no injury results. On the contrary, some excellent tenors and basses—one a distinguished operatic artist—"sang through the break" in the Paulist Choir and served several seasons as counter-tenors before confining themselves to their natural ranges.

There are three major points to be studied in the technique of this undertaking:—

1. The symptoms which indicate the beginnings of the change process.
2. The range in which the youths may safely continue to sing.
3. The vocalizations which will bridge artistically the space between the treble and bass clefs.

1. It has already been remarked that added brilliancy on high notes is frequently advisement to the choirmaster to watch for the appearance of other symptoms. Many boys do not achieve the added brilliance, but when it is suddenly achieved, and is not due to forcing, it may always be accepted as a reliable cue.

Changes in a boy's appearance are also dependable warnings of con-comitant laryngeal developments. Widening of the features—particularly of the nose—an increased fullness of the lips, clumsiness of legs and arms, the appearance of hair on the face, and above all, the protuberance of the thyroid cartilage, commonly termed the "Adam's apple," are un-mistakable proofs that the glands are busy making the boy into a man. Considering the fact that the growing prominence of the thyroid cartilage is a symptom of great significance, a choirmaster should fre-quently investigate its development in all boys over fourteen years of age, to keep check on their condition. Sometimes boys show symptoms of change earlier, but the average lad retains his boyish attributes until after his fourteenth birthday. Sometimes, too, the advanced age of a boy fails to prove the activity of the factors by which nature accomplishes the process of mutation. I have had many boys in my chorus, who retained all the characteristics of pre-adolescent boyhood including vocal properties, until sixteen and in some cases later. I remember an unusually talented solo-boy who reached his nineteenth birthday before there was any good reason to withdraw him from the soprano section.

The boys of a highly trained unit can generally be allowed to sing without danger on the top soprano line longer than the boys who have not enjoyed expert vocal training.

But only choirmasters of extensive experience will find it wise to postpone the development of the counter-tenor voice, after the symptoms enumerated above have manifested themselves.

2. The first step of importance is to prescribe the range in which the boys with symptoms should sing. Among the other physiological changes in progress, is the gradual lengthening and thickening of the vocal cords; these will lengthen one sixth of an inch to permit the utterance of sounds an octave lower than the soprano register.

It seems clear that if boys be permitted to sing such high notes as to require the extreme tensing of the cords, needed for the upper notes, the practice will be in conflict with the development which nature is essaying to effect.

Therefore, it is my conviction that the boys must not be permitted to sing above the treble staff. The range in which they may safely con-

tinue to sing soprano is  until another symptom reveals

itself probably a few months after the discovery of the preliminary signs. During the period in which the boys are allowed to sing in this restricted soprano range, the *OO* and *EE* sounds, especially the former, should be eliminated from their vocalizations; this, for the reason that the retained middle soprano register is to be the important factor of the counter-tenor voice, and only such vowel sounds as will tend to maintain the richness rather than the elasticity of the middle register should be employed. The most serviceable vowel sounds at this juncture are *AH* and *OH*. It is important to prefix a labial or a lingual consonant to the vowel sounds, in order to keep uppermost in the boy's mind the necessity of forward focus, lest in the very unsettled condition of his larynx, he swallow his tones, thus burdening very delicate membranes and ligaments, and inviting chronic faults of vocalism.

Boys here should be ultra-conservative in dynamics. It is safe—until the appearance of the next symptom—to permit them their customary *crescendos* from 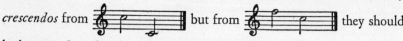 but from they should be kept on the soft side of the *mezzo-forte* panel.

The principle of apposition[1] should still be applied; in fact, with all types of voices, after the preliminary elimination of defects, no system of vocal exercise is academically sound or practically efficacious which is not based upon this principle.

However, it is profitable to use vocalizations of wide intervals, rather than exercises of consecutive steps, in order to prepare the boys for the "feeling" of different registers which will be a valuable asset in the counter-tenor's control when he is called upon later to mix two types of utterance, i.e. the upper (falsetto) and the lower (natural) baritone. Thus:—

Fig. 1

3. Generally, when the boys give the first evidences of vocal restlessness, they cannot sing with tonal authority, but after some weeks or maybe months, this note will appear in their voices as a definite and easy intonation. The choirmaster must be vigilant to discover its

[1] See Chapter IV, "The Positive Development."

first appearance, for this is the proper moment to apply vocalizations specially designed to develop the bass clef range, retaining a modified range in the treble and simultaneously establishing a working continuity between the tone colors of the two qualities. Of course, there can never be a real continuity of vocal colors between a falsetto alto and a baritone timbre. The former is artificial, the latter natural, but, to achieve a practical end, at the same time guaranteeing vocal safety, candidates may be so exercised as to achieve a very acceptable if counterfeit continuity of tone, at least sufficiently conformable to aesthetic canons to solve the alto problem for liturgical choirs and the tenor problem for choruses in Junior High Schools.

Immediately upon ascertaining that a boy can sing a fairly authentic tone in the baritone range, his compass on the treble staff must be further

restricted to this:—

The space between the treble and bass clefs is the "no man's land" of the changing voice and care must be taken to avoid all attempts at singing there until the upper and lower ranges have been well practised in juxtaposition.

Thus, a vocalization in the falsetto range should be mated with an exercise in the baritone range, e.g.

Fig. 2

Per-Per etc.

Mah Mah etc.

This juxtaposition of the vocalizations tends to serve the two-fold need which confronts the choirmaster at the moment. The use of the *PER* sound in the treble clef exercises is important, as the physical movement by which it is uttered facilitates the unencumbered vibration of the true vocal cords, the false vocal cords, or muscular tissue adjacent to the true cords, tending to dissociate themselves from the latter, when the *ER* sound contracts the base of the tongue. Samuel Brenton Whitney, the great choirmaster of the Church of the Advent, Boston, in the late nineteenth century, claimed that no other vowel sound could accomplish the same smooth and easy falsetto phonation, and my personal experience for many years confirms his opinion.

The use of the open and reedy *MAH* sound in the bass clef exercise is obviously to assure free and facile expression to the natural timbre of the baritone notes.

This manner of exercising both the natural and falsetto voices is generally sufficient to assure the retention of a smooth flexible quality, which, employed on the alto line, will blend readily with the tenors and sopranos; and when used on the lower lines, will coalesce satisfactorily with the mature tenors and baritones.

The features which distinguish the conserved falsetto alto from the type which is developed only after the adult voice has definitely become settled, are the superiority of the quality of the tone heard by itself, and the easy blend which it achieves with the other voices. The thin, piercing timbre of the made *alto* cuts through an ensemble, except when the soprano part lies low, with an effect akin to Shakespeare's "vile squeaking of the wry-necked fife."

On the other hand, it has been objected by some that the tone of the conserved falsetto is so flaccid and wanting in vigor as to fail to delineate its choral line. This objection is well taken in some circumstances which will be discussed presently, but in practically all circumstances the timbre can be pointed-up and indued with sufficient concentrate energy to make it adequate for polyphonic as well as homophonic service. The outstanding objection to the made alto is that it delineates too clearly, thrusting the part so far that it becomes dissociated from the integrity which the texture of polyphony bespeaks.

There is a suggestion of the eerie in the squeaking utterances of the made alto which tends to upset the aesthetic serenity of listeners. I found the experience of hearing this type of falsetto so trying that I have consistently refused to use the voice, except for a definite reason and seldom. The weird intimations of this querulous ventriloquism challenge the bleating of high muted trumpets for first place among the foes of ensemble-artistry.

The art of preserving the treble staff registers was highly developed by the Spaniards during the Renaissance and Post-Renaissance Period, and in the seventeenth century, adult Spanish sopranos as well as altos were in great demand throughout Europe. In spite of much effort, I have been unable to discover the precise technical processes by which the Spaniards succeeded in retaining the treble pitch and timbre, but the technique must have been fundamentally the same as that indicated above except that the lower adult timbres were probably undeveloped. Facility in the use of falsetto depends on the tranquility of the heavier tissues of the false vocal cords, while the true cords are in vibration. Probably the quality of falsetto alto which I have been disparaging results from the quietude of *all* the membranes adjacent to the true cords, the phonetic vibration occurring only in the thinnest, marginal, edges of the latter. The thinner the string of cartilage involved in vibration, the thinner the resulting tone. The quality of the conserved alto, on the other hand, indicates that a slight portion of the false cords is active as well as the true cords. Furthermore, the law of habit prompts a youth to approximate the tone quality which as a boy-soprano was habitual. The imagination, —that insistent agency of influence—sets before his inner sense of hearing the accustomed timbres and invites the larynx to co-operate in preserving them. Whatever the explanation, the tone-quality of the *conserved alto* is much rounder than that of the *made* alto, and is thus more suitable for the ensemble. This very roundness is the characteristic of the conserved alto which gives trouble sometimes. It is an elliptical roundness suggesting the hoot, and two or three times during a season, the choirmaster should give it point and incisiveness. The tendency of this tone to spread, if not checked, will make the alto line murky, and in polyphonic music, the lack of clarity on any line is a serious defect. The scheme which I employ in this circumstance, is to use the vowel sounds, in exercises which are most analogous to the double-reed and string tones, i.e. *MAH* and *MEE. PER* must, of course, be used as well, to maintain control of the falsetto. It is serviceable also to accompany these exercises with *oboe, salicional* and even *gamba* stops on the organ.

Sometimes, when these devices have not checked the spreading tendency adequately, I add a made alto to the ensemble for a few weeks, finding the very defect of this voice a curative for the other. This is the only circumstance in which I use the made alto, but I concede its efficacy in setting before the tonal imagination of the counter-tenors the clarity of timbre desired, although it is too piercing for use by itself.

Many choirmasters are timid about "bringing the boys through the break" and developing the counter-tenor alto. But the process is simple, and almost guaranteed. After the first group of lads has established a tradition of correct tonality, there is even less difficulty in guiding the changing boys to their new vocalism, for these, having a definite exemplar to imitate, accommodate their voices to the pattern with a minimum of instruction.

The two major responsibilities of a choirmaster, in this phase of choral technique, are the timely restricting of the soprano range and the opportune introduction of exercises similar to that given at Fig. 2. If one be inattentive to these responsibilities, he will have little success in maintaining an alto choir which can function *pari passu* with the other choral lines.

In order to assure to the falsetto choristers an adequate development of their baritone or tenor voices, the choirmaster should assign them to their proper lines in compositions for T.T.B.B. Choirs which include Gregorian Chant in their repertoire offer splendid opportunity to these choristers, for the frequent singing of the chants in unison with the adult members exercises the natural timbres to great advantage.

The counter-tenor altos prove to be good substitutes for real tenors in Junior High School choruses, as supervisors who have become proficient in developing them attest. They can give a passable performance of an extensive and varied repertoire. Of course, the absence of the real tenor is felt, especially in madrigals and other polyphonic styles, and therefore an ensemble, having only substitute tenors, cannot give strictly idiomatic performances, but such a unit satisfactorily attains the ends of school music. Teachers of music in the public and parochial schools have long been perplexed as to the treatment of the changing voice, but many are beginning to appreciate the value of the conserved falsetto, largely through the influence of Mr. John Dawson and Miss Elizabeth Van Fleet Vosseller, the founder of the interdenominational Choir School at Flemington, New Jersey.

A clearer understanding of the laryngeal changes which nature is effecting during adolescence will tend to deter supervisors from forcing the unsettled voices of youths into the tessituras suitable only to the settled voices of adults. With the technique of training the counter or alto-tenor available to all, excuses for recruiting a *soi-disant* tenor chorus from a group of lads of sixteen or seventeen years, who can but struggle perilously and inartistically against the demands of *open* natural tenor timbres, will be thin, inadequate, and indefensible.

The futility of depressing adolescent voices to the profundities of adult bassos, by guttural gymnastics, to provide the lowest line for an ill-advised school programme, is the supervisor's penalty for offending against the fundamental principles of vocal hygiene. The innocent victims frequently sustain a grievous and enduring mishap—the forfeit of a possible plenitude of vocal distinction in maturity.

CHAPTER IX

The Alto Line—Continued

Mezzo-Sopranos and Contraltos

In Chapter VII of this treatise, two of the seven principles of tone color were established for the alto line:

Principle No. III: "Mezzo-Sopranos are preferable to contraltos for the alto line in polyphonic singing."

Principle No. IV: "The ideal alto tone-quality is not merely an extension downward of treble quality, but a distinctive vital coloring, sufficiently self-assertive to arrest attention to itself, and possessed of elements not common to other voices."

1. Mezzo-Sopranos

As pointed out in Chapter VII, many directors are notoriously indifferent to the requirements of the alto parts. Some are quite content if only the number of singers assigned to the alto line be sufficient, frequently recruiting them from the sopranos whose upper range is limited or valueless.

In some compositions, notably of the French School, the second line is designated "Second Soprano" and can be effectively sung by sopranos, but, obviously where the alto line is a bona-fide independent part descending to *A, G,* and *F* below the treble clef, the thin utterances of the soprano voice are altogether inadequate.

On many occasions, as guest conductor of mixed festival or oratorio choruses, I have found make-shift alto sections one of the chief obstacles to effective performance.

The mezzo-soprano voice is a richly endowed medium. It borrows elasticity from the higher soprano and solidity from the contralto. It can be dramatically convincing in emotional music, contributing impressively to mass effects and energizing climaxes, and, with proper direction, it can assume the lyric character proper to the music-poetry of *a cappella* polyphony. The timbres of the mezzo-soprano are multiple. Using the familiar analogy of orchestral instruments, the mezzo-soprano may be said to intimate the plaintive loveliness of the English horn and the broader melancholy of the middle and lower registers of the clarinet. It has the sturdy vibrancy of some alto notes of the cello, and in robust passages the color of the treble brass instruments. This voice can supply all the tone-color required for a satisfying performance of many styles of music.

The contralto voice is of greater effectiveness in dramatic music, when the part lies low and the structure of the composition is chiefly homophonic. But in contrapuntal styles, where elasticity and vibrancy are of paramount importance, the dark heaviness of the contralto is not only less effective than the mezzo-soprano but it destroys the explicit clarity essential to polyphonic forms. I am not recommending that contraltos be debarred altogether from polyphonic ensembles, but I am convinced that they should be in the minority, and trained to employ a lyric timbre. If their voices cannot be lyricized satisfactorily and made to function with lightness and definitiveness, they must be eliminated.

The soprano voice begins to lose dramatic efficacy at [musical notation] downwards while the contralto shows signs of tonal awkwardness from [musical notation] upwards. Considering the fact that the polyphonic demands of the alto postulate a range of at least [musical notation] and the modern demands a compass [musical notation] it is evident that the foregoing contentions about counterfeiting the alto line with sopranos or obfuscating it with contraltos are well established.

The mezzo-soprano generally has an easy range of an octave and a sixth [musical notation] in which all the distinctive attributes of the voice can be presented. This range can be readily extended to [musical notation].

Therefore, if its salient potentialities of elasticity and breadth be properly adjusted to each other, this voice can serve an ensemble of mixed voices with admirable felicity. Its variable color-timbres make it adjustable to the tonal tints proper to any style of composition.

It is the only voice that can always assure symmetry, balance and grace to the alto line.

Masters of liturgical choirs must regret (unless they be hopeless faddists) that no type of male-alto can be evolved, with the information available today, that simulates even vaguely the vocal virtues of the mezzo-soprano.

Acute tenors, male-altos and counter-tenors require adroit manipulation to be brought happily into such blend and balance with tenors as to establish the alto-tenor axis, around which the outer parts in polyphony must turn. It is true that the polyphonists composed for the male-alto voice. As we know it, this voice is thin; it is too fine a thread to serve substantially in the warp and woof of the other voices.

Perhaps the technique, which influenced the vocalism of the best ensembles from the days of Dufay (1400–1474) of the Netherlands School to the solemn finish of the polyphonic period (in the early 17th century) gave to these great masters of choral effects a male-alto voice richer in tonal gifts than our modern substitute.

I have often thought, while rehearsing various personnels in the great music of the Polyphonic period, that if Palestrina, Vittoria, Tallis, Byrd, Aichinger, etc., had at their disposal only the contraband, spurious, anaemic intonations, by which even the utterances of the least undesirable male altos must be described, the marvellously balanced and perfectly co-ordinated independent lines of their rich polyphonies probably would not have been conceived.

I am not arguing—(diplomacy alone gives assurance of this)—that male-altos and counter-tenors be discarded from liturgical choirs, and that their choir-stalls be assigned to bob-haired *mezzo cantatrices* amusingly disguised as singing levites, in cassocks and surplices. Some choir directors have naively tried the experiment of trifling thus with liturgy, history, and the general aesthetics of ecclesiastical *mise-en-scene,* by dressing up young, middle-aged, and veteran females in the choral insignia of males. It is not difficult to understand the urge of such directors to avail themselves of the mezzo-soprano quality and to be rid as well of the nerve-racking job of converting small, wriggling, noisy and generally undisciplined male sopranos into media of aesthetic expression, but I cannot applaud the travesty to which they have committed themselves for relief. It is almost true that a "choirmaster who has faithfully trained boy-choristers for a decade should be canonized a Saint," but it is lamentably untrue and absurd that a black soutane and a stiff white cotta can transform the self-conscious, romantic daughters of Eve into liturgical choristers, which canons require to be males. When I listen to a choir of men and women, vested carefully under the supervision of a scrupulous (ritualistic) sacristan, the masquerading ladies seem more Gilbertian than Gregorian, making over every antiphonal response into "and so do his sisters and his cousins and his aunts."

No, I am not arguing for the replacement of falsetto males, by un-liturgical females, I am merely emphasizing the extraordinary choral values of mezzo-sopranos for the alto line in non-liturgical choruses.

Every master of a male liturgical choir should organize, train and direct in public, a chorus including female voices. Otherwise his choral experience will be incomplete.

There are definite circumscriptions which limit the artistic useful-ness of liturgical choruses of boys and men. These find their origin chiefly in the relatively meagre variety of timbres in the boy-soprano voices, and in the monotony of the one ever present color of the artificial altos. If a conductor wishes to become a real master of chorophony, he should deal with the art in all its phases. Studious direction of a standard chorus of men and women will reveal more principles and facts of choral ex-pression in one season than a decade's wading in the shallow waters of boys' and men's choruses. The application of the technique acquired in training the former to the general conduct of the latter will bring about notable improvement in many fundamental features of choral singing.

The chief points to occupy the attention of the director in the prepara-tion of mezzo-sopranos for effective participation in the choral ensemble, in addition to the general principles of correct vocalism analyzed in preceding chapters, are:

(*a*) the elasticity, natural to this voice, but sometimes sacrificed through much over-singing.

(*b*) the tempering of a too pronounced reed or string-vibrancy which is one of the natural characteristics of the voice.

(*c*) the avoidance of guttural quality in low notes which mezzos sometimes affect in imitation of the natural murkiness of real contraltos.

(*d*) the training of these singers to relate their voices chiefly to the tenors, in polyphonic music, in contrast with their probably habitual sense of sup-porting the sopranos.

(*a*) The rudiments of correct vocalism must be invoked here as in most cases. In particular, the use of *staccato* in rapid passages balanced by *legato* in sustained phrases, is recommended, for it practically guarantees an increase of fluency. Attention should be given, also, to ascending passages starting below the staff, since elasticity is immediately forfeited if the weight of these low notes be dragged sluggishly up on the ensuing tones.

The following vocalizations include the factors most likely to promote the buoyancy sought:

A variety of vowel sounds should be used in these exercises, always with consonants. They should be sung with a feeling of ease, first softly and later *mezzo forte*.

(*b*) It is easy for the natural vibrancy of the mezzo-soprano voice to degenerate into a penny-trumpet stridency. This, as other defects, is due usually to too much loud singing. Obviously the first remedy to be applied, then, is *pianissimo*. A further treatment of the condition is found in the elimination of the *AH* (reed) and *EE* (string) vowel sounds and the consonant *M,* until the condition has been corrected. The vowel sound *a* as in *Tat*, resembling the bleat of sheep, is usually disastrous to pleasant vocalism, bringing to mind the vapid plainness of some coloratura soprano tones which have not been properly rounded; but the bleat is an excellent means of reducing excessive vibrancy, and I incorporate it in the special vocalizations designed to that end.

In *a cappella* music, the tendency to dramatic expression must be restrained. The mezzo-soprano singer, having the most eloquent and emotional of the female voices, is affected by every indication of agitation contained in the music itself or read into it by the conductor, and is urged by every *subito-forte*, every *accelerando*, every *crescendo e animando*, to express herself too forcibly. Even the slight increase of quantity required in certain polyphonic phrases by the swaying undulations of *arsis* and *thesis*, and the delicate single note *crescendos* and *diminuendos* of the Brahms' School, frequently tempt these singers to intrusive emphasis. Exercises which will develop control in these matters should frequently be practised by mezzo-sopranos even if the symptoms of this sharp pungency have not become acute. For example:—

(This exercise is conducive of control of curve lines requiring only *slight* increases of quantity)

1. (Use *VOO, VOH, VAT* successively)

2. The following is from the alto line of a motet "Oculus non vidit" by Orlando di Lasso, and is typical of the writing for altos in the polyphonic school:

3. The following exercise should be sung without *crescendo* or *diminuendo*, in all the dynamic panels. The singers should be on guard lest an unwitting *crescendo* be made from the second to the fifth measure.

In the *forte* and *fortissimo* panels, the tendency to emphasize their vocal brilliance, is restrained by the use of *TAT*. After they have become accustomed to control the quantity in these measures, the exercise should

be tried on all the vowel sounds including *MAH* and *MEE,* but these
latter only after all hints of stridency have disappeared:

Tit Tat Too   Tat Tat Tat   Tit Tat Too   Tat Tat Tat Tat.

4. The following vocalizations are phrases from the "German Requiem" of Brahms, and will help to inculcate a sense of volume proportions. In the first two phrases (Chorus No. 1) the tendency to push too
much tone aggressively through *crescendos,* which were clearly conceived
by Brahms as scarcely perceptible dynamic movements, usually impedes
at the outset the "counterpoint of quantities" which has always seemed
to me, as integral a part of Brahms' lovely score, as the counterpoint of
notes and the mosaic of orchestral colors.

This next excerpt is the conclusion of Chorus No. IV in the same
opus. Throughout this chorus, the mezzo-sopranos are prone to allow
undue keenness of tone to challenge the serenity which should mark the
progress of this extraordinary composition. Having exercised the singers
on the vowel sounds, the notes should be sung with words:

(*c*) To prevent the affectation of true contralto density, which mezzo-sopranos are wont to attempt in low notes, vocalizations in upper and lower octaves alternately are prescribed. In the opening choral measures of Chorus No. II of the "Requiem," Brahms has written the very form which usually invites this tendency. A few measures later, the same phrase (with some alterations) is assigned to the alto line an octave higher. I find it an effective practice to use this theme as a vocalization first in the upper and then in the lower octave, warning the singers to make no more effort in the second case than in the first, preserving as far as possible the same sense of forward focus and easy utterance in both areas. Thus first:—

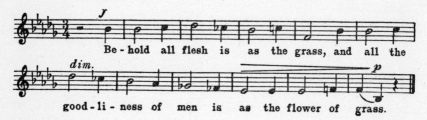

And then:—

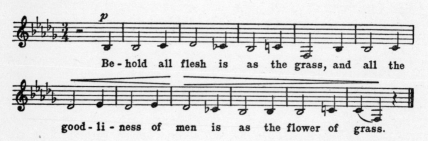

The following vocalize is offered as a corrective for throatiness which will prove specially effective if sung on *PEE*. The 2nd, 5th, and 6th measures will probably show murkiness. If this be pronounced, *legato* should be temporarily abandoned in favor of *staccato,* and the tonal quantity reduced. In the 3rd, 4th, 7th, and 8th measures, the attempt to simulate the natural consistence of the true contralto will often produce a graceless grunt. The *caveat* to be stressed here is to guard against exceeding the natural powers of the voice. Frequent and regular practice of these and similar exercises will gradually extend the natural amplitude of the mezzo-soprano in low notes:

The following exercise, taken at fast and slow tempos, is efficacious in habituating the singers to avoid guttural excess especially in addressing low notes suddenly without preparation, as in the third measure:

(*d*) A sense of tonal and contrapuntal kinship with the tenor choir usually impresses mezzo-sopranos after sufficient application of the point of view and the exercises submitted under the caption "The Alto-Tenor Axis,"[1] but sometimes choruses give evidence of meagre attention to such minutiae of artistry, and perhaps a director will find it necessary to rehearse the mezzo-sopranos, contraltos, and tenors, apart from the rest of the ensemble, frequently, until subconsciously each of these three sections finds its choral orientation in the others, and makes tonal alliance accordingly.

The requirements of Principle III[2] of the color scheme are met with signal completeness by the well schooled mezzo-soprano. The quality of this voice is distinctive, for, although sharing some tonal elements with the soprano and the contralto, it is not merely a synthesis of these. It possesses its own differentiating characteristics, which, in summation, are an exotic richness of color in the middle register; a poignancy which gives to the best tessitura of the alto line a clarity of delineation most satisfactory in choral ensembles; and a vocal personality at the same time notably individual and readily fusible with the other voices.

2. *Contraltos*

Although the foregoing considerations unmistakably favor mezzo-sopranos as generally more suitable to the demands of the alto line, and

[1] See Chapter XI, "Blend and Balance of Parts."
[2] See Chapter VII, "The Color Scheme."

as particularly apt for polyphonic music, it must not be concluded that the contralto voice is therefore to be held in low regard.

As a solo voice, it is a medium of peculiar effectiveness and charm, and in certain styles of choral composition it contributes a tonal viscidity and opaqueness which enhance the compactness upon which mass effects sometimes depend and which a good conductor tries to develop.

Furthermore, having traits which it shares only and in part with the basso-profundo, its very individuality intensifies its dramatic value, especially in operatic duets, trios, quartets, etc., where the histrionic portrayal of moods is the first objective rather than a mere lovely intertexture of musical elements.

The fact that this unique voice began to be appreciated at its real worth, only in the middle of the 19th Century, is additional evidence that music as a medium of dramatic expression had achieved only inchoate development during earlier centuries. Music's previous growth had been zealously, if ingeniously and piously, impeded by the conservative criteria of lyric decorum. Rigorism in music antedated by centuries the full blooming of the puritanical philosophy that was to come. Perhaps, if the 15th Century exiles from across the Aegean had sought a new orientation for music as they succeeded in re-orientating the other liberal arts, when after the fall of Constantinople they swarmed into Florence, setting up the banner of the Renaissance at the Court of the Medici, the history of intimate emotional expression in music would have begun then.

But the custodians of music did not permit the art which had been nurtured for so many centuries by levites and monks to stray into the luxurious and effeminate environment of these Sybaritic Neo-pagans who would have divested it of its spiritual raiment, and, long confirmed in its lustrous perfection as a medium of converse between men's souls and God, have inclined it to mere humanistic or cultural purposes.

From 1428, when Guillaume Dufay began his service to the art of music, to about 1460, the previously unsuspected possibilities of counterpoint only commenced to bud and blossom. The prodigious richness of melodic, rhythmic, and polyphonic ingeniousness which was to achieve its full effervescence almost two hundred years later, had to wait upon Josquin, Campere, Willaert, and their illustrious pupils, culminating in the great Giovanni Pierluigi da Palestrina.

The interpolation of these considerations here is in partial explanation of the delayed development and appreciation of the contralto voice. If the emigrés from Constantinople or their disciples had been versed in the true technique of music, they would probably have wrested the art from its ecclesiastical allegiance, and wedded it to their revived epicurism. The contralto voice would doubtless have been assigned the stellar role in music's new service.

It is the most beguiling of the female voices and the composer who understands its sorcery provides the best songs and arias for it. Rossini, who was the first notable composer to write important parts for this voice, was probably made aware of its peculiar endowment by the extraordinary timbre of Marietta Alboni's singing. If not the first, she was at least a pioneer contralto, and it is with her name and that of Sofia Scalchi who succeeded to her laurels, that the art of using this voice most effectively is associated.

The pre-eminent characteristic of the contralto voice is its density. It is not a semi-transparent quality, through which the lighter emotions may gleam. It is a thickly woven texture of vocal velvet which is appropriate vesture only for the sturdier emotional urges.

The conception of *alto-quality* which continued to prevail through the first quarter of the nineteenth century, was the same, practically, as that of the polyphonic period. *Alto* seemed to have connoted the idea of acuteness, a clear reediness, or a vibrant string timbre, rather than the murky bourdon-like cumbersomeness of the female contralto voice. The history of opera throughout the eighteenth century shows that the singing *dramatis personae* were usually cast in one pattern—3 women and 3 men —and occasionally a fourth man. Two of the female voices were high sopranos, the other being the equivalent of the modern mezzo-soprano. Two of the male singers were soprano or alto, the third an alto or tenor, and the occasional fourth a bass. Even in Gluck's celebrated "Orfeo e Eurydice" the contralto part, sung nowadays by a woman, was assigned to a *male-alto,* and for one occasion of an important performance, a suitable *male-alto* being unavailable, Gluck re-wrote the part for a tenor rather than permit a woman to sing it. Music even in Gluck's and Piccini's era had not progressed to the point where density, compactness, and opaqueness were appreciated as tonal assets. Music had long been horizontal. It was only when it became definitely vertical that lower voices, acting as "props" for the sopranos, began to need substance. It was this need that gave the contralto her start.

Modern music has definitely appraised these qualities as very important assets, invoking them frequently in the constitution of its most forceful compositions. But, it must be insisted, the *contralto voice* is a relatively modern voice. Its use in ensembles which include the older forms in their repertoires, is therefore deprecated, unless the contralto can be made to sing with a different timbre in the older styles. Succinctly, the density, compactness, and opaqueness, must be temporarily lightened, loosened and made transparent. Such an operation cannot be successful in a chorus whose alto section is comprised chiefly of contraltos.

If the majority be mezzo-sopranos, the minority contraltos can be made to borrow some lightness from the former.

Frequently, choirmasters of small units choose the voices for their suitability as solo-voices, but if the unit is to give idiomatic interpretations of *a cappella* music, the ultimate criterion in the selection of voices must be their aptitude for participation in the choral ensemble, rather than their solo possibilities.

The simplest procedure for fitting contraltos for satisfactory polyphonic singing, is to induce them to copy the tone-quality of the mezzo-sopranos and to display in their singing as little as possible of their characteristic guttural timbre. The alto-line parts of the repertoire should be used as vocalizations on various vowel sounds, the mezzos and the contraltos singing together, the latter using less voice than the former. Special exercises containing the factors most likely to promote elasticity and edge to the tone should be employed.

Staccato of course is a reliable agency for reducing weight in heavy ascending passages.

MEE (string) and *MAH* (reed) forbidden to over-vibrant mezzo-sopranos, intensify the higher frequencies which the throatiness of the *contralto* tends to obscure.

These factors, therefore, tend to promote buoyancy in the latter.

The following two-part vocalizes, with the string or reed timbre of the mezzo-soprano coloring the fundamental note, tend to develop an affinity of quality in the contraltos who sing the harmonics * on the accented beats:

I

II

Exercises in dissonance, the mezzos on the lower part, are helpful in directing the vocal imagination of the contraltos to a simulation of mezzo-pointedness.

A prepared dissonance suggests that the voice which brings in the dissonant note should make the color of its tone cognate to that of the first. The dissonant singer should therefore strive to duplicate the timbre of the preceding note. Establishing the mezzo-soprano in the antecedent or preparatory role, the contraltos will find the following type of vocalization profitable:

There are few choral ensembles of mixed voices in this era which can boast of elegance or symmetry in their alto choirs. Certainly the alto line is, as a rule, either inadequate or obtrusive; inadequate when its personnel is recruited among sopranos who prefer to sing in the low register rather than to retire; obtrusive, when the vibrancy of the mezzo-sopranos has been magnified to acute stridency or the breadth of contralto tone, robbing it of clarity, renders it inert and heavy laden.

One of the major re-constructions to be undertaken in almost every modern choral society of women and men, is the re-building of the alto chorus. Celebrated oratorio choruses, as well as the more humble singing aggregations, annually proclaim this need in their onsets upon the fugal choruses of "The Messiah." This yearly subversion of the Handelian concept is accomplished, of course, by all the constituent parts singing lamentably out of the composer's idiom, but the boisterous and un-disciplined vociferation or the amorphous flaccidity of the singing on the alto line is so great a stumbling-block to idiomatic interpretation that even finely attuned sopranos, tenors and basses could not overcome the handicap. If one seeks a real test for the tonal rectitude of an alto chorus, he will find it surely in the choral fugues of Handel, Bach, Mozart and Beethoven. The great compositions of these masters, and of those who followed their style, constitute the substantial repertoires of most choral organizations. And yet every performance of these compositions is a *reductio ad absurdum* of the notion that the composer's tonal intentions are faithfully fulfilled. Fanciful nonsense!

Many singers in oratorio societies can sing the principal choruses of the standard works from memory; they can "sing them backwards" (and frequently a *cancrizans* impression is in reality conveyed); therefore they are free to give their undivided attention to the *vocal color* which they are creating.

If it were my privilege to guide the aesthetic efforts of such an organization, I should assign a generous portion of the first season's rehearsal time to blending the mezzo-sopranos and contraltos, in such fugues as "For Unto Us a Son is Born" (Handel); "Kyrie Eleison" (Requiem, Mozart); "All Breathing Life" (Sing Ye to the Lord—Bach) "Sanctus" (Requiem, Verdi); etc.

This fact cannot be too eloquently or too frequently recalled: *the alto line is generally minimized, neglected and frequently ignored in all ensembles, choral and orchestral.*

CHAPTER X

Tenors, Baritones and Basses

As a general rule, a standard S.A.T.B. chorus which has been prepared to meet the demands of *a cappella* singing, can give a convincing performance of the greater part of the important choral repertoire. With particular tonal adjustments, here and there, chiefly in the addition of robust timbres, such a chorus is equipped to sing the entire library. But if, on the other hand, a chorus has been trained primarily to sing the dramatic and epic forms of opera and concert, its acceptability for the polyphonic style is improbable.

An outstanding thesis of this volume has been that highly refined lyric utterance is the distinguishing feature of praiseworthy polyphonic singing. In the technique of voice training this conception has been the fulcrum for all movement. In the selection, modifying, and blending of voices it is the principal influence, and provides the criteria by which the seven principles of the color-scheme [1] are ascertained and established.

Therefore, in discussing the preparation of the tenor, baritone, and bass choirs for participation in the choral ensemble, principles (*) V, VI and VII are consistently invoked as constitutional canons of chorophony.

The general principles of the vocal technique sponsored in the preceding pages are of course applicable to all voices. But, obviously, modifications and special prescriptions are required to develop the distinctive timbre proper to each species of voice. Thus the lyric high soprano is given a course of vocalization which would be probably in part unsuitable or inadequate to the needs of a mezzo-soprano. Likewise, mezzo-sopranos, contraltos, and counter-tenors, although assigned to the same choral line must be guided to their best usefulness, each by a different scheme.

And so with tenor, baritone, and bass voices, the general principles of tone-production are the same as for sopranos and altos while specific treatment is indicated to prosper their special characteristics.

Primary defects are eliminated by the processes of the Five Stages and

[1] See Chapter VII.

a normal development of tonal resources is accomplished by the plan of apposite vocalization.[1] *Pianissimo, downward vocalization, staccato,* and *prefixed vowel sounds* effect the same magical cures, correcting undue throatiness, weight, rigidity, and stridency with equal promptness and dependability for all voices, high and low, lyric and dramatic.

Naturally, certain modifications must be made in the application of the corrective exercises to the several categories of voices. The proper pitch and vowel sounds must be selected at the outset.[2] The adult male voices are usually sturdier mediums than the light voices of boys and female lyrics. The latter, for their very frailty must be brought to artistic maturity slowly and with infinite caution. While great care must be exercised with men's voices, too, their more robust laryngeal anatomy permits more rapid progress.

The essential differences (considering acoustical features) between boys' and female lyric voices, on the one hand, and adult male voices on the other, are the length and consistency of the vocal cords and the size of the resonator.

The average length of the true vocal cords among women is 5/12 of an inch—the average length among men 7/12 of an inch.

The resonator, among men, is generally 20 percent larger than among women and boy-sopranos.

The muscles, membranes, and cartilages which together with the cords and resonator constitute the sound-making mechanism of the voice, are naturally all more ample in men than in women. The thyroid cartilage (Adam's apple) in men is much more of a protuberance than in women. This cartilage is engaged by the cricoid which in turn must be proportionately larger. The arytenoid cartilages engaging the true cords must similarly be more ample and sturdier.

Therefore it is not unsafe to introduce dynamic variations during the curative stages, in the training of adult male voices. Conservatism should restrain the choirmaster, however, for while he is justified in allowing these males voices to graduate earlier from the *pianissimo* phase, it is easy unwittingly to permit loudness (the most insidious foe of good vocalism) to effect disastrous results.

Lyric tenors are of three general types, and a well balanced tenor line requires a blend of these. (1) The thin, reedy type, particularly effective and sometimes over-assertive in the upper register; (2) the string type, having adequate resonance in the upper but meagre resonance in the

[1] See Chapters II, III and IV.
[2] See Chapter III, "The Five Stages" (Part II).

middle and lower registers; (3) the sturdy middle register type (though not *robusto*) whose upper notes are probably inelastic and without the delineating qualities of string or reed timbre.

The first type is admirable in many respects for choral service; but alone it is inadequate. The other types must be introduced as well, otherwise thin, piercing vibrancy will delineate the tenor line too poignantly, and, as in the case of the made male-alto (q.v.) prevent the rapprochement of each choral line to the other, and all to the unity of the ensemble concept, which polyphony aims to establish.

This thin, reedy type of tenor is generally mobile, true to pitch, and especially effective in the *arsis crescendos* of Palestrinesque phrases. Directors who cannot recruit sufficient of these voices to guarantee elasticity, accuracy of pitch, promptness, and clarity to the tenor chorus, usually fail to produce good polyphonic effects, for the tenor line has the honor of precedence (*primus inter pares*) in the fraternity of the polyphonic parts, and the four vocal virtues just listed are indispensable to the dignity of the *Cantus Firmus*.

Like the mezzo-soprano, this type of tenor voice inclines to excessive vibrancy. In its upper register it achieves a pungency which sets it out in front of the other voices. Just as the oboe often cuts a ruthless path through the treble ensemble in the orchestra, banishing strings, flutes, and clarinets to the threshold of inaudibility, reedy tenors sometimes commandeer undue attention to their voice-line.

The director, then, must first bring this natural vibrancy under control, and then blend it with the other types of tenor quality, the final synthesis of timbres being admirably suited to polyphonic music. The *AH* vowel sound should be used sparingly by tenors of brilliant reedy quality, since this sound intensifies the reedy timbre; likewise the *EE* sound should be seldom employed. *VOH, VAW* and the bleat[1] are recommended as effective in tempering the over acute piquancy of this voice.

In vertical music, the need for modifying the high frequency vigor of the reed-tenor is less urgent, for in S.A.T.B. choruses, the tenor part is usually contributing to the harmonic support of the tune-laden sopranos, under a sonorous alto choir, while in T.T.B.B. compositions the first tenors are usually the "honey-sucking bees."

In the latter case, directors frequently succeed in "taking-up" the undue shrillness of the top-tenor line with the rounder quality of the accompany-

---

[1] See Chapter IX, "Mezzo-Sopranos and Contraltos."

ing voices, but in the open spaces of contrapuntal frankness, the lower voices will fail to palliate an excess of vibrancy. Only at points where polyphonic parts proceed in coincidental rhythms are the effects of vertical music hinted and the disguises of homophony effective.

At the risk of over insistence, it is emphasized here again, that each voice line must be itself tempered and balanced within itself before admission to its stratum in polyphonic society. The untempered reed-tenor is a tonal pariah (in vocal ensembles, not necessarily as a solo voice) and cannot properly be granted vocal franchise in the *a cappella* autonomy.

Nor is the second type of lyric tenor sufficient by itself to delineate satisfactorily, with color and adequate resonance throughout its compass, the *Cantus Firmus* tenor line of Palestrinesque or Tudor music. This type of tenor voice gives intimation of much vitality and authority in its upper portion but loses so much of sturdiness in the medium and lower registers as to need reinforcement by other types. The medium register of such tenors can always be amplified to a certain degree, but the lower register does not respond to treatment with notable success.

The style of vocalizations suggested for the expeditious development of this type of voice is the style forbidden to the reedy-tenors. The quickest and safest method of increasing the potential activity of a "lazy" voice is to animate it with the keen, lively pungency of the natural reed and incisive string caliber. Therefore, the vocal exercises should be chiefly sung to *MAH* and *MEE*.

Conductors who in spite of being thoroughly convinced that the robust baritone-tenor is ill suited to the needs of polyphony, sometimes inadvertently drift to the extreme of having practically no audible contribution from the tenor line below . In nontransposed positions, the *Cantus Firmus* of the Dorian, Phrygian, Lydian and Mixo-Lydian modes, especially in their plagal or *hypo* forms, requires voices of good consistency in the middle and lower registers. Thus, for example, the octave in which the tenor line usually functions in the Phrygian mode is and considering the fact that idiomatic modal writing finds the *Cantus Firmus* frequently descending to the final note *E* and pursuing a curve line around its Gregorian dominant *C,* an authoritative quality is required from *C* to low *E*. In the Hypo-Phrygian mode, the tenor line would have even lower tessitura since the hypo-scale descends a fourth below the final. In such tessituras it is evident that the tenor line needs greater amplitude than the notably light string type can furnish. Therefore, if the synthesis of all the lyric tenor timbres available has failed to produce an adequate quality, it is my custom to add one or two light baritones, to the tenor choir to maintain the authority of the tenor *Cantus Firmus* in its low reaches.

If the third type of lyric tenor, the sturdy middle register (though not robusto) voice be available, it can be made the important substratum for an effective and altogether acceptable tenor contribution. The voice to which I am referring, usually has limited range and meagre endowment as a solo voice. It is inclined to be "dry" and therefore creaky in notes above  In ascending passages it frequently requires attention in the matter of accurate pitch. Perhaps the likeliest way of identifying this voice to the reader is to state that it is the type usually as-signed to second tenor parts, and is a very reliable, satisfying tonal agency, but altogether undistinguished. For choral purposes it needs lubrication, as it were, so that it may lose the stiffness with which it seems generally to proceed.

Rapid, *staccato* passages, with intervals spaced far apart are effective with this particular type of voice, as in the following exercise, especially if due attention be given to the *diminuendo* and *portamento senza-rallentando* of the cadence:

Bah etc.

One should seek to copy the tonal texture of the clarinet playing

. There is strength in this contexture but not obtrusive

vigor and the lighter high string timbre and more acute characteristics can be woven into it so deftly as to make the synthetic tone a desirable quality for choral use. The beautiful, pliant, adaptable, and convincing tone resulting from the unisonous synthesis of violoncello, clarinet, bassoon and the *piano* notes of the French horn in a passage like the following,[1] is the orchestral analogy of the amalgam of tonal elements which are needed to set forth the honorable part of the *Cantus Firmus* in polyphonic sing-ing, and to counterbalance the alto timbres in the choral axis.

The three types of lyric tenor herein discussed should therefore be blended and merged by much unison and two part vocalizations. Unison

[1] See tenor line, Fig. 6, p. 182.

vocalization with the baritones and basses tends to reinforce the middle and lower registers of tenors, while the tenors give lightness and point to the heavier voices.

Generally, there are two classes of baritone voices eligible and available for choral service, just as there are two distinct types of bass voice. These are adequately discussed in the following chapter to which the student is referred.

The different hues of baritone and bass color must be co-ordinated and blended as the various tenor qualities already discussed.

The string baritone is the effective voice for low polyphonic parts, and for all homophonic music, but the round *clarabella* type is more suitable for medium and high contrapuntal parts.

Obviously, another of the director's many responsibilities is to exercise the baritones and basses, separately and together, so carefully that the thin voices borrow roundness from the full, and the full borrow lucidity from the former.

A disposition of baritones, basso cantantes, and basses to spread tones without focus in this area will promote more defects in the bass line of a chorus than almost any other tendency. Spread tones lack definitiveness, and in the range indicated a conspicuous lack of clarity plays havoc with pitch, blend, balance, and polyphonic symmetry.

Adult male singers seem to err more conspicuously in the matter of too great impact with first notes of phrases, than boys or women. Given a fresh start, tenors and basses find difficulty in keeping the quantity in its proper relation to the nuances of a piece. Thus often the lovely effect of a *diminuendo* is interrupted or neutralized by the men pressing on the first notes of a new phrase or the first to be sung after a breath.

In the vocalizations of the men's choir, special attention should be directed to this tendency, so that facility in applying a well regulated even quality and quantity become second nature.

The men's choir is the substratum of the chorus, and according to the validity of its constitution, training and balance, will the voices of the superstructure find more or less, much or little, of incentive to sing beautifully the rhythms of the Muses, the verses of the poets, the polyphonies of the mystics.

CHAPTER XI

Blend and Balance of Parts

With vocal defects eliminated as far as possible, and the tonal timbres suitable for a varied repertory developed, the choral conductor must proceed to synthesize the single lines of his chorus in a composite unity.

The blending of all choral lines into a unified ensemble is the second undertaking of choral technique.

There must be no single elements, either individual voices or groups of voices, so prominent as to attract attention to themselves. The raison d'être of the broader phases of choral singing is to create effects by the subtle mixture of diverse elements, which cannot be obtained by soloists or by small groups of choristers singing in unison with one prevailing timbre. Just as the richness of symphonic effect depends upon the set-off of strings against woods, woods against brasses, etc., each orchestral choir fulfilling or complementing the suggestions of the others, so the consummate art of chorophony depends upon the correlation of polychrome voices, lyric flute-sopranos trading with lyric reed-sopranos, giving lucidity to dark contraltos, borrowing harmonic authority from solid basses or a quasi-vibrato from high cello-tenors.

The timbre-euphonies of a chorus must be more varied but not less cognate than the seven colors into which a ray of light is separated by the prism.

Each vocal color must be readily discernible but only in its proper relationship to other prismatic tints. The choral lines must be distinct enough to assure the independences of rhythm, melody, and dynamics upon which *a cappella* polyphony is based. And yet they must not be so distinct as to seem dissociated from one another.

Obviously, then, the conductor's problem is to work out a technique by which all the voices submit themselves to the oneness of choral mass-tone, at the same time conserving their respective identities. This technique does not involve an effort to accomplish two contradictory ends. Furthermore, it is simpler than might be anticipated.

The aim is merely to provide a certain aura between the choral lines. For instance, the soprano line, maintaining its treble clarity and all its other characteristic qualities, can be brought close to the alto line. There must be no tonal-vacuum between the lines. Similarly the alto line can approach the tenor and the tenor the bass line.

My experience with large choirs of women and men and liturgical choirs of boys and men has convinced me that the simplest means of achieving the proper commingling of vocal resources is:—

1. To blend each part *with itself* first.
2. To blend the extremes, i.e. the sopranos and basses.
3. To establish the altos and tenors as the choral axis.
4. To establish the baritones as the comptrollers of blending modifications.

This process of course implies the proper balance of voices in a chorus and includes consideration of special points to be encountered in four-part singing and in low-pitched *a cappella* numbers, especially in the minor-mode.

I. To Blend Each Part with Itself

It seems clear that before any single line can be successfully merged into the ensemble, it must be itself a thoroughly blended unit. For instance, in a chorus including fifty sopranos, if there are a half-dozen voices which always assert themselves to the disadvantage of the soprano section as a unit, the director will have no success in his general undertaking until he has subdued the conspicuous singers and brought their individual vocalism into the uniformity achieved by the others. Eccentric voices must be normalized, or eliminated. His first point of attack here is, as it has been so often, *quantity*. Differences of quality do not usually mar the blend of any choral line. On the contrary, they tend to enhance its musical value. But the undue amplitude of a few voices tends to rob the other voices of effective participation in the ensemble, substituting the singing (which thus seems to be forced) of a few for the relaxed and fluent contribution of many.

It is rarely safe to allow the very broad voices to make a *crescendo* to their full possibilities, for they outsing the others and of course arrest attention to themselves. For the same reason, it is rarely safe to allow the light lyrics to sing their softest *pianissimo*, for the broad voices will not usually diminish so completely, and thus again be heard outsinging the lyrics.

A safe rule here is:

Precept XII. "Gauge the proper amplitude of one notably broad voice by the amplitude of two normal light voices."

In pursuance of the plan to bring each choral line as near as possible to its neighbor by producing an *aura,* two-part vocalizations should be used in each choral part. Frequently, there are double-lines in all the parts, especially in polyphonic music. Therefore, the voices should be equally divided and exercises devised to give both divisions equal opportunity on the higher and lower parts, thus:—

FIG. 1

The groups should alternate on the upper and lower lines:

Exercises of this type should be sung at all comfortable pitches. The keys indicated are obviously for sopranos and tenors. The corresponding pitches for altos and basses are a fifth lower. All the vowels should be used with prefixed consonants.

The first aim in such vocalizations is to establish a parity of tone-quantity between the two lines *in all the dynamic panels* from pp. to ff.

Attention must be given to each part as it crosses over and above the other; for example:—

Exercise A, the second part will tend to overbalance the first in the second half of the second measure and in the first half of the third, while the first part will incline to outsing the second from this point to the finish.

The choirmaster has a specially good opportunity for observing and adjusting the balance when the mediant is the lower note of the two. There is so much satisfaction accruing to modern ears from a nicely modulated third of the tonic chord that instinctively one judges the virtue of associated notes by their dynamic relation to the mediant. Therefore, as a matter of practice, I usually direct the higher part to make a slight diminuendo to give the mediant a chance to produce its best effect, which is just as notable on singers as upon an audience.

Vocalizing in thirds is invaluable in establishing a blend of all the voices on a single line. The very instinct which finds gratification in harmony impels singers unconsciously to make more beautiful sounds themselves so that the harmony may be more satisfying. Therefore, the singers, vocalizing thus, mentally approach the notes sung by the other part, setting their own sounds in juxtaposition with the others. In this way, a kind of tonal aura is developed between the two lines, and while maintaining their own individuality, they appear to be merely two emanations, as it were, of the same thing.

In exercise B (the harmony here is clearly a dominant ninth), an excellent opportunity for creating this tonal aura affords itself at the tied half-notes. The *crescendo* suggested should be perfectly balanced and gradual, followed by an equally careful *diminuendo* (beginning on the second beat of the measures indicated) with a dallying *portamento*. The two minor thirds lying between the two major thirds and the dissonance between the dominant and its ninth, which are the structural features of this chord, while admittedly banal and cloying if used frequently, stimulate a sense of harmonic appreciation in singers, and tend to promote a feeling for the *aura* which will associate their voices more closely with the whole chord. A feeling of intimacy with other voices usually develops a kinship with them which is manifest in a suave blend of timbres. On the contrary, if singers feel aloof from an integral harmonic instance, sensing little or no affinity with the essence of the concord, their voices remain too cold to coalesce with the others.

A proper fusion of elements depends first upon the heat of the elements themselves. Alchemy and metallurgy attest this fact. And what is necessary to the commingling of metallic substances is necessary, at least by analogy, to the cohesion which the diverse components of ensemble music must achieve for artistic effectiveness. Therefore the warmer elements of music must be frequently invoked in order to keep the voices *fusible*. Only those factors in music which serve to make it glow, flare, and incandesce can help the blending of many voices into one great musical instrumentality.

The stimulation of reactions to harmony, the promotion of a sense of kinship with the vital contents of the music itself, the warming of one voice line by the tonal *aura* emanating from another, these and other processes of choral-alchemy must be applied before any single choral line, soprano, alto, tenor, or bass, can be naturalized as a suitable member of the ensemble fraternity.

Another effective form of exercise for the blending of the voices in any one part is the use of the drone key-fundamental and the fifth. The usefulness of this type of vocalization can be deduced from the fact that the part chanting the drones immediately invests itself with the harmonic authority; it is the genetic influence of the phrase, and although the motion of the upper part will incline singers to arrogate prominence, it is easy for the director to hold them in check, especially if he signals a *diminuendo* from those carrying the melody, and a slight *crescendo* from those supplying the drone. It is a law of acoustics that whenever the fundamental or principal harmonic notes are emphasized other synchronous sounds tend, like obedient children, to make themselves less conspicuous.

FIG. 2

The parts should alternate

I have frequently played the tonic and the dominant alternately, without other notes, as the accompaniment to vocalizations for this very reason, and usually with a quick sensing by the choristers that they should make their melodic meanderings a mere embroidery of the tonality established at the keyboard. This was in fact merely an insistence on the principal ideal of blend, i.e. that no single factor of an ensemble should challenge the atmosphere of the whole (in this instance the pre-eminence of the tonic and dominant). It is easy for the choirmaster to point out the difference between the prominence which interpretative requirements give sometimes to one line over the others, and the mere disruption of musical atmosphere which occurs when individual voices carelessly assume 'the position intended for a more important musical factor.

The two-part canons and rounds of Beethoven, Haydn and Mozart, now available in excellent editions, can be used most effectively as blending vocalizations, and I recommend choirmasters to have them handy at rehearsals. For balancing two soprano-lines or two tenor-lines in the middle and lower registers, the canon of the third "Agnus Dei" by Palestrina (*Missa Brevis*) is exceptionally good material.

Although it has been indicated in this Chapter that differences of quality do not usually mar the blend of any choral line but tend to enhance it, it is profitable nevertheless to vocalize reedy voices in apposition to flute and string voices as suggested in Chapter V, page 94. It must be remembered that one voice takes quality from another in some subtle, almost inexplicable manner, and the chorus master can prosper the rapport of his different types of voices by exercising the opposites together. Thus a twangy-reed soprano can *point-up* the comparative paleness of a flute-soprano, while the latter is at the same time reducing the pungency of the reed. These opposite types find, as it were, in common, a tonal-mentor while practicing together and by its influence are adjusted and readjusted to one another.

A master of orchestration knows the exact amount of woodwind tone necessary to balance the string tone for the effect he conceives, and the virtuoso organist is guided by a similar sense of balance in selecting his registration.

The chorusmaster, too, must effect a nice symmetry of vocal colors in each line, if it is to be a perfectly blended unit suitable for interlacing with the other lines.

The exercises given at Fig. 1 are helpful to this end if the director assigns the string voices to one line and the flute voices to the other—or the reedy to one and the horn-type voices to the other.

Just as the violin choirs of the great orchestras acquire their suave tonal-style by daily playing together *a deux,* so the single vocal choirs of a choral ensemble must sing together frequently in two parts to acquire a convincing choral style.

In effecting a proper blend of the altos, with themselves, or the basses with themselves, the director must often soften the darker voices, allowing the string or reed type to contribute more in the exercises. In order to compensate for the sluggishness with which the deep contraltos and basses reveal their respective tone-colors, the more readily discernible timbres of the mezzo-sopranos in one case, and of the baritones and basso-cantantes in the other, should be emphasized. After much vocalizing with exercises like those suggested at Figures 1 and 2, both the alto and bass chorus will sense the proper relationship of the lighter and darker timbres. And more important than this is the resulting information to the choirmaster as to which voices must be kept under strictest surveillance and control to conserve the tonal balance.

When the single choral lines have developed adequate uniformity, the director can proceed profitably to the next step in fusing all the lines in an integral ensemble. However, it must be insisted that if he has not succeeded in establishing uniformity within each constituent group, all efforts to blend the unblended groups must necessarily fail.

II. *To Blend the Extremes*

The next step forward is to blend the extremes, i.e. the sopranos and basses. One might raise objection here, offering the thought that it is just as important immediately to blend the sopranos with the altos, the altos with the tenors, etc., as to balance the sopranos and basses.

It is important first of all for the director to proceed systematically; if he fails to determine upon a logical scheme, his procedure will be haphazard and success only "the accident of an accident." Therefore, I suggest that he essay to balance group by group in orderly fashion. And I have found by long experience that the sopranos and basses require first attention. They are the top and the bottom, the terminals of the entire structure. They are the measure of the ensemble, and the most rapidly apprehended factors in the unit.

I have selected the sopranos as the first choral unit to study because it is reasonable to conclude that the voices with the highest frequencies, i.e. the greatest number of vibrations per second, under normal circumstances, are appraised first. But I do not therefore select the altos, having the next highest frequencies, for immediate blend with the sopranos because the alto as well as the tenor is an inner part, and except in open polyphony, i.e. when the alto or the tenor part is the highest part actually singing, neither of these voice parts reveals its adequacy or inadequacy as quickly as the bass part. Good orchestration and good organ registration balance the treble and the bass before adjusting the sounds lying between. Furthermore, while it is true that polyphonic music gives equal importance to all parts, it will be seen presently that the alto and tenor parts are tonally cognate and were obviously conceived as such by the polyphonic composers. The consideration of this point will debate the suggestion that the women's voices should be blended together before seeking a balance with the male voices and vice-versa.

It would be logical here to introduce some consideration of the numerical balance of parts, but since the numerical proportions of a chorus must properly and ultimately be determined by the quantitative ratios between the parts, I shall postpone the study of numerical balance to the later pages of this chapter.

If the sopranos and basses have been properly blended in their respective choirs, and there is a notable lack of affinity between these two units, it is because:—

1. One of the units is quantitatively disproportioned to the other; or because:—
2. The prevailing soprano timbre is incompatible with the prevailing bass timbre; or because:—
3. There is an over-assertive tone in the bass and baritone choirs singing together in this range.

Generally, the lack of quantitative parity between the soprano and bass choruses is the explanation of their tonal incompatibility.

Probably there are few conductors of wide experience, who have not sometime faced the difficult task of inducing a top-heavy chorus to sing with evenly apportioned energy.

In America, and perhaps elsewhere, it is frequently a problem to secure enough good male voices to balance the sopranos and altos. Therefore, it is important for American choral conductors to know how to achieve an equivalent, if artificial balance, under untoward conditions.

Personally, as guest conductor for choral societies in many parts of the country, I have found the constant necessity of keeping the treble quantity conformable to the par indicated by the basses, an unpleasant handicap, frequently requiring modifications and serious changes in interpretation. If one were free to dispense with the services of superfluous sopranos, the problem would cease to be, but frequently a conductor must accept the personnel as he finds it assembled and established, on a social perhaps more than on a musical basis.

One of the most trying experiences of my musical career was an occasion when I essayed to conduct a highly idiomatic performance of Palestrina's *Missa Papae Marcelli* with sixteen basses struggling for contrapuntal equilibrium against the exigent activity of one hundred and twenty-five sopranos. Considering the primary requirement of polyphonic conducting, i.e. the maintenance of dynamic parallelism between all parts, the plight in which I found myself can readily be imagined.

The first and principal remedy for such lack of balance is, of course, to reduce the quantity of the soprano chorus. The dramatic sopranos must be kept throughout in the *piano* panel, *crescendos* being taken only by the lightest lyrics. The basses may be brought-up, but very conservatively, for any degree of forced quantity immediately attacks the ensemble choral quality.

The conditions which sometimes confront a guest conductor do not generally prevail in the choral ensembles over which a director regularly presides. Usually he can maintain a working balance of voices, but even when there is a proper ratio between the parts, the need of blending them carefully is always present.

Exercises like the following are profitable in establishing a tonal-poise between sopranos and basses.

Fig. 3

(From the Credo (Missa Papae Marcelli)—Palestrina)

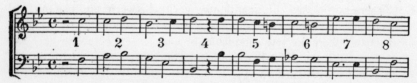

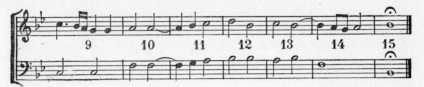

This should be practiced at various pitches, with all vowel sounds and in all the dynamic panels.

The open fifth in measure No. 1, if sung not louder than *MF,* will reveal immediately the tonal relation which will generally prevail between the sopranos and basses of a particular chorus, unless modified by the conductor. Nothing serves more effectively to indicate lack of blend and balance, than a bold fifth. Usually the fundamental is not adequate, and must therefore be brought-up or the soprano note reduced. Sometimes, on the contrary, the bass is too sturdy and needs softening. Before proceeding with the ensuing notes of such an exercise, it is well for the conductor to direct the singers to sing the opening chord *firmato,* for if he makes the necessary modifications in the first measure, it is clear that the rest of the exercise will be more profitable.

In measure No. 3, one must be on the alert lest the bass part give undue prominence to the *Eb,* which is a tendency, since this part moves a full beat before the soprano part. Frequently in such cases, the third beat of the soprano note is inaudible.

On the other hand, the soprano may disturb the balance by a too notable *crescendo* in this and the fourth measure, for upward progressions naturally suggest an increase of tone. (Interpretatively of course, a *crescendo* is indicated in such a Palestrinesque passage, but interpretative requirements should be waived when an excerpt from a composition is being used merely for general blending purposes.)

In measures Nos. 5 and 6, the accidentals must be kept carefully in the tonal-panel established in the rest of the exercise. Here again a natural tendency to emphasize, or *underline* the accidentals will assert itself. The choirmaster is seeking to blend and balance the tone quality and quantity of the extreme parts, so that under any and all circumstances there will be suave commingling of such diverse vocal characteristics as those proper to sopranos and basses. The appearance of an accidental in a measure is usually an invitation to singers to step out of the dynamic panel momentarily and draw attention to the alien factor.

Some commentators on polyphonic singing favor the underlining of accidentals even when they constitute false relations. Personally, I am opposed to any emphasis of foreign elements, except under special circumstances. But this matter will be discussed fully from the interpretative angle, in Volume II. A choir which cannot preserve its tonal balance against the appearance of homeless accidentals can never give a performance in which continuity, dependability and control will be notable virtues.

One rarely hears a chorus or even a quartet, which has been adequately disciplined to resist the lures of the stray flat or sharp.

Perhaps the psychology of the singers as mere human beings is revealing itself again: there is a subtle if lamentably perverse satisfaction in the irregular, and even the innocuous irregularity of accidentals seems to offer its enticement.

The tenors in the old college glee clubs always welcomed every chance to sharp the fifth as the bass would start a new chord on the third, with such satisfaction, that rarely did the composers of part-songs deny them recurring opportunities.

In measures Nos. 8 and 9 the bass part will draw too much attention to itself if a slight decrease in quantity is not indicated in the $B\flat$ to F and the C to F. The point involved here will be discussed fully in the paragraphs of this chapter devoted to the special recommendations for blend in four-part singing.

By means of such an exercise as that given at Fig 3, the director can quickly determine the tone-colors to be brought-up or subdued, as well as the quantity to be contributed by each part. Frequent practice of such a vocalization for the compound unit will establish the appraisal of his or her proper contribution in the mind of each singer. This appraisal will soon become the subconscious influence in all music that does not call for special effects, i.e. where one part must dominate dramatically, or subdue itself to an unusual softness.

Two other types of exercise should be practiced as well, to secure a satisfactory blend of the extremes in a choral ensemble.

Fig. 4

(Excerpt of Hymn "O Food the Pilgrim Needeth" by Alfred Young)

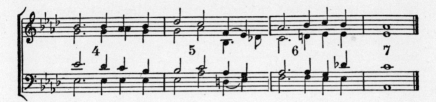

It has frequently come to my attention that choruses, adequately blended and balanced in music of parallel motion lose their parity of tonal energy in contrary motion, especially when the extremes start relatively close together as in measure No. 2 of Fig. 4 (sopranos and basses a major sixth apart)—and separate rather widely as in measure No. 3 (here they are separated by almost two octaves).

In this exercise, the director must be alert lest the basses force the tone on the Db in measure No. 2 and having made a stentorian start, carry an over-blown quantity-quality through to the next measure. Also, he must dissuade the sopranos from a too ample *crescendo* in the upward progression of measure No. 2.

I have selected this excerpt as a model exercise for accomplishing a blend in contrary motion, because it presents in those two items a real difficulty to a chorus, and if the difficulty can be overcome here, the choirmaster will have little trouble with other passages in contrary motion.

For tonal balance, I have found the hymn of which this excerpt is a part the most difficult in the extensive repertoire of the Paulist Choristers, and therefore I propose it as an excellent paradigm for the rehearsal room.

Another style of exercise must be used to achieve parity between soprano and bass choirs in passages where one part is moving rapidly and the other part is less active, or sustained. No more fitting source for vocalizations to this end occurs to me than a great choral masterpiece almost every performance of which is marred by lack of tonal parity in such circumstances, viz. the *MISSA SOLEMNIS* of Beethoven.

Early in the work, namely during the *Christe Eleison* movement, an ensemble reveals whether or not the sustained vs. the mobile parts have been properly established. From the ninth measure of this movement to the twenty-seventh, there is plenty of evidence for the critic to foretell the degree of success to be expected from the later efforts of the chorus at the *Cum Sancto Spiritu* of the *Gloria* and the *Vitam Venturi Saeculi* of the *Credo*.

Usually, even in the highly applauded performances of the *Missa,* the choral ensemble—and frequently the orchestra, too—makes a sorry burlesque of what Beethoven conceived as transcendent expressions of spiritual understanding, for rarely are the moving parts so related to the phrasing of the slower lines as to show forth the grandeur of infinite eons intimated by the former and the abiding unchanging verities of God announced by the latter.

The whole motet *Singet den Herrn* of Bach also depends in large measure upon the correct distribution of tonal energy in recurring passages of like structure. The *Hosanna in Excelsis,* too, of the *Sanctus* from his *B Minor Mass* cannot be promoted to its full emotional appeal unless careful attention be given by the choirmaster to the mutual adjustments of the substantial and the ornate elements in the score.

FIG. 5

Obviously the chief purpose of an exercise of this type is to promote control of the fast moving phrases. The progressions of the first two measures in the bass part and of the concluding measures in the soprano part invite agitation and display, which if not subdued, will altogether muffle the principal content of the four measures, which is the descending melody from the Soprano *G* to the Bass *G*.

As in all such exercises, facility in maintaining control must be achieved in all the dynamic panels.

When the choirmaster is satisfied that both the soprano and the bass line have established a normal energy-relationship in the exercises suggested at Figs 3, 4, 5, it will be profitable to practice these vocalizes with *crescendos* and *diminuendos* distributed variously, even capriciously between the two choirs in order to prepare them for the independent nuances which the polyphonic repertoire will demand.

But first he must have made certain that in the three types of music intimated at the Figs. 3, 4, 5, his choristers have accomplished a balance of soprano and bass contributions which permits the former to float about like, as it were, choral-harmonics, over the solid but not stolid fundamentals of the latter.

Much experimenting may be required before a director finally discovers the most effective treatment for a chorus in which there is a frequent lack of quantitative parity between the trebles and the basses, but if he studies the symptoms assiduously he will eventually diagnose the case aright and prescribe accordingly.

Sometimes this lack of quantitative parity is due to the second cause of misrelation indicated on page 173. If the prevailing timbres of soprano and bass choirs are mutually incompatible, it is clear that the processes suggested at Figs. 3, 4, 5, will not suffice to effect a rapprochement.

Usually, the adjusting of quantitative elements completes the task of conforming the top and bottom lines, each with the other, but occasionally a mal-adjustment arises from the effort to throw voices together in contravention of the seven principles of choral tone-quality established as a substratum of chorophony in Chapter VII. For instance, light lyric sopranos, including boy-sopranos, can rarely be blended with the string-staccato type of bass-voice. If this latter type dominates in a bass chorus, it will cut through the ensemble and show the fluty quality of the sopranos to be inadequate and incompatible.

There must be a kinship of colors in all the lines, especially in the soprano and bass lines. Therefore, in this circumstance, the director must cultivate more string tone among the sopranos, and at the same time try to broaden the timbre of the basses. If he cannot supplement the personnel of his unit with additional voices of the required timbres, he may face the alternative of requesting some resignations.

Probably most choral directors have permitted the balance of their choruses to be disturbed, at some time, because of reluctance to dismiss members who would be serviceable choristers if there were not too many of their type. Personally, I upset the blend of the Paulist Choristers for two seasons by allowing too many basses, of exceptionally acute string-timbre, to sing in the ensemble. It is often difficult to escape the claims of kindness, in selecting the roster of a chorus, but one must remind oneself that the first purpose of the organization must be fulfilled—an aesthetic purpose —and that fraternal considerations must be weighed in the light of the musical criteria which prosper this fulfillment.

Just as the vocal amalgam of light lyric sopranos and stringy basses is not a serviceable choral mixture, so there is a lack of affinity between the broad, ringing utterances of dramatic sopranos, especially in f and ff panels, and the inert timbre of heavy somber-hued bass voices.

Such incompatibilities can rarely be rectified by vocal exercises à deux.

Theoretically it is possible, of course, to promote certain resonant qualities in the more ponderous bass voices, but practically, the undertaking is not feasible in the average chorus which has meagre rehearsal time to accomplish its aims.

If the ratio of lyric to dramatic sopranos and of stringy to somber basses be about the ratio of two to one, the choirmaster will have little difficulty in commingling the timbres of these important lines.

In Chapter IV the principle of apposition was applied in determining the allocation in the choir of boy-sopranos. The same principle may successfully be invoked here; two lyric sopranos should sing with one dramatic soprano, and a somber bass should be flanked on either side by a stringy bass, or a reedy basso-cantante.

A third and common reason for the absence of *entente musicale* between the sopranos and basses is the unwitting vocal arrogance of the

latter when they find themselves in the pleasant area

where they sense that full-toned, very masculine and stentorian utterance lends authority to the whole performance and makes the rest of the ensemble obviously of lesser importance.

There are few bass choruses which find it easy to discipline themselves in the range indicated. But they must be kept under strict surveillance, and a choirmaster must be ready to subdue the line as each passage in the range approaches. This is a *caveat* of great importance. The point will be discussed later in this chapter when special technique for maintaining balance and blend in four-part singing is under consideration.

Another step preliminary to the profitable vocalizing of the complete ensemble is the establishment of the alto and tenor choirs as the choral axis of the unit.

III. *The Choral Axis*

The quality and balance of the combined alto and tenor sections are important factors in determining the degree of mobility attainable to an ensemble. The mutual infusion, insinuation, and interposition of alto and tenor qualities into a sort of duality make of the inner parts a tonal conjugation which promotes the strength, grace and the more esoteric charms of *a cappella* polyphony.

In the music of the 15th, 16th and early 17th century, the tenors are, as a rule, faithfully engaged with the *cantus firmus* which is the modal custodian of a composition, while the altos are functioning rather as super-tenors than as sub-sopranos.

The *cantus firmus* being the modal pivot of the number, structurally, the alto part being its primogeniture and favored ramification, it follows that the other parts should, in the actual singing, seem to be moving circumferences of tonal color rotating around the central tone-color of the tenor.

Thus, the tenors and their germane neighbors, the altos, should be established as the polyphonic axis around which imaginary vocal centre the soprano and bass movements are finessed.

In the mechanics of balancing and blending a chorus for *a cappella* polyphony, therefore, the adjusting of alto and tenor qualities and amplitudes is of pre-eminent importance.

In another volume, treating of the interpretation of the polyphonic schools, this interesting phase of choral musicianship will be set forth at length. The purpose here is merely to outline the scheme by which the choral axis can be established in effect. The student is referred to the anthem "Turn Our Captivity, O Lord" as an excellent example of a composition requiring a vocal centre for tonal definition. This number is rarely sung with good effect, because directors fail to take cognizance of this necessity. I struggled in vain during many rehearsals with this motet, but as soon as I realized the need of coalescing the tenors and altos, the obscure intentions of the number became apparent.

If the voices have been chosen with discrimination according to the principles of the color scheme, and have been properly cultivated, the director can profitably proceed with the following plan. There must be symmetry of both quality and quantity in the contributions of both parts; they must be so well matched as to be readily convertible, the alto to take the tenor notes and vice versa; they must function steadily even under these awkward circumstances:

1. When both parts are low.
2. When both parts are high.
3. When the alto is ascending, the tenor descending.
4. When the tenor crosses the alto, becoming the superior part.

(1) *When both parts are low.*

The following exercise is serviceable both for diagnosing the case, as it stands between alto and tenor lines, and for bringing about the proper relationship of color and quantity:—

Fig. 6

Probably the tendency of the singers on the alto line will be to adopt the open baritone tone, if they be falsetto altos, or to allow an excess of guttural quality if they be mezzo-sopranos or contraltos. The tenors, if they be lyric will tend to thin out, or if robust to surrender a forced basso-cantante quality.

The necessity of maintaining an "edge" on all tones in polyphonic singing requires in this instance that there be a minimum of baritone timbre and no guttural quality in the alto part. If these undesirable qualities be present, not only does the alto line itself deteriorate, but it almost completely eliminates the thinning out tenor line below. If the robust tenors, to compensate for the low-range and the threat of subjection by the altos be permitted to amplify their utterance to simulate basso-cantantes, their line becomes too open and assertive, as it were, reversing the threat balance.

In employing the vocalization to the best effect, it is important to maintain a string effect with the altos and a reed effect with the tenors. The profitable vowel for the altos is *MEE,* while *MAH* will serve best for the tenors.

In the first and third measures, the tenors will probably make a *crescendo* out of proportion. While it is true that in polyphonic music, *crescendos* are generally employed in passages like that of the third measure, the director must accustom the tenors to keep the *crescendo* within the dynamic limits necessary to assure the efficacy of the alto line.

When the alto descending and the tenor ascending, sing the unison *G* in the third measure, the coalescence of the two timbres should be perfect. Modifications of quantity should be made in both voices, until neither is more audible than the other. When the director has become satisfied with the coalition at this point, he should persuade the singers to note their respective contributions and to make these their standard in similar passages.

Having achieved a nice balance of timbres and quantity on the unison

G, the director should have little difficulty in extending this excellence throughout the vocalization.

The particular purposes of this vocalization will be achieved only at the written pitch and in the keys of *B♭, B* Natural, *D♭.* It should be sung *P, mf, and f. Pianissimo,* and *fortissimo,* being the extreme dynamic panels, offer less likelihood for profitable exercise when the parts are in extreme tessituras.

(2) *When both parts are high.*

F<small>IG.</small> 7

This exercise will probably discover those on the alto line unwittingly outsinging the tenors.

Counter-tenors (the *conserved* falsetto) tend to force into their flaccid quality a kind of strained Viola timbre which immediately produces a blatancy on the line. They must be warned against forcing. The tessitura of the alto line in this exercise is uncomfortable for counter-tenors and they should sing the notes *p* and *mf* on *per* and *poh.* If much practice has not brought their quality and quantity into equation with the tenor-line, and if there be no other types of altos in the choir, the director should give such alto passages to second sopranos.

The *made* falsetto altos also find it difficult to avoid a too conspicuous and obtrusive quality in this exercise. This quality suggests the piercing timbre of an over-blown oboe. If not carefully tempered it declines affinity not only with the tenors but with the sopranos as well. With an alto unit composed entirely of such falsettos, the efforts of the director to develop a kinship of timbre with the tenors in such passages will probably be futile, in most instances. However, careful practice of the exercise here suggested, on *FOO* and *FOH* at *p* and *mf,* will help considerably to modify the shrillness. Second sopranos are suggested again as substitutes in this tessitura. Mezzo-sopranos can be more readily blended and balanced with the tenor line here than the other types used for alto parts. It is easy for the mezzo-sopranos to bring the vibrancy of their notes in the tessitura of this exercise under control. They tend always, of course, to undue brilliance in such passages, but the practice of this exercise with *FOH,* will bring speedy results.

As in the first exercise, the unison *G,* appearing here in the second measure, gives fruitful opportunity for auditing the contribution of the two parts. The unison must not only be a unison of pitch, it must be a unison (amalgam) of timbre and a unison of quantity.

The heavy contralto-tone, if unaided by associated mezzo-sopranos, throws weight as well as murkiness into this tessitura, and if they cannot easily acquire a lyric tone, by singing this exercise with *MEE* and *MOO,* they should be instructed to remain silent during such passages.

Lyric tenors will find little difficulty in adjusting their contribution to this two-part vocalize. The "oboe" type, however, must favor the softer dynamic panels, because the high frequencies of this type of voice easily "cut through" at such spots, preventing a tonal rapprochement with the altos.

(3) When the alto part is ascending, the tenor descending.

Rising phrases in polyphony usually demand a slight *crescendo,* while descending phrases require a *diminuendo.* This undulation of rising and falling is one of the most graceful features of polyphony, and must therefore be attended with special care. An ensemble, in which the altos and tenors have not been balanced to meet such an interpretative requirement, therefore, definitely lacks a principal facility. By careful vocal exercise together, the two parts should be brought to feel the precise degree of dynamic change which will produce the undulation without disturbing essentially the equation between the parts.

The following notes are from the alto and tenor parts of Tomasso Vittoria's celebrated motet "Ecce Dominus Veniet" (second part). It is a typical example of the reciprocal arsis and thesis phrases which abound in the polyphonic style, constituting a resource of interpretation which shall be presented in another volume under the title of "Counterpoint of Dynamics."

FIG. 8

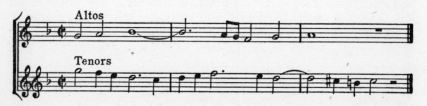

There is no technical problem to be discussed in this connection. The director must simply secure the undulating balance by faithful exercise. The tendency will always be among moderns to stress the arsis *crescendos*. The director must therefore listen carefully for the diminishing thesis and protect it from too zealous and competitive a *crescendo*. Striking passages in the repertoire should be practised separately with the purpose of confirming an appreciation of this choral nicety in the subconsciousness of the singers.

(*4*) *When the tenor crosses the alto, becoming the superior part.*

This polyphonic device is, of course, kindred to the resource just considered. The tenor in an extended arsis reaching to the top note of the mode while the alto is working out a figure below, gives opportunity for eloquent effect frequently. The exchanging of higher and lower positions in the contrapuntal texture *almost* invariably upsets the tonal balance between the parts, unless the director has trained the singers to a high degree of sensitiveness about the matter, and unless in the actual performance of such passages he be on the alert to regulate the dynamics of the participants. The *crescendo* of the tenors, in this instance must be kept well in check, and the altos, singing below, should not carry their *diminuendo* to as soft a degree as under other circumstances. The crossing of the interior parts offers opportunity for subtle choral effects, but the singers must be well drilled in maintaining tonal equality. Frequently one hears altos purling out to a vanishing murmur while the tenors, elated and superior, ascend to grandiose sonority.

The following exercise is of benefit in securing a dependable evenness of inverse correspondence in this exchange of positions.

FIG. 9

This exercise makes an auspicious start, the tenors and altos finding immediate and graceful opportunity to set a standard of balance in the thirds of the first measure. If a correct balance has thus early been established, it will be easy for the director to detect any deviation therefrom, when in the ensuing measures, the tenor crosses to the superior position.

The unison *F* in the third measure is obviously the point of departure to the exchanged positions and the director will find it beneficial to survey the balance here, as in the unison *G* of the preceding exercise. In the ascending tenor part, care must be taken to prevent an excess of tone, while the altos must maintain an adequate contribution in the descent. The tenor note in the fourth measure being the octave of the alto note, it is good musicianship to consider it as the first harmonic of the altos *B♭*, and since harmonics are naturally softer than their fundamentals, to direct the tenors to diminish quantity, at least after the first beat. The altos are equivalently becoming tenors and vice versa, as far as their natural singing relations are concerned, so one might epitomize the counsel thus: let the altos pursue the noiseless tenor of their way while the tenors strive not with much chortling to be altiloquent.

The best results in this exercise will be obtained if a rapid tempo is used, because the elasticity and facility which come with movement assist the singers to sustain, in awkward circumstances, the normal balance. When ease in the "crossings" has been developed, the tempo of the exercise should be slower. Obviously, the ranges of both altos and tenors restrict the pitches at which the exercise can profitably be practiced. Usually it should not be lowered more than a tone. It can safely be raised to the key of C, although for the needs of polyphony, such high practice is superfluous.

The next step in co-ordinating the many tonal elements of a choral ensemble is to blend the sopranos with the tenors and the altos with the basses. This is a simple undertaking, for if the sopranos and basses have been properly correlated, and the alto and tenor sections adjusted with finesse, the director will experience little trouble in smoothing out the other tonal relations.

The best exercises for quick results here are phrases from the choral fugues, in which the sopranos and the tenors usually sing from the tonic, the altos and basses entering at the dominant or sub-dominant, or vice versa. The relationship of these parts to one another in fugues is determined by mathematico-musical formulas, and any defect of balance is immediately detected.

If the conductor experience difficulty in bringing the soprano-bass unit, which he is presumed to have already suitably blended, to parity with the alto-tenor axis, likewise presumably well established, he should advert to the relative size of the two units. One should be increased or the other decreased. Obviously, the axis must be of proportions adequate to carry the circumference parts. Also it is equally clear that the axis must not be over-sized.

The conductor should listen carefully to the complete ensemble, first, in the hall in which the ensemble will sing most frequently, and, according to opportunity, in halls of different acoustic properties. It was only after I had begun to conduct extensive tours, which placed my choristers in halls of different structure and accoustics, night after night, that I was enabled to diagnose serious flaws of balance and blend which had not revealed themselves so clearly in the home auditorium. After a few years of concertizing, I adopted a certain unaccompanied number for the first motet, as a sort of acoustic "range-finder" which afforded opportunity for immediate discovery of the chief idiosyncrasies of the hall, thus indicating, among other things, the dynamic readjustments to be made between the parts to assure a balance.

IV. The Baritone Comptroller

One of the most influential agencies for steadying the tonal balance of a standard chorus is what I have come to refer to as the "baritone comptroller." This involves nothing more than the vocalization of the group with the baritone singing the dominant above the bass. This relationship of baritone and bass has already been recommended in another connection.[1] The following exercise will do much to solidify and enrich the blend of all the voices and tend to create the mystical *aura* which should hover between all the choral parts.

FIG. 10

The *D* in the baritone part should be underlined clearly, so that all parts feel its influence in the chord. The affinity which this exercise

[1] See pp. 107 seq.

establishes between the two most obscure notes in the chord (the *G's* of second sopranos and second tenors) reveals to a conductor the importance of keeping the octaves of tonics meticulously balanced. It has become habitual for me to listen to the second tenors in such positions, for I use a harmonized setting of liturgical responses, almost identical with the above progression. In each recurring response, I relate the baritone *D* to the quantity of the treble and tenor *G's*.

An interesting experiment in the use of this exercise, is to have it sung first without the Baritone *D*. The eventual appearance of this note not only gives great satisfaction to the singers, but it establishes a greater compatibility among the parts, promoting a consonance of elements that is the primary aim of superlative chorophony. The exercise is of course a simple progression popular as a basis for harmonic strength in 19th century Russia. My choice of the progression for certain ecclesiastical responses was due not only to the solidarity and richness of the effect itself, but because of the excellent reaction it stimulates at every repetition on the singers.

"Number of Voices"

Integral and essential to the blending processes of the choral lines is the tonal balance which generally is determined by the number of voices on each line. It may be conceded at the outset that a numerical balance of voices is impossible to debate because of the great disparity of volume between voices even of one category, which are available to volunteer choruses. In paid professional units, however, a numerical balance is possible of achievement. This latter item may be adjudged too academical to arrest attention here; at any rate the subject of tonal balance, being much more important, is forthwith examined. Years of hyper-critical examination of my own views and practices and much observation of those of others have convinced me that the modern chorus is ostentatiously and ineffectively large. The personnel must be determined by its audibility. To North Americans, the importance and probable effectiveness of a choir has long depended upon the size of its personnel.

First among the questions which for nearly thirty-five years I have been answering about the Paulist Choristers has always been and still continues to be "How large is your choir?" Americans applaud bigness, extensiveness, and amplitude. These congenial qualities seem to be native to our vast open spaces, our thrilling mountainous reaches and our great expanse of fecund and kindly prairies. Of course we are keenly interested in the realities of art, too, quite as much as our European friends.

But the very philosophy of the people, so mightily expressed in the Constitution of the United States of America, frets at narrowness, inferiorities of scope or size, paucity of resources, and unnecessary restriction of opportunity. The American ideal of ensemble singing units, therefore, in order to be characteristically American, would almost necessarily include sizableness as a fundamental virtue.

In its elation at escaping the social rule of castes and the civic oppression of oligarchies, it was natural for a great free country to emphasize magnitude temporarily.

Therefore, the deplorably large dimensional designs of our choral societies and church choirs can reasonably be imputed a national exuberance, an enthusiasm and elan of an untrammeled people, which time will moderate and regulate.

Our choruses have been excessively large. They have over-burdened the acoustical capacities of our churches and auditoriums, so that one could "scarce hear the singing for the singers." Gradually, the sense of evaluating an ensemble for its essential qualities and its fitness for the acoustical attributes of a particular place will supersede the rating of worth by size and quantity.

Already, there has been some indication that appreciation of the smaller ensembles, both choral and orchestral, is growing. Radio, both directly and indirectly, is responsible for this: directly, because of the proved value of small units for broadcasting: indirectly, because of the study of acoustics which the engineering needs of the wireless has stimulated.

Past and present meet in the musical arena with this striking tenet in common:—ensembles of few participants are preferable to those of many. The record of music sets forth this fact as a conviction of mediaeval and even post-Renaissance musicians. The historical choirs that carried music from the moment it entered the fraternity of the arts through all its phases of development to the high Parnassus of polyphonic achievement, were of limited personnel.

The practice of the ages favored small choirs, although the musicians did not probably allege a scientific reason for this. Even in the great basilicas of the Continent and in the Cathedrals of England, the regular service-choirs probably averaged not more than twenty-five voices. The full quota of the Sistine Choir at the zenith of its glory was thirty-two.

The most ingratiating and convincing choral music which I personally have heard was rendered by groups of fifteen or sixteen voices, with the exception of one occasion on which a mere sextet of carefully balanced voices presented a programme of *a cappella* music with extraordinary effect in a Cathedral where normally a chorus of sixty voices struggled to find resonance. Large numbers of voices can easily challenge the acoustics of a building, come into conflict with them, and defeat an artistic purpose easy of accomplishment by smaller groups.

The old masters knew this, even if they did not explain the phenomenon. Palestrina had not more than a half dozen soprano-boys in the choir at St. John Lateran. He and Annimuccia initiated the "Laudes Spiritales" which later developed into the oratorio style, with a double quartet. And personally, on one occasion, in a hall of great dimensions, I was able to produce a vibrant vital effect with a group of twenty boys and men immediately after a chorus of approximately one thousand voices had failed to catch the acoustic wave length of the hall.

It has been recorded that for his first London performance of the "Messiah," although all the vocal resources of the metropolitan district were at his disposal, Handel chose fewer than a dozen sopranos. It is amusing, in contrast, to note the composition of the choir at the celebration at Westminster Abbey in 1784 of the centenary of Handel's birth: 59 sopranos, 48 altos, 83 tenors, and 84 basses. Also be it observed that some degree of "Americanism in Music" wafted across the Atlantic to London during the latter half of the nineteenth century, for in 1874 the Handelian Choir and Orchestra comprised a personnel of 3500, and in 1926 this number was considerably augmented by Sir Henry Wood.

The latter half of the nineteenth and the current century to date, have been a quantitative era, for ensemble expression. But the acousticians, those academically annoying mathematicians of sound-waves, are urging us to adopt the sometime practice of our musical ancestors.

Two major points may be noted as the salient features of their criticisms, first: choruses and orchestras are excessively large; and second: there is too much treble to allow a proper balance between bass notes and the chordings.

Anent the size of our ensemble units:—the general advice administered by radio engineers and applauded by physicists making research in sound-recordings is not to overload the acoustical "hearing capacity" of a hall or a microphone. This is practical counsel, and needs no debate, since it has already been insisted that the notable choirs of history have been numerically small units.

Another point relevant to this general item of advice is that only a certain percentage of the playing or singing participants of a group contribute any audible sounds to the sum total. The rest may mark

over their parts "tacet" for their efforts are futile,—at least so says the
spokesman of the vanguard of the musico-physicists, Mr. John Redfield.
His theory, acceptable to many of his colleagues, is that voices or instruments of the same quality and amplitude, sounding in true unison, increase the quantity of a first player or singer as follows (as it were, in a
ratio of diminishing returns)

the second—21%
the third —10%
the fourth— 6 5/10%
the fifth — 4 8/10%
the sixth — 3 8/10%

If the 2nd, 3rd, 4th, 5th and 6th performer contribute a total of 46 1/5
percent to the increase of the first performer's tonal-unit, and if, as the
Redfield position has it, 27 performers are required to increase the original
unit by 100%, it is clear that twenty-one performers, on a diminishing
scale, make inconsequential, negligible and finally useless sounds.

In the laboratory, one sixth of the participants is practically non-
contributory, while in concerts the percentage increases to one fourth.
The theory is predicated upon the absolute unison and the absolute
equality of dynamic force among the players. Such absolute unisonance
never obtains in practice, for the natural *vibrato* of singers and string
players, each "celesting" the notes with individual differences, and the
improbability of securing from each participant an absolute uniformity
in a volume expressible in decibels, prevent the theory from being
verified fully.

But granted that absolute unisonance cannot be achieved by singers,
and that therefore the diminution of secondary and other additional contributions will not be in precise agreement with Mr. Redfield's table, it
is fair to conclude (if Mr. Redfield be scientifically correct) that a certain
undetermined number of the voices in a church choir or singing society
are never heard, belonging to the sixth, the fifth, or the fourth or whatever portion of the whole may constitute the aphonous unavailing section
of a chorus.

I admit that the immediately foregoing considerations cannot be
turned to valuable account readily, until the Redfield theory will have
been verified practically under diverse circumstances, and an exact table
of the logarithmic quantity-relationships among participants will have
been compiled.

Meantime the Redfield theory and other kindred points of view tend to emphasize the futility and artistic uselessness of large orchestras and mammoth choruses.

I have personally experimented, during the last three seasons, with a large group on one strophe and a small group on the other. If several of these pairs of strophes be sung consecutively, the director has splendid opportunity for ascertaining and almost judging the extent of the tonal efficacy of the two groups. Thus, in the great Church of St. Paul the Apostle, New York City, I frequently keep a half dozen singers in the chancel, to sing the alternate verses of a recessional hymn, while the main chorus delivers its assignment from the processional platform. I carry the experiment further along, sometimes to divergent styles of music and to varying conditions and circumstances. Thus, a semi-chorus (ten voices, approximately) sings a complete movement of a motet followed by the complete personnel on the repetition.

At first I was surprised and probably somewhat chagrined, to discover that the smaller groups, frequently gave as satisfying a delivery of the verse or movement as the larger, and in some instances, a more gratifying effect. It may be reasonably commented here that perhaps the small group was singing *forte* and the large group *piano,* thus making the comparison disingenuous. Answering this comment, I am pleased to relate that I have tried the two groups at all possible points of contrast, employing all the dynamic panels from *PP* to *FF*.

The addition of a few more voices to each choral line sometimes seems to add a shimmer to the tone of the smaller group, but I hazard a conjecture that I would produce about the same degree of tonal and dynamic applicability with a choir of thirty adults as with a choir of fifty.

At the present writing, it is unwise to insist upon definite criteria by which to estimate the decibel strength and the probable numerical strength needed and adequate for the performance of specific music styles in specific music auditoriums. As the research into the arcana of physics continues under the interested and capable guidance of radio and cinema sound engineers, more of the esoteric dogmas of acoustics will be revealed, and a definite creed proposed for practical guidance.

Meantime, it is safe and desirable (even outside the radio studios) to tend in the direction of the smaller rather than the larger ensemble unit. "Little" symphony orchestras, sinfoniettas, and small singing groups are gradually becoming the vogue among the connoisseurs of the finer phases of music; but some decades must pass before the general American public will believe a smaller group to be potentially as convincing as a larger group.

I remember a case in my own experience which illustrates this North American skepticism and reluctance where numbers are involved. In one of the greatest concert halls of this continent, I conducted the Paulist Choristers in an interesting and relatively easy programme. There were one hundred and ten choristers, strikingly garbed in French uniforms, and an ingenious *mise en scene*. The audience was enthusiastic, and the professional critics of the journals most eulogistic. A year later, the choristers, having been reorganized with a new adult personnel, revisited the city and with fifty-five singers, minus the eclat of military uniforms and *mise en scene,* gave a concert of much more significance. It represented a more important and difficult repertoire than the earlier concert. Vocally, the choral lines were as smooth as zephyrs in the groves of Diana, and the balance, blend, and aesthetic obedience of the group were notable. But the public felt that the organization had deteriorated, and the critics, while not committing themselves to such misjudgment, contrived to "damn with faint praise." The organization was reduced in size, therefore it had sacrificed something substantial: it did not look the same, therefore it could not sing the same.

There had been a definite reason for travelling with a large personnel the first year: the organization was on a long patriotic tour during the war, and extra choristers were included in the group to guarantee at least a quorum of singers when the ranks would be thinned out (as they often were) by illness.

I have occasionally been challenged by questioners who knowing my convictions about the relative merits of larger and smaller groups, to explain the large personnel of the Paulist Choristers in New York City. My reply is always to insist that the singing choir is not actually but only seemingly large.

This season (1936–37) there are fifty soprano-boys in the choir, fifteen counter-tenors, six real tenors, three baritones, and seven basses. A choir of 81 voices, and distributed according to what curious plan?

In reality there are in the singing balance, as probably measurable in decibels,

8 sopranos
5 altos
4 first tenors
4 second tenors
4 baritones
5 basses
30 singing voices

Analysis of the personnel which is observed to occupy choirstalls in the chancel, shows the following synthesis of vocal elements:—of the fifty soprano-boys, twenty-six are juniors just graduated from the probationers' choir, vocally ineffective and unacquainted with the major part of the repertoire; during their juniorate, the boys contribute practically nothing to the tonal fabric:—

the treble quality of the Paulist Choristers has been traditionally restrained, disembodied, and almost translucent; individual boys are never permitted to use their voices in dynamic panels where the organization's diaphonous soprano tone might be in jeopardy, and so, normally, three boys are required to compound a lyric tone of the amplitude proper to one average female lyric voice. Thus with twenty-four out of fifty boys contributing conservatively to the totality of soprano tone, there are equivalently eight lyric soprano voices in the Paulist Choir:

of the fifteen counter-tenors, only five are used on the alto line, and three only, as a rule, in the open compositions of four part harmony. The falsetto character of this voice gives it such prominence on the alto line (not so much on the tenor line) as to interfere seriously with the unity of the chorus that a minimum quantity of counter-tenor quality should be used. The remaining counter-tenors are usually distributed among the tenors and baritones to reinforce and bring these sections up to the required balance:—

of the seven basses, two are so light as to be absorbed by the others; these, like the extra counter-tenors, are frequently useful as emergency substitutes.

I have taken these few paragraphs to show that in a boys' and men's choir, the personnel is usually much in excess of the actual singing forces. But one should be careful not to be misled into believing that this is always the rule in boys' and men's choirs, or that in mixed choirs it is even frequently the case.

If the sopranos of a boys' choir be allowed *individually* to sing great *fortes,* make bold *crescendos,* and generally to deliver the treble line as women might artistically deliver it, the choirmaster should count each boy as a woman, aye, and more than woman, for he can out-sing, quantitatively (especially if the *chest-tone* quality be employed as it is so generally) any save a great dramatic soprano.

A general critique of the balance of *voices* and instruments in their respective ensembles is that there is usually too much treble. Soprano notes, being high and above (*sopra*) the rest, assert themselves with great poignancy.

The rapid vibrations which produce the high tones disturb the modern microphone in the same way as they disturbed the needle of the old phonographic recording devices, i.e. by overloading the mechanical ears of the instruments.

Therefore in broadcasting, the careful engineers are on the alert to keep the soprano contribution the lightest of all. In some studios, provided over by real physicists, not only is the quantity of the soprano tone restricted to a minimum, but the soprano singers themselves are assigned to places most remote from the microphone.

The research of radio engineers has done much to enlighten musicians as to balance of parts, and while admitting that such conservatism in the use of high voices and instruments, as has been mentioned above, is prescribed on account of the two dimensional limitations of the broadcasting and tone-reproducing machines, it must be insisted that in churches or on concert stages, the aesthetic and well balanced effect of orchestral and choral music would be enhanced by a considerable reduction in the treble contributions.

The error of unduly stressing treble parts is essentially modern. Even at the memorial concert commemorating the centenary of Handel's birth, when a chorus of dimensions inconceivable to Handel or his contemporaries was assembled, the grievous blunder of over-emphasizing the soprano line was avoided, for witness the balance: 59 sopranos, 48 altos, 83 tenors, and 84 basses! But an outstanding defect in modern music is its weakness for treble effect. The rust of antiquity has obliterated many of the memorabilia of mediaeval music, but none more thoroughly than the Guidonian Hand. The monk of Arezzo found music functioning at its best in a certain range, and in that range he placed his three hexachord scales and their four duplicates with Gamma-ut (G, do) as a starting point one note lower than the old Greeks descended, and E^2 la as the top note, establishing the termini of effective compass.

Music has traveled upwards through many leger lines since Guido's era, perhaps sacrificing both substance and charm. The added brilliancy that accrues to the orchestra when the higher instruments are well scored for and well played is without doubt an asset in certain styles of orchestration, and the lovely ripplings of rapid and light scale and arpeggio passages in the upper octaves of the piano are dainty and delightful, but full loud chords on piano or organ or in the orchestra, in the high registers, soon begin to irk and presently to make listeners thoroughly uncomfortable. Loud rapid vibrations impinge unpleasantly upon the ear.

And so it has seemed wise to bring the treble writing under careful scrutiny. If, in either the choral or orchestral parts, this modern penchant for aviation be notable, the conductor must reduce the number or the dynamic contribution of the sopranos, or the treble instruments,— perhaps both.

The average choral society of men and women seems top-heavy, the sopranos being as two to one. The personnel of an amateur chorus can be assembled sometimes only with great difficulty, especially in the men's sections; therefore, it is easy to understand why there are often so many more female than male members of an organization, but in the case of paid or otherwise compensated choruses, the director should have little trouble in choosing a balanced unit.

If a quartet S.A.T.B. can be nicely balanced and blended, why, as the size of the paid, carefully selected group increases, not determine the increase on the basis of additional quartets? This plan might not prove to be feasible always, but it would at least tend to improve the balance so essential to ensemble organizations.

If a string quartet can give so ingratiating an impression as to have lured the great composers, including Beethoven, to write for it, it seems unreasonable to increase the number of first and second violins, out of proportion to the increase of violas and cellos, in the selection of string players for the symphonic ensemble.

Personally, I am usually conscious of an excess treble and a penury of alto, tenor and bass in the string choirs of orchestras, and in all mixed choruses. In boys' and men's choruses, the lack of low voices is a general defect.

As a guest conductor, at festivals, it has often been my experience to find the single choirs of both chorus and orchestra disparate in equilibrium, and generally the remedial strategy has been directed mainly to sopranos and first violins.

If I were to be given opportunity to effect as perfect a balance of parts as my artistic sensibilities could dictate, I think that I should add the sopranos last; sweeten to taste, as it were. Most conductors put the sugar in first, and usually so lavishly, that the other ingredients are neutralized or attenuated to a serious degree.

The *sopranos* are the *above* (*sopra*) voices and should be assigned to the ensemble only when the lower parts, having been reconciled quantitatively among themselves, indicate by their mutual balance just what measure of *sopra* quality is required to "point-up" the mass-tone, and to make it buoyant.

Harmony is preoccupied first with the bass. So too is organ registration, except in the selection of solo-stops.

The preoccupation of orchestra conductors frequently, and chorus directors generally, seems to be with the trebles. The more I experiment with different plans of vocal balance, and the more I observe the indifference of many conductors to the need of such experiment, the more I am convinced that the subject of balance of parts is one of the most interesting, profound and important phases in the twin arts of the orchestra and the chorus.

Radio will do much to readjust the sometime orchestral and choral balances to the findings of acoustics. Doubtless, the readjustments will be towards the softer side. Perhaps female sopranos will be tonally reduced to the three-to-one ratio of the Paulist Choir. Perhaps the dramatics will soon have sung their swan-songs, handing over their tinsel and laurels to the lyrics. Perhaps, *loud* trumpets, pungent strings and the nasal yapping of oboes will be modified by treble agencies of more congenial timbres. Perhaps, quantity is writing its own obituary.

And, perhaps, finally, musicians will again burn sweet smelling incense before Apollo and Euterpe.

CHAPTER XII

The Control of Dynamics and Tempo

I. Dynamics

Consistently, throughout this thesis, the necessity of being on guard against quantity as an insidious foe of artistry has been emphasized. One of the convictions from which the writer's plan of choral technique has evolved is that excessive loudness in playing instruments and in singing have seriously impeded the growth of music towards more aesthetic ideals.

But the fact that the music-philosophy of this book is so premised, does not permit the corollary to be drawn that quantity is not, if disciplined, a valuable asset to music. It is in fact one of primary features of music determining, with quality and pitch, its aesthetic validity. Therefore it must be brought under control and made to serve properly as a co-efficient.

The degree of amplitude which must be applied to tones is fittingly determined by the style of a composition, the character of a particular movement or even the mood of a particular phrase. Sometimes, too, the circumstances of the performance or the exigencies of the moment require immediate alterations and readjustments in the application of degrees of dynamic energy. Exact variations in quantity cannot be prepared in advance, nor can a general plan of interpretation always be followed, in this matter of quantity. A particular need may suddenly present itself, calling for the instant substitution of a compromise for the more correct interpretation of a number, such as the need of emphasizing a particular part, if a deviation from pitch be indicated, or diminishing a single line's contribution if the acoustics or other conditions would be thus better served.

The use of dynamic and tempo variations, as a general resource of interpretation, will be discussed in Volume II. In this chapter the mechanics of control comprise the subject matter, and suggestions are offered to expedite the acquisition of facility in applying all the nuances of expression which the needs of performance may indicate.

Quantity is discussed in the first, and tempo in the second division of the Chapter. Study of the control of and elasticity in altering degrees of quantity begins with the examination of the dynamic panel diagram, and proceeds to consider:—

(*A*) Maintenance of steady pressure in all panels.
(*B*) Different types of quantity-variations.

1. The slight or considerable change of dynamic level required by the beginning of a new series of phrases, or a complete new movement.
2. *Subitos,* both soft and loud—and *rinzforzando.*
3. The long *crescendo* or *diminuendo,* throughout all the *panels,* during several measures, or quickly.
4. *Crescendo* and *diminuendo* between adjacent panels.
5. The *loop crescendo* and *diminuendo.*
6. The arsic and thesic undulations of Gregorian Chant and polyphony.
7. *Animando: accelerando senza crescendo: diminuendo senza rallentando.*
8. *Crescendo* and *diminuendo* in single parts.

The first step towards the developing of facility in this most important item of quantity control is the acquisition by the conductor himself of skill in accurately appraising the intensity and amplitude of the sounds he directs.

Many conductors have admitted to me personally that, although recognizing the importance of appropriate dynamic variations, they had never adverted seriously to the subject and had therefore failed to acquire appreciation of the finer discriminations of quantity-nuance.

There is a gamut of dynamic intervals just as definitely co-ordinated as the gamut of *DO RE MI;* there is an unwritten syntax of aesthetic intensities as prompting as the written grammars of harmony; there is a counterpoint of nuance, which like the counterpoint of color is yet to be codified in a book, as appurtenant to the integrity and perfection of music as the counterpoint of notes in the Gradus ad Parnassum.

The authoritative musician is convinced of this, and his use of this rich resource of interpretation is determined by studied criteria of artistry.

There is no phase of music over which caprice has held sway so conspicuously and diastrously as its quantitative phase, and conductors must teach the regulation of this as a primary principle of true musicianship.

At the outset, it is well to offer here a diagram of dynamic panels which is serviceable both to conductors and singers. I have used the plan with notable success, not only at my own rehearsals but at the rehearsals of choruses of which I was the guest-conductor, and which were so few as to require the most expeditious methods to meet the needs. This diagram has been accepted as a valuable aid to the proper control of dynamics, by many orchestra conductors and bandmasters, as well as by choral directors. The diagram is a sort of decibel-graph which indicates to the eye the general progress of a sound, from its *pianissimo* threshold of audibility to its maximum *fortissimo* quantity.

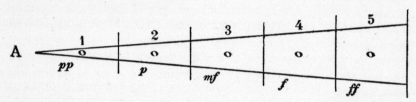

The diagram presents, of course, only the cardinal panels, since it would be profitless and confusing to indicate the minor degrees by which they are related, as:

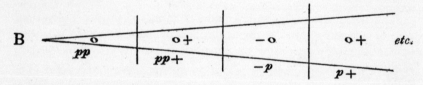

However, although not designated *nominatim* in the paradigm, the conductor must note that these minor degrees through which nuances proceed are very definitely involved, and that in reality there is a *minus* and a *plus* side to each panel.

With the diagram before their eyes the singers can readily fix their attention upon whatever feature of quantity-control the conductor is emphasizing.

It is urgently necessary for them to direct their full undistracted mental energy to the item proposed for improvement, and concentration upon a sort of optical dynamometer is an easy means to that end.

A

The first virtue to be acquired is the maintenance of a steady unvarying pressure in all the dynamic panels.

Obviously, it is futile to rehearse singers in the subtle motions to and fro which are involved in *crescendo* and *diminuendo,* until they have become adept at holding a given quantity with stability, but a critical study of the *status quo* of orchestras and choruses indicates that only a minority of conductors habituate their groups to this primary requirement. Judging from results, one cannot escape the impression that the average conductor adverts only casually to the need of stabilizing the quantity produced, for it is a common experience to hear ensembles straying back and forth between *piano* and *mezzo-forte* or between *mezzo-forte* and *forte,* without artistic intent and without being aware of their oscillations.

The ability to sustain tones through several consecutive measures without involuntarily modifying the quantity of the tones is the result of much intelligent practice, rather than a natural gift.

For the maintenance of an imperturbable dynamic level in spite of the five hazards which menace such equilibrium is a mark of well drilled craftsmanship.

These five hazards are somewhat inter-related, but any single one may readily countercheck the steady pressure needed for even utterance.

The first is the irregular address of breath to the cords, which may be due merely to carelessness or fatigue, or which may be associated with the second hazard, i.e. the mental condition of the singers (apprehension, uncertainty of pitch, intervals, note values, entrances, etc.) or the unevenness of breath pressure may be sometimes ascribed to the third hazard, i.e. the emotional reaction of the singers to the text or music. Excitement, fervor, enthusiasm, pathos, etc., all affect the quantity of voice used. The fourth hazard is found in the structure of the phrase or the curve-line of the melody, for these by requiring greater or lesser intervallic skips stimulate a sense of more or less vigorous intonation. The fifth hazard is the hazard of distractions which is a menace always, but a particularly annoying menace when and where it promotes inattention to that which is in progress. In the performance of music, inattention discloses itself first and immediately in heedless meanderings from one dynamic panel to another without purpose or pattern.

Perhaps a few leading singers on the right become interested in the entrance or departure of a party, or a few on the left become engrossed in the orchestration or a solo-obligato, and immediately their attention is diverted from the quantitative control of their own parts, and the equilibrium of the unit is imperilled!

It is unnecessary to examine these hazards in detail. They are easily circumvented by consistent practice with the diagram.

To keep a series of notes at a steady dynamic level requires concentration. An ideal of perfect stability must be set, and frequent stress put upon the fundamental worth of developing physical sensibility to all degrees of quantitative change. A high standard of dependability in this connection soon communicates itself to other features of choral team-work, and will be found to be an invaluable influence generally.

I remember two concerts of the Paulist Choristers at which disaster suddenly seemed imminent. On both occasions the service fuses of the electric light system blew out, leaving the auditorium in the blackness of Erebus. A few exit lights twinkled like the remote stars of distant solar systems. The conductor was invisible to the choristers, but the organization continued to sing with no perceptible sign of perturbation or anxiety, the dynamic variations being altogether in accord with the demands of the piece. They were singing by memory, of course, but the relevant point here is that even so unusual and intimidating an oc-currence could not distract them from their habitual, second-nature con-trol of the dynamic panels.

Probably it is immaterial whether the practice is begun in the lower or the higher panels, although this treatise consistently favors the lower panels for practically all rehearsing. But since *mezzo-forte* is the panel in which most speaking and much singing are done, it may be well to select it as the logical place for starting.

At first only sustained tones should be used. Having determined what strength of intonation is reasonably denoted by *mezzo-forte,* the singers should focus their attention upon it and identify this degree of amplitude as belonging in the centre of panel No. 3 of the diagram.

With the aim of learning to maintain this degree steadily, the singers should practice exercises like the following (here pitched for sopranos) :—

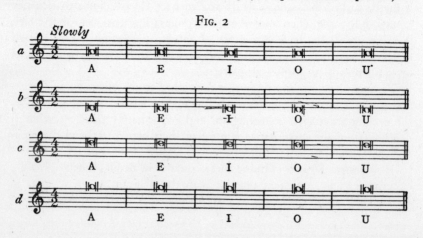

FIG. 2

Let the director place the point of his baton upon the dot in the centre of the panel, and indicate every slightest variation detected in quantity by moving it to the right or left. This is a most effective method of checking oscillations.

The erratic movements of the baton, indicating the unsteady, fluctuating tones, plague and mock the singers who quickly try to bring the tones under discipline. Inviting the eye to participate in the making of music, as an observer and mentor, is excellent pedagogy, as I discovered in my personal experience. In this matter of steadying the quantity, the baton and diagram contribute to immediate results just as the moving of a finger across the top of the piano music-rack helps to inculcate a concept of steady pitch to beginners.

As soon as it is evident that the sustained tones have become stabilized, the singers should modify the exercise at Fig. 2 as follows:—

FIG. 3

Pay Pee Pie Po   Pu   May Mee Mei Mo   Mu

Tay Tee Tie To   Tu   Bay Bee Bei Bo   Bu

It is more difficult to keep a stable equilibrium with the shorter than with the longer notes, for the former, marking the beats of a measure, stimulate the feeling of greater or less accent. At first it is well to disregard accentuation altogether; let each note be sung without reference to a rhythmic pattern, slowly and presently with increasing speed. In the upper register portions of the exercise, the tendency to increase the volume is sometimes almost irresistible. The baton and the diagram should serve here also as the mentor. When the virtue of steadiness in a series of equal notes has been acquired, the time value of the notes should be diversified so that the choristers may cultivate uniformity in various rhythmic patterns. Thus:—

FIG. 4

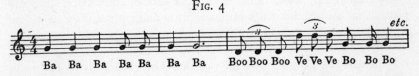

Ba Ba Ba Ba Ba   Ba Ba   Boo Boo Boo Ve Ve Ve Bo   Bo Bo

In order to develop full control of quantitative steadiness it is profitable to interrupt the progress of an exercise with a measure of rest; the tendency, upon resuming the vocalization, will be to add quantity to the tones, especially in the impact with the first note. Thus:—

FIG. 5

Pah Pah Pah Pah Pah Pah Pah Pah　Pah　Pah　Pah

It is opportune at this juncture to apply the principle of "accentuation by diminuendo."[1]

The rhythmic requirements of measured music demand refined differentiations between strong, weak, and unaccented beats. Practice in modifying a steady tone to meet these requirements is necessary. One of the most annoying and persistent duties of the artist-conductor is the achievement of an aesthetic refinement of these subtle differences, which escape the notice of many. Solo-singers of international repute, concert-masters of celebrated orchestras as well as their subordinate colleagues, and chorus-singers especially, are amazed and fretful when a strict disciplinarian insists upon meticulous cognizance and punctilious exemplification of these differences.

The majority of conductors is content with a decisive "down-beat." Many strum out the time in such fashion as to indicate an impression that all pulsations are "down-beats." The possibility that a composer has deliberately chosen a four-four instead of a two-four form, or a six-eight instead of a three-eight, or an *alla breve* instead of common time, has not impressed the average modern musician. Thrum follows thrum; stress denies itself to no note; binaries and ternaries are closer than twins, their respective time signatures being seemingly out-moded and meaningless!

It is not uncommon to find good musicians deceived by such specious formulae as:—

"Start a measure with a strong beat, and the rest will follow along amicably! Learn to bring the baton down vigorously every two, three, or four beats, and the art of the conductor is accomplished!"

In reality, the "down-beats" take good care of themselves. It is important, of course, that their responsibilities and prerogatives should be conserved, but the periodicity of rhythm is so punctuated by natural law that the authentic accentuation of first beats is *nolens-volens* unescapable.

The mystery of music is in the up-beat. This thought is an important

[1] See p. 45.

substratum of the principles of interpretation which are debated in Volume II.

A conductor who fails to sense the latent poetry and drama of unaccented beats, or the obeisance which in quadruple forms the third beat must pay to the first, probably has little understanding of Ruskin's philosophy, that in rests is the making of music.

Many conductors are merely metronomic leaders, their batons moving up and down with the mechanical indifference to rhythmic patterns of a Maelzel pendulum. But those who appraise at its true worth the value of taking weight and stress off weak beats, unless special accentuation be indicated by the composer, are probably instrumentalities of convincing music, and genuine masters of the lyricism of the art.

Rhythm is the motion of sound waves marked off into symmetrical periods. Motion, like cause and effect, is a vivid reality, and its relationship to melodic lines furnishes a topic for much study. The universality of motion is conceded by philosophers and scientists alike, and its importance as the corner stone for both metaphysical and empirical inquiry is unchallenged. Therefore, since the periodicity of impulses,—motion according to a pattern,—is the differentiating quality between music and mere noise, musicians must take cognizance of its implications.

The great composers, at least, chose their rhythmical forms deliberately. Mendelssohn was not confused when he selected a four-four instead of a two-four form. He felt the lesser accent of the third beat. Neither was Beethoven writing at random when he chose the time signatures for his symphonic movements.

I am quite conscious that many instances can be cited to show that composers frequently disregarded the first beats as necessarily stronger than the others. There are plenty of examples at hand, in symphonic as well as choral compositions, of first beats being moments of repose. But it has often occurred to me that the composer might more properly have chosen a different time signature, or started his phrases on a beat which would make the majority of his effects coincide with rhythmic patterns. Generally, in modern music, the first beat is the authoritative active agent of each measure.

Thus it behooves the modern conductor to address his attention seriously to the subject of rhythmic forms and patterns, and to perfect his organization in the skill required to present these forms.

The exercises suggested at Figs. 3, 4, 5 should now be practiced with this end in view. Still using panel No. 3, the choristers should learn to control and employ the slight fluctuations of quantity necessary to establish the rhythmic sequences. The conductor may successfully direct the practice by the same method followed in inculcating the sense of steadiness. With his baton on the centre dot for the first beat, he should move it somewhat to the left for the second and fourth beats, marking a point not quite at the centre for the third beat. The choristers find little difficulty in following the suggestions of the baton, and after a few earnest rehearsals, the conductor will be gratified with the gracious rhythmic flow of notes which the organization can produce.

Ternary and compound ternary forms should be practiced in the same manner, as well as the two-four and six-eight (two counts) forms.

Having practised these exercises consistently in one panel, the singers should be rehearsed according to the same scheme, in all the panels.

B—1

The next undertaking in the acquisition of control of quantity deals with the change of dynamic level indicated at the beginning of a new phrase or movement. For example:—a phrase or sentence or movement has been concluded *piano;* the ensuing measures are marked *mezzo-forte.* In this circumstance, the universal tendency is to begin the new phrase *forte.* The tendency to leap at the chance of louder expression tempts the majority of singers and orchestral players to advance to a higher panel than the composer intended. Even with highly trained and sensitive units this temptation has constantly to be checked. Therefore, the chorus must be drilled, with diagram and baton, to apply only the extra degree of amplitude indicated. Material may be profitably chosen from the repertoire, or an exercise like the following may be proposed:—

FIG. 6

Here again the "listening-eye" will keep the *mezzo-forte* of the new phrase in proper accord with the *piano* of the preceding notes.

The need of cultivating a fine sense of the ratio of increase permitted by aesthetics in such a relationship of *piano* and *mezzo-forte,* or of any adjacent panels, yields place only to the major necessities of singing the right notes with the right tone-quality.

If the first four measures of Fig. 6 were marked *mezzo-forte* and the ensuing measures *piano,* the conductor would find his singers reluctant to abandon the *mezzo-forte.* Therefore the exercise should be practised with these markings also.

The exercise at Fig. 6 should now be sung with the first four measures at *piano* and the new ¾ phrase at *forte.* Immediately, the average chorus and orchestra will produce a lusty *fortissimo.* The same process of correction is prescribed as in the preceding cases.

Fresh starts, even in closely related measures as well as in the initial notes of different movements, always urge the singers, subconsciously, to deliver the notes with added assurance and authority, which of course means simply with considerable increase of quantity.

In perfecting a unit in a highly refined control of dynamic relationships, this exercise is suggested as an infallible means of tempering fresh starts with the conservatism which must prevail if the interrelation of the dynamic panels is to be preserved.

FIG. 7

The alertness which must be exercised in order to keep these measures properly at the very centre of the panels indicated will in a short time display itself without conscious effort on the part of the singers. The habituating of choristers to sense dynamic relationships subconsciously while in the conscientious hurly-burly of technical, vocal, and pitch demands can be accomplished only by a systematic pedagogy which promotes this sense to the rank of an intuition.

But there is reassurance in the knowledge that systematic and painstaking instruction and rehearsal with baton and diagram inevitably develop intuitive control. In this connection I find myself impelled to refer to the subliminal regulation of the subtlest dynamic nuances by the Paulist Choristers, especially on long tours. It has been my experience to find the choristers responding to the whole gamut of dynamic variations by a mere shrug of my shoulders on the conductor's platform.

Just as an intuition for correct pitch and intervallic skips must be made a dependable asset, so the instinct of dynamic propriety must be developed as an unconscious apperception.

B—2

The next topic for study is the radical difference between *subito* changes and the gradual processes of *crescendo* and *diminuendo*. The average chorus singer fails to distinguish clearly between these resources of expression. The art of the *poco a poco* increase or decrease of quantity will be discussed presently. At first it is profitable to drill the chorus in the proper delivery of *subito fortissimo* and *subito pianissimo*. Having become skillful in addressing the *subitos* artistically, the singers develop a keen consciousness of the difference between them and the gradual nuances.

The *subitos* frequently convert dramatic intentions into burlesque. The *sforzando* introduced sometimes in a generally quiet number can easily upset the artistic continuity altogether. A sudden over-done *forte* is not a grace of expression; it is an explosion, a detonation, an unexpected salvo which removes it from the category of musical expedients. It is the impact itself which determines the artistic rectitude of a *sforzando* or a *subito pianissimo*.

The safe rule to follow, in order to assure seemliness, is to address the *sforzando* at the extreme left side of panel No. 5 instead of at the centre, and the *subito pianissimo* at the left side of panel No. 2 instead of hushing the voices to a whimsical whisper. Exaggeration in either case is sure to distort the composer's intentions and to produce a false representation of the dynamic contour of a number.

After the instant of impact a slight increase of pressure may be effectively applied in the *sfz*, and a further decrease in the *subito-pianissimo*.

The following paradigms are suggested as useful: —

FIG. 8

Rinforzando is akin to *sforzando,* except that it is applied usually to a single part in the ensemble and involves more than the single notes which are stressed by the *sforzando.* Furthermore it seems to connote the idea of reinforcement rather than the mere quantitative impact of *sforzando.* It is frequently a sudden stressing of a subordinate part. Personally I have found it most effective when interpreted as the French indication *en dehors* which of course means merely to give a single part more prominence than the rest of the ensemble. It is a mistake to interpret *rinforzando* as calling for the same quantitative increase as *sforzando.*

The single part applying the *rinforzando* must be held carefully within the general constitutional pale of the ensemble phrase, otherwise it would claim such attention as to destroy the tonal shapeliness of the whole. Any number in the repertory will furnish the material for practice in this connection. A simple hymn tune is excellent, for the various choral lines can take their turns at applying the *rinforzando* to their respective parts. The *rinforzando* is very similar in effect to the *crescendo* and *diminuendo* in single parts which are considered as item No. 8 in this Chapter. The difference lies in the gradual process denoted by the latter, for the former like *sforzando* connotes the idea of abruptness.

The art of applying *rinforzando* to subordinate or interior parts constitutes one of the richest and most subtle resources of interpretation. By its felicitous and opportune use a vitality is frequently imparted to a phrase which transforms it from an inconsequential congeries of notes to a sparkling effervescent episode.

The structural idiom of much Russian music of the nineteenth century requires the *rinforzando* for effective performance. And the well liked "Ave Maris Stella" of Grieg depends upon it. Conductors will find this number an outstanding example of the efficacy of *rinforzando;* they should try the first eight measures first with all parts singing in the same panel, and then with the baritones delivering the *D* and *E* in a higher panel. The difference is marked and most convincing.

In Volume II this valuable interpretative factor will be studied thoroughly.

It is vitally important here for the choirmaster to accustom his singers to the frequent and correct use of the nuance. The majority of the exercises suggested for blend and balance [1] can also profitably be employed to develop a sense of and facility in applying the *rinforzando,* and notably the exercise at Fig. 10.

There are no particular difficulties to be confronted in mastering the

[1] See Chapter XI.

use of *rinforzando* but it is essential to fix the importance of it in the minds of a new group of singers, and to renew the appreciation of veterans by occasional practice.

The principal point to be emphasized in such practice is the necessity of adding only the degree of re-enforcement indicated by the conductor. Such indication may be simply and clearly made through a code of signals.[1]

B—3 and 4

We proceed now to study the most effective and the most frequently recurring of the quantitative nuances, the gradual increase and decrease of tonal amplitude. *Crescendo* and *diminuendo* are the major means of securing rhetorical effect with music. They are also the most difficult of the interpretative graces to master. One rarely hears a perfect *crescendo* or *diminuendo* from soloists, orchestras or choruses. The slightest offence against the fundamental principle of gradation interrupts the progressive continuity which is the essential feature of the increase or decrease designated by these terms. Growth of tonal strength is determined by a definite increment as it passes from one dynamic panel to another and similarly its attentuation is determined by a definite loss of amplitude as it subsides to the threshold of audibility.

The average musician, at some point in an attempted *crescendo* or *diminuendo* fails to regulate the ascent or wane of the quantity, thus introducing irregularity and an impression of *subito* in the movement.

Crescendo means to the average chorus: "Sing louder"; *diminuendo*: "sing softer."

Among the most trying tasks of the artist conductor are the efforts to inculate a feeling for gradual movement, to develop control of this during rehearsals, and to invoke it successfully at performances.

I remember the disappointment which I experienced in the performance of a very subtle composition, when after many weeks of meticulously careful attention to an extended *poco a poco* growth from *pianissimo* to *fortissimo,* the organization yielded to its agitation and unwitting impatience and leaped from the minus side of panel #2 straight to the centre of No. 5. Such an experience is most disconcerting to a painstaking director, but he must not be discouraged. He must revise his pedagogy and teach the unit to overcome its dramatic impatience. For in the matter of substituting a *subito* for a gradual increase,

[1] See Chapter XV, "Baton Technique."

impatience and an excited enthusiasm to deliver a telling effect are usually responsible for the singers' eagerness to be free from restraint.

Restraint is the quality which must be developed. This can be accomplished only by faithful, constant, and enlightened efforts.

Only in the greatest of the symphony orchestras does one hear bona-fide *crescendos* and *diminuendos,* and only when these are directed by notably sensitive artists who insist, at rehearsal, day after day on the *poco a poco* elements. If the reader be skeptical about the almost universal imperviousness of groups to the basic character of the *crescendo* and *diminuendo,* let him propose a single chord to his organization to be sung gradually from *pianissimo* to *fortissimo* and vice versa. The first chord of the exercise at Fig. 10 in Chapter XI serves the purpose admirably. From my experience with many choruses, large and small, it is my conviction that, unless the director has forewarned the singers to be on guard, he will find the unit proceeding from panel No. 1 to No. 3 to No. 5 on the ascent, and from No. 5 to No. 3, concluding in No. 2 on the descent. In fact, this tendency has long been a menace to artistic continuity. It so disturbed Hans Von Bülow as to cause him to focus his attention upon it for a considerable period of time. Finally he produced a formula which is most effective if carefully applied. The formula is a paradox, which means that it is good pedagogy, for there is nothing more striking than a paradox to impress the mind. His formula, freely translated, is: "To make a good *crescendo* think of *piano;* to make a good *diminuendo* think of *forte.*"

Naturally the notion of *crescendo* suggests singing louder, but Von Bülow prescribes the mental image of softness. Likewise *diminuendo* certainly connotes the idea of softness, but Von Bülow insists on *forte* as a guarantee of its correctness. Von Bülow probably decided to add this paradoxical tenet to his musical creed because of the very widespread indifference to the second panel in the *crescendo* and to the fourth panel in the *diminuendo.* The second panel is *piano;* singers and instrumentalists ignore it, proceeding directly from No. 1 to No. 3. Therefore the wisdom of Von Bülow's counsel. Similarly, the fourth panel is *forte,* which usually escapes the attention of musicians in *diminuendo;* therefore they must advert to *forte* in order to soften their tones gradually. The same suggestion is applicable to *crescendos* and *diminuendos* which do not extend through the entire length of the diagram. In these less extensive variations, Von Bülow's counsel may be stated thus:—

at the beginning of every *crescendo* or *diminuendo,* fix the attention immediately upon the adjacent panel.

Using a simple chord at first, the conductor should insinuate, with baton moving slowly through the panels of the diagram, the gradual growth of tonal strength and its gradual decrease.

On account of the artistic impatience already referred to, it is imperative for highly trained and experienced units to be checked-up frequently, for upon the accuracy and authority with which they maintain control over these resources of quantitative expression, depends, in no inconsiderable degree, their rating as a convincing instrumentality.

Two lesser defects present themselves usually in the accomplishment of the *crescendo* and *diminuendo*. One is the "fall-off" at the end of the *crescendo*. This means simply that the singers do not sustain the *maximum* quantity to the end of the *crescendo* section. It is easily remedied, if the conductor, by a definite gesture, will hold their attention to the point. The other defect is the "push-up" which tends to disfigure or at least to impede the loveliness of a *pianissimo* at the end of a *diminuendo*. This defect is also readily curable. An excellent signal to warn the singers against this "push-up" is the gradual sliding of the left fore-finger down the length of the baton as the *diminuendo* approaches its completion.

An important point for all choral directors to keep in the forefront of their minds is the value of never allowing the singers at rehearsal to extend themselves to the full power of their *fortissimos*. The reaction involves a twofold evil. It is a temptation to force their voices, which must be given no quarter lest it injure the tone-quality, and it develops too much enthusiasm for loudness, which always and under all circumstances must be restrained by the discipline of art.

Most of the practice should be done with simple chords. The exercise at Fig. 10, Chapter XI, after the initial chord has been perfected in *crescendo* and *diminuendo,* should be sung in its entirety, the conductor indicating nuances at various points.

In the preparation of the *crescendos* and *diminuendos* of compositions, it has been my habitual practice for many years to direct the singers to "think" the nuances, the while singing the music *pianissimo*. In this method, the choristers are intently studying the moods of the composition and simultaneously vocalizing to advantage. The psychological effect on the singers is striking, while the physiological advantage of such procedure is to *keep their tone-quality* out of jeopardy. In the public performance of the composition, the singers are mentally well prepared for the nuances, and if the conductor have a simple code of signals for indicating degrees of amplitude, the rendition will be gratifying both in quality and quantity.

B—5

The loop *crescendo* and *diminuendo* are niceties of expression which are beyond the skill of the average chorus, but which can readily be cultivated in the greater choral units.

The *loop* involves the relationship between rhythm and progressive increase or decrease of quantity. The preservation of rhythmical patterns which depends upon proper accentuation and the steady growth of tone implied by the *crescendo* present a problem which can be satisfactorily solved only by the application of the loop to the progressive increase. By the loop I mean the circling round, as it were, of unaccented beats. Since the first instant of impact establishes the quantitative rating of a tone, it is simple to preserve the rhythmic pattern by beginning the unaccented slightly softer than the accented beat in binary rhythms, and immediately looping around it, so to speak, with a *crescendo*. In ternary rhythms it is necessary to loop the *crescendo* only on the second beat since the slight *decrescendo* there—for the fraction of a second—is adequate to present the rhythmical form. The singers must be taught to feel the first beat of each ensuing measure of a *crescendo* and to give it mental stress. The loop process with the *diminuendo* is of course the inversion of what is suggested for the *crescendo*. The impact with the accented beats must be slightly louder than the quantity of the preceding subordinate beats, with an immediate resumption of the *diminuendo*—a loop thrown around the note to bring it back quickly into the *diminuendo* line.

The slightly softer impacts of the loop *crescendo* and the slightly louder impacts of the loop *diminuendo* are so meagre as to be next to imperceptible. They are almost entirely mental modifications with just enough physical confirmation to indicate awareness of the rhythmical sequences.

The *loop* is the most involved nuance among the many resources which the conductor may invoke to impart life, lustre and loveliness to music, but it is futile to attempt it unless the chorus be super-excellent in its mastery of choral technique. It is recommended, however, to select units as a contrivance of great artistic value. It is a subtle design, commingling and adjusting elements which seem to be in conflict. Subtlety is of the nature of music and its employment by a master craftsman underlines the mystic, mysterious and magnetic elements of the art. Call the loop an artifice, a subterfuge, a maneuver if you will, but in spite of nomenclature it secures to the periodic pulsations prescribed by the time signature a definitiveness which is a primary need of rhythmical utterance, at the same time permitting the growth line of the *crescendo* to be delineated satisfactorily. The diagram of the panels including the loops presents this appearance. The loops will naturally be at the points indicated by the rhythmical structure. I place them here at the right of the panels merely for convenience and simplicity.

The top line indicates the *crescendo,* each loop at an *unaccented beat*
The bottom line indicates the *diminuendo,* the loops at *accented beats*

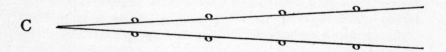

In short episodes of gradual change, the device is not effective enough to warrant the extra practice entailed. In the long *poco a poco* developments from one extreme panel to the other it proves its worth and will justify much intensive rehearsing.

B—6

The arses and theses which give rhythmical pattern to Gregorian Chant and to all the polyphonic styles up to the latter part of the seventeenth century demand moderate *crescendos* and *diminuendos* for idiomatic performance. The chant and polyphony are strangely but strikingly ineffective when conductors fail to take cognizance of this requirement. Many leaders of Gregorian choirs are expert in applying the proper variations to arsis and thesis, but there is probably not one among a hundred conductors who, undertaking to interpret the classical *a cappella* polyphony, recognizes an arsis or knows what to do with it if he does chance to identify it.

There are certain very definite, precise, and altogether distinctive lineaments which must be clearly outlined if polyphonic music is to escape the amorphous monotony with which the modern world is being forced to identify it. These features will be set forth and discussed fully in Volume II.

One of these is the underlining of the arses with a slight *crescendo,* and the subtraction of some quantity from the theses. An arsis is of course an upward progression suggesting the raising of the voice; a thesis is the recession from a top, intimating a "fall away" with the cadence. The curve line of polyphonic music indicates it to be an almost regular wave line of alternate ups and downs. Rarely, if ever, are there two wide consecutive skips in the Continental or English compositions of the classic period.

One of the real beauties of the polyphonic style is the interlacing of rolling *crescendos* with ebbing *diminuendos,* which is effected by the distribution of arses and theses at different points in the various choral lines. These arses and theses must be considered broadly in their relationship to a complete phrase, and the arses which set forth the highest and the largest notes and the most important progressions must of course be emphasized more than the subordinate movements of the phrase.

The general technical need in this connection is facility in making the slight increases and decreases. The movement of the polyphonic music is undulation, the rise and fall of the waves. The *crescendo* and *diminuendo* processes are therefore light and graceful. The chorus should be exercised with vocalizations to this end until they have developed an intuition for the aesthetic balance of increase and decrease.

The only place in polyphonic music where a considerable increase of tone is indicated is at the top of the curve line of the most important part of a phrase.

The choral lines of any composition of the Palestrinesque, or Byrd School furnish excellent passages for practicing undulation, except perhaps pieces written in the "stile famigliare" like the "O Bone Jesu" and the "Alma Redemptoris" of Palestrina.

The following exercise suggests the relationship of arsis and thesis which must be conserved:—

FIG. 9

The final *diminuendo* is in consonance with the principles of interpretation which I find essential to the polyphonic style.

B—7

Animando: accelerando senza crescendo: diminuendo senza rallentando.

These eloquent means of convincing musical expression, like the loop, are highly refined measures. But they are much more readily mastered than the loop and are quite well within the capabilities of the average chorus.

Animando is effective in three forms. Most often it includes *accelerando e crescendo*. Even when not thus indicated, the majority of conductors so interpret the direction. Another form is the *accelerando* with a delayed introduction of the *crescendo,* possibly after several measures.

The third form is the *accelerando* without increase of quantity.

The relative value of these forms of *animando* and the opportuneness of their use is not discussed here since this aspect of the subject belongs more properly to the academic development of the subject among the "Resources of Interpretation" in Volume II.

The acquisition of the technique appurtenant to a facile control of the three forms is relevant to the purposes of this volume, and the choral director should proceed as follows:—

The normal *animando,* which includes synchronous *crescendo* and *accelerando,* depends upon the elements already discussed for its efficacy, plus the factors which characterize a good *accelerando.* These factors are discussed in the second division of this Chapter.

The director must be on guard when an increase of speed is added to the *crescendo,* for the reaction to a more animated tempo is a feeling of greater excitement which usually tempts singers to disregard the restraining canons of *poco a poco* increase of quantity.

The postponement of the *crescendo* until after the *accelerando* has been in progress for a few measures, intensifies the dramatic progress to a climax, and is one of the subtlest and most admirable of all interpretative effects. There are several compositions in the repertoire which I regularly conduct which owe their popularity to this manner of setting forth some of the climactic clauses.

It involves no difficulty for the chorus. The director has merely to accustom the singers to sing phrases with increasing speed without increasing the quantity until a signal is given. The director who conducts with a definite code of signals will have no trouble in indicating the precise moment at which to initiate the *crescendo.*[1]

The charm of *accelerando senza crescendo* in certain types of compositions is intriguing, and the conductor should not fail to include this in the art of his chorus. Much practice and patience are required to win control to the extent of preventing increase of quantity altogether while the tempo is gaining speed, but since the delicate elegance of the embellish-

[1] See Chapter XV, "Baton Technique."

ment depends upon this, the director must not be satisfied with casual attention to the item.

The *diminuendo senza rallentando* belongs to the same species of dynamic ornamentation. It can be used effectively more frequently than the *accelerando senza crescendo,* and should be added to the assets of any chorus that aspires to virtuosity. The gradual softening to a *pianissimo* without any slowing of the tempo is most ingratiating, and perhaps rather naive because so seldom employed. I have used the grace even in the standard oratorio choruses which are so generally hurdy-gurdied in untinted dullness by choral units.

The chorus will give evidence of sensing a *rallentando* during a long *diminuendo,* and the only point, beyond the requirements already discussed, which the director must stress is the adherence to metronomic exactitude while the quantity abates and the mystic quality of a lovely *pianissimo* appears.

B—8

Another facility to be acquired by the chorus, is the art of responding to the conductor's baton with short or long *crescendos* and *diminuendos* in one or more parts while the rest of the ensemble maintains an unvaried quantity. The interpretative effects which such variation makes possible are most satisfying and, like the *rinforzando* are frequently indispensable. The ease with which a chorus can follow the conductor's guidance in producing these effects makes it difficult to understand why only a minority of conductors is prone to employ them. There is scarcely a type of harmonized music, including hymn tunes and carols, which does not offer frequent opportunity for the ingratiating underlining of harmonic or contrapuntal features which, though latent and perhaps because latent, can enhance the comeliness and strength of a musical contour. Many conductors are satisfied to have the entire chorus, *tout ensemble,* sing louder or softer together *en masse.* But the esoteric character of ensemble music requires that its hidden content be revealed, and explained, as it were, to the comprehension of the listeners. One reason for the ineffective delivery of strict forms like canon and fugue, is that the conductor fails to increase or decrease the quantity of the single choral lines at certain points. The mathematical structure of canon and fugue requires the single line *crescendos* and *diminuendos* for true representation as insistently as the computations of trigonometry require the logarithmic functions.

A modicum of practice will suffice to bring this particular form of nuance under control, for there is only one special point to be emphasized, i.e. that when one part is singled out for a dynamic variation, the others must not permit themselves to be affected, sustaining their proper dynamic level without change.

Carelessness and much singing under indifferent conductors frequently distract singers from the discipline and culture of dynamics which they have acquired under the tutelage of their chief conductor. In order to counteract the demoralizing effects of singing hither and yon under unfavorable conditions, with low standards of artistry prevailing, it is necessary to deliver earnest allocutions occasionally, especially to professional singers who make their livelihoods by adapting themselves genially to the amateur vagaries of "popular" conductors.

The bona fide master of choral artistry demands sincere acceptance of the best sanctions of musical excellence, and in the matter of dynamics as well as of tone-quality, he must be always vigilant and *semper paratus* to hold his forces close to the high line of perfection.

II. Tempo

Before engaging himself seriously in the task of inculcating the fine points of pace control, the conductor must address himself to the basic need of securing accuracy in the time values of notes and rests. If his system of teaching sight reading start with the counting of time beats,[1] he will already have habituated the singers to precisions, thus prospering the interests of rhythmic patterns. Even among professional singers an amazing degree of slovenliness prevails, due to carelessness rather than to lack of knowledge, and chargeable to the inadvertence of conductors.

The full value of each note must be accorded to it, except when it is necessary to shorten a note by an imperceptible fraction in order to take a "catch breath." Frequently singers release half-notes, dotted-halves, and whole notes too soon. Less often they extend the quarters and halves beyond their proper duration. Dotted and double dotted quarters and eighths are not infrequently confused, while slow triplets and the awkward pulsations of 5/4 time are incorrectly delivered. Many choristers have a definite complex about rests, some tending to sing through major portions of these, others to rest too often and too long. I have had singers who under varying circumstances would reveal first one tendency and then the other.

An accurate baton technique assists the singers to exactness in these

[1] See Chapter XVI, "Sight Reading."

items, but the dependable guarantee is practice and more practice in cultivating conscientious orthodoxy and scrupulous punctuality.

The habitual singing of compositions from memory, especially if the conductor as well is directing without a score, is sure to develop unperceived irregularities. After a long tour, during which the programmes were sung from memory, when the business of serious rehearsing was resumed, I have often been surprised and chagrined to discover that many modifications had substituted themselves for the notes of the written score. The "listening-eye" must frequently investigate memorized music for without its impartial observations, the imperceptible growth, day by day, of inexactitudes will eventually distort and rewrite a composition.

The chief reason for the existence of so many editions of Gregorian melodies[1] is that the melodies were learned by ear and passed orally from one generation to another. Only after notation was perfected could the "listening eye" detect discrepancies. When France, Germany, Belgium, and Italy finally committed to the Gregorian four lines and three spaces the Masses, hymns, antiphons, etc., which had been transmitted down the centuries, the divergences were so many and great that only after much scientific research and patient comparisons were the Monks of Solesmes and their Benedictine colleagues elsewhere satisfied to offer a probable authentic edition of the original melodies. Oral tradition and singing by memory inevitably influence accuracy, frequently to the extent of radically altering the original contours.

After approximately two hundred and fifty performances of an *a cappella* fugue from memory, I decided to check the rendition with the written notes, discovering to my confusion that the altos had been gradually re-composing their line in the stretto, changing progressions and time values. The metamorphosis probably had been in progress for a long time, the alterations making their appearance so stealthily as to escape notice.

It is, therefore, of paramount importance to call upon the "listening-eye" for co-operation to the end of serving authenticity and unerring precision.

With his chorus well established in these essential virtues, the conductor must proceed to develop resourcefulness in the control of tempo which shares with dynamics the major responsibility for effective interpretation.

[1] The official edition now is the Vatican edition, all others having been abrogated and ordered withdrawn from use.

It is superfluous to dilate upon the need of precise attack and release, each voice of each line being synchronized to accurate rhythmic entrances and exits. The average chorus can safely boast of fair technique in this matter.

But the average chorus lacks—(1) dependability in sustaining a steady *tempo* without any quickening or retarding of the pace; (2) elasticity in the application of the *accelerando* and *rallentando;* (3) appreciation and control of *rubato.*

1. To abide by a fixed rate of speed through many measures, involves a sense of stability which sometimes is a natural gift, but which is usually the reward of earnest practice. In some compositions the voices will show a tendency to hurry, in others to lag. Sometimes, especially in *a cappella* music which lacks the helpful accompanying pulsations of instruments, one line will show excitation while another is unmistakably sluggish.

In processional hymns, the sopranos are apt to increase speed and the basses to slacken. If the hymns be accompanied, the organist can correct the aberrations by playing a pedal note *staccato* on each beat of the measure until the *tempo* has become steadied. This plan is most effective and some years ago was known as "bunting the pedals." The value of the practice was brought to my attention by pupils of the late Harrison Wild, distinguished conductor of the Apollo Club and organist of Grace Church, Chicago.

In *a cappella* hymns the chorus will have to depend upon its acquired sensitiveness to steady progress in a fixed *tempo.*

One of the conductor's most important tasks—never altogether finished—is the inuring of a chorus to a constancy of pace which will remain imperturbable under all conditions.

Practice with the metronome is invaluable at different rates of speed.

It is advisable to begin the practice with slow sustained notes separated occasionally by rests. The rests will tend to render the progress somewhat sluggish and thus furnish a hazard which the practice is designed to overcome. The exercise should be written out on a blackboard (some schools are now using yellow boards with blackened chalk) and the conductor should beat the time on the board in the measure which is being sung. The "listening eye" helps here as it does in the acquisition of *crescendo.*

The indication of the time beats on the board, while the metronome clicks steadily, is the counterpart of the movements of the baton in the diagram of the dynamic panels.

Sustained *adagio* and *largo* numbers should be chosen for practice, and exercises similar to the following:—

FIG. 10

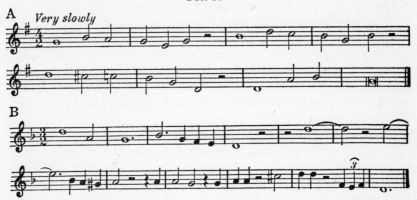

Paradigms should then be proposed to the chorus which call for faster *tempos* and in which runs or many consecutive short notes abound. Such exercises are intended to restrain the tendency of the singers to abandon a steady *tempo* to follow the lure of the short notes into a wayward acceleration of pace.

FIG. 11

Boy-sopranos are inclined generally to hurry the *tempo* in styles of composition which stress the reiteration of accents. Triplets in the accompaniment in *moderato* or faster *tempos* almost invariably tempt the boys to hie through the measures oblivious of their racing speed. A vigorously restraining baton is usually required to keep them under control. The "Jerusalem" chorus of Gounod's "Gallia" is a favorite opportunity for sprinting. Basses, on the other hand, are inclined to reduce speed, especially in long downward progressions of generally equal notes. With sopranos hurrying on one side of the chancel and basses lagging on the other, the director is occasionally hard pressed to synchronize their conflicting movements.

Boy-sopranos, however, show the opposite tendency in slow-moving polyphonic motets, especially if the choir be divided in the liturgical mode. The horizontal style lacks the incisive measure-beats of vertical music, and the boys, separated from their adult colleagues, are under the necessity of proceeding by "dead reckoning," sometimes in a dense fog, and therefore conservatively. Conservatism in *tempo* among boys soon becomes sluggishness, and persistent practice under the promptings of authoritative conducting is indicated as an essential feature of routine rehearsals.

If the choir be undivided, these tendencies are much more readily controlled, but in the liturgical choir, the director must take cognizance of them as major difficulties.

After conducting a Mass by Palestrina in the great Church of St. Paul in New York City, I have frequently been utterly exhausted, the effort to maintain equilibrium between the two widely separated sections of the choir drawing extravagantly against one's reserve of energy. But a performance of the same Mass in a choir gallery or on the concert stage is much less of a physical tax.

A few unsatisfactory renditions of polyphonic music, the choir placed *modo liturgico,* in the matter of steady *tempo,* are sufficient sometimes to produce a complex against this style of composition. The complex may persist throughout an entire season. At the date of this writing (March 1937) I have just succeeded in dismissing such a complex from the minds of our leading boy-sopranos. A notable part of our repertoire is chosen from the masterpieces of the sixteenth and seventeenth centuries, much of this music requiring two evenly balanced soprano choirs. In the early autumn, 1936, sluggish entrances by the sopranos disfigured the renditions twice. The boys then became timid; they lost assurance. After five months of the most painstaking efforts in the choir-hall, their confidence is restored, and once again they can sing the most involved polyphonies with the accuracy of a metronome. In fact they regained assurance and competent steadiness through much practice with the metronome.

The metronome should be used frequently at rehearsals, with meticulous care on the part of all the singers to synchronize with its every click, no attention being given to *accelerandos* or *rallentandos* until the steadiness of the piece as a whole has been substantially, stubbornly, and fixedly confirmed. During the rehearsing which ignores the indications for variations in *tempo,* I call the attention of the singers to the quickening and slackening which will occur eventually at certain points, recommending them to "think" the variations, while singing through all the measures with uncompromising obedience to the metronome.

2. The effect of *accelerando* or *rallentando* applied to an unsteady *tempo* is fortuitous. The deliberate variation of the pace presupposes that a prevailing pace be generally maintained. Therefore, only after a chorus has proven its reliability in this connection, is it opportune to introduce modifications. Like the agencies of dynamic increase and decrease, *accelerando* and *rallentando* connote the idea of alterations being effected in gradual process from one status to another. The director then must accustom the singers to a steadily increasing or decreasing speed through the indicated area, until the resumption of *a tempo.*

In the following diagram the pace-grades are shown in the same relationship as the panels of the dynamic diagram:—

(Following the Maëlzel conventions)

1	2	3	4	5	6
40–69 very slow	70–99 less slow	100–125 fairly slow	126–153 moderate	154–183 fast	184–208 very fast
Largo	Larghetto	Adagio	Andante	Allegro	Presto

These Italian designations of the pace-grades are not infrequently interpreted by conductors to indicate different degrees of speed, notably *adagio* and *andante* which are commonly read more slowly. However the nomenclature is inconsequential since the metronomic number of beats per minute is indicated in each grade and constitutes the safest guide for determining the *tempos* of modern music.

The task of the conductor is to train the chorus to proceed gradually through the grades, first to the right and then to the left, using the baton to trace the progress for the "listening-eye."

Von Bülow's paradox for the concatenation of the dynamic panels may be paralleled with an apt version for *accelerando* and *rallentando*. The tendency to ignore adjacent pace-grades originates in the same impulse to respond too eagerly to the impetus of animation which interferes with the regulated progress of dynamic movements.

Thus, to co-extend the formula of Von Bülow:—To make a good *accelerando,* concentrate on *slowness;* to make a good *rallentando,* concentrate on *fastness.* This, like the original formula fixes the attention on the adjacent grade and promotes the graduation of progress through contiguous steps.

3. *Tempo-Rubato* involves the modification of the steady rhythmical flow of a passage by the prolonging or acceleration of certain notes. It is the employment of *accelerando* and *rallentando* in miniature form. The occasional retardation of prominent notes or parts of phrases is an excellent means of stressing important features. Such retardation must be compensated for by the acceleration of less important notes or parts of phrases. This acceleration is an equivalent "robbing" from the time value of these notes and should be accomplished at least before the conclusion of the period to which the *rubato* phrase belongs.

The prolongations and accelerations are slight. The degree of increased intenseness which *rubato* is designed to convey, is meagre, and if a conductor permit its factors to exceed narrow limits, the effect is not of an artistic grace but of erratic caprice. Skill in the use of *rubato* will develop almost automatically as a corollary to the general control of *tempo* modifications which the unit has been cultivating. Its effective application is chiefly a responsibility of the conductor who must be on the *qui vive* to protect it with the restraint of aesthetic propriety.

In conclusion, the worth of invoking the aid of the "listening eye" may be profitably reiterated.

The use of the diagrams of the dynamic-panels and the pace-grades is an invaluable help in teaching choristers an appreciation and control of the subtle movements of music which depend so largely upon the modifications of quantity and pace for their potential effectiveness.

Tone-quality, blend and balance, steadiness, plus elasticity in applying the elegances of interpretation—these are the compass points by which the choral art must find its musical orientation.

CHAPTER XIII

Diction

The majority of concert-goers is unmoved by the performances of the average chorus. Finding little of beauty, magic, or elan in neutral music, they have no interest in the policies, plans, and programmes of choral societies. But there is a minority still fostering an appetite for ensemble singing. Perhaps the most clamorous and insistent criticism offered by these faithful devotees is directed against the diction of the singers.

The text is hidden, disguised or distorted, they complain; except in the programmes of small units which specialize in the elocution of music, the hub-bub of vowels and consonants which parodies the written texts might as profitably and with as much fruitfulness be assembled from the names in a telephone book, or from a page in the Farmers' almanac as from the greatest lyrics in Daniel's Thesaurus Hymnologicus.

The criticism of the devotees is justified in the fact; poor diction prevails. There is a notable lack of clarity in the phonations and articulations of choirs and concert-choruses. The utterance is opaque, a coalescence of diverse sounds inhibiting the lucidity of expression which makes words intelligible. Whole phrases are shapeless behind the murkiness which a fusion of vowels, with the ligatures of a great imaginary diphthong, necessarily produces.

Nevertheless, the inadequacies and faults which mar choral diction may not fairly be charged altogether against the choruses and their conductors, for a large number of choral conductors have given earnest attention to this problem, devising sundry ways and means of improving the utterance. In my survey of choral standards throughout this country, Canada, and England, I have been impressed with the serious efforts of the majority of conductors to make the text intelligible. But the results are not in proportion to the efforts.

There are real difficulties involved, and there are natural defects to be eliminated. On the other hand, there are remedies available which can render some of the major difficulties less formidable.

Probably there are many difficulties to be encountered in the process of bringing lucidity to choral enunciation. Some of these are general, others are personal to individuals. It seems sufficient for the purposes of this treatise to call attention to the four major sources of trouble, proceeding then to consider some curable defects, and concluding with three recommendations.

1. One source of serious difficulty in making choral utterance comprehensible is the complex structure in certain styles, of the music itself. In homophonic music, there is usually synchronous delivery of consonants and vowels by all the parts, but in contrapuntal compositions, this is impossible. Counter-point is concerned with the relationship of notes, making no concessions to texts, except when these do not trespass upon its mathematical rights. Each contrapuntal line is an independent integer with its own melodic, rhythmic and dynamic figures. These independences postulate separate entrances and exits and the weaving of separate textual continuities which frequently discover each line emitting a different vowel sound at a given moment. Obviously the jumble which must result from such a fusion of vowels is an obstacle to diction inherent in the polyphony itself.

The fact that each line might form its vowel sound with signal clearness would not prevent the mixture from becoming a medley-diphthong. One might suspect, rather, that notable distinctness in the forming of the various vowel sounds might, on occasion, increase the babel.

Incidentally, it may be noted here that there are two ways of listening to polyphonic music. One is to concentrate attention on a single part and follow its progressions with a minimum of attention to the other parts. Musicians, and of course polyphonic specialists, listen often in this manner, but the other method of listening, i.e. hearing the tonal fabric as a whole, is more common. If one isolate a single part for observation, the enunciation of its vowels may be detected, but if one be listening to the unified ensemble, the identification of phonations as they are tossed about, mixed, and confused in the whirlpools of polyphonic singing is about as simple as the deciphering of a code without a key.

Many of the polyphonic writers made valiant efforts to synchronize the vowels throughout the parts. Frequently they succeeded, and there are scarcely any compositions in which coincidental expressions fail to appear. But the style itself, unless restricted to the simpler forms, necessarily disregards the allocation of words. Josquin des Pres left unwritten many labyrinthine polyphonies, according to legend, rather than garble the sacred text of Masses and motets. Palestrina, when called upon to compose a model Mass for the Ecclesiastical Commission which was debating the withdrawal of polyphonic music from liturgical use, was careful to confine himself in the "Missa Papae Marcelli" to such figures as would not interfere seriously with coincidental phonations. He was not always so conservative, however. Witness the phonetic confusion developed by the altos and basses in the following excerpt from "Ascendo ad Patrem" Mass.

	1	2	3	4	5	
Altos:—Quoni —— am	tu	so — lus	sanc — tus
Basses —————— quo — ni — am	tu	solus	sanctus

The first and third combinations are *AH–O*, the second *OO–EE*, the fourth *OUS–OO* and the fifth *AH–OUS* and *AH–U*.

The union of these different vowel sounds challenges the science of phonetics for a prescription which will prevent resultant diphthong effects from substituting for the single vowels. "Dominus," "Deus," and "Sabaoth" pronounced synchronously necessarily produce a chaos which no technique can put in order. And yet Palestrina in the "Sanctus" of the same Mass calls upon the sopranos for "Dominus," the first tenors and basses for "Deus" and the altos and second tenors for "Sabaoth." It is needless to multiply examples of the sacrifice of vowel individuality required by polyphony, but this example from the Bach B Minor Mass is offered to show that the difficulty was not confined to what is known as the polyphonic era:—

1st Sopranos	A	A	A	A	Men	Et	Vi	Tam		Ven	Tu	Ri
2nd Sopranos	A	A	A	A	A	A	A	A	men	En		Et
Altos	A	A	A	A	A	A	A	A	men	Et	Vi	Tam
Tenors	A	A	A	A	Men	En		Et	Vi	Tam		Ven
Basses	Men	Ven	Tu	Ri	Sae	Ae	Ae	Ae	Ae	Ae	Ae	Ae

A glance down the columns of this excerpt from the "Et Vitam Venturi Saeculi" fugue should convince even a tyro that such a mixture of vowels through the parts constitutes, in effect, a crazy-quilt of phonetic patches stitched together with contrapuntal threads.

2. Another source of difficulty inherent in music itself is the velocity of the vibrations required for high soprano notes and the languor of low bass notes. Variations of vowel sounds are accomplished actually by the resonance of the fundamental of the vowel and its overtones. If the fundamental of the vowel itself be lower than the fundamental pitch of the note

sung, it is obvious that the vowel cannot be pronounced without distortion or at least some modification. There is, in this circumstance, a conflict between two fundamentals with their respective harmonic re-enforcements.

Sopranos, essaying to sing certain vowels, or pitches, above the staff find themselves helpless to reconcile the differences, and both vowels and tone-quality are disorganized. The resonance of vowels belongs to both the mouth and the neck cavities acting together. Beginning with the English vowel *A*, pronounced as in *hat*, continuing through *e* as in *set*, *a* as in *hate*, *i* as in *pit*, and *ee* as in *meet*, the fundamentals resounded by the cavities below the glottis, in the resonator scale of whispered sounds, are (for sopranos) all lower than $E\flat$ on the third space, treble staff. It is clear then that sopranos singing these vowels on notes above the staff must unconsciously modify their phonations. Even with the help of well articulated consonants, good diction with these vowels is almost impossible.

Similarly with basses on very low notes; the fundamental of the pitch may be so far below the fundamental of the vowel, that its slow vibrations will take all the buoyancy from the vowel, its heavy inertia so encumbering the tone as to achieve only a grunt.

A third source of difficulty presented by the music itself is encountered when many vowels and consonants must be sung rapidly on short notes. A note for a syllable in *allegro tempos* is a serious obstacle to clear diction. The rapid formations and re-formations of the resonance chambers above the glottis, and the quick interrupting of the vowels by consonants at varying points in the oral cavity, concur to bevel the edges of clear enunciation. The skill of the artists who amaze their audiences with the patter songs of the Gilbert and Sullivan operas, is beyond the accomplishment of the average chorus. Frequently the mechanical art of the robot is indicated in vocal scores which, crowded with unsympathetic consonants and vowels without affinity, come from the pens of composers who should rewrite their faddle for fiddles and flutes.

The fourth major difficulty against which a chorus must often contend is the noisy accompaniment, ordered or permitted by the conductor and served unctuously by pianist, organist, or orchestra, with jejune understanding of and regard for the ratios demanded by art. Frequently it is well nigh impossible to catch more than a vague idea of what a soloist or a chorus is struggling to project above the din of the accompaniment, which usually has been conceived by the composer as an accessory to the vocal lines. One of the most celebrated choirs of England was buried for at least a decade under the thunderings of an organ which not only made texts unintelligible but the carefully rehearsed repertoire practically inaudible. The performance of an *a cappella* motet interrupted the onset semi-occasionally, when the charms and graces of beautiful singing and painstaking diction justified the reputation of the choir.

Perhaps the average modern conductor does not realize the extent to which clangorous accompaniments challenge the effectiveness of their choirs. Organists draw the full battery of diapasons, reeds, and piercing mixtures, and choirs try vainly to send the words of the Psalter through the charivari. There is scarcely a devotee of Grand Opera who does not frequently wonder what the principals are declaiming, their facial motions testifying that they are trying to sing, while snarling trumpets and torturing reeds throw up a parapet which only Gargantua could scale.

I remember a performance of Boito's "Mefistofeles" at Covent Garden, London, where a tenor, celebrated alike for voice, diction, and exquisite phraseology, exerted himself to the limit of effort, but hopelessly and in vain, to transmit over the reverberations in the orchestra pit, a hint as to what the music-drama was unfolding.

The use of excessive quantity in accompaniments is clearly a blot on the escutcheon of the general musicianship of the current era. Its effect on diction is disastrous, neutralizing the most carefully planned efforts in its behalf.

3. The defects of enunciation which are due to the ignorance or carelessness of singers rather than to acoustical or idiomatic factors, are the (*a*) improper phonation of pure vowels and their differentiations, and (*b*) indistinct articulation of consonants.

It is beyond the purpose of this treatise to discuss these defects in detail. A cursory examination will suffice to focus the student's attention upon them. For precepts and exercises which will be of invaluable aid, conductors are referred to the excellent monograph by Thornfield "Lip and Tongue Training."[1]

There are five parental vowels in English, but each of these submit to modifications which make a total of over eighty. The shape of the resonators above the glottis determines the authenticity of their respective sounds. Using the whispered scale, as given below, one can observe in a mirror the shapings of the mouth required to produce the true vowel. One can approximate these shapings when, after sufficient practice, they are used in actual singing. Some physicists insist that the vocal cords are not in vibration during the absolute whisper; some laryngologists, on the other hand, hold the opposite view. This point is irrelevant here but may

[1] Edward Schuberth & Co., 11 East 22nd St., New York City.

be of interest to students who wish to investigate the subject. Personally, I am inclined to believe that the vocal cords are at rest during the whisper and that the modifications in the shape of the resonators control the pitch of the whispered vowels. The resonators of men are generally twenty percent more ample than those of women, and the whispered vowels of the former are a minor third below those of the latter, while in vocal-cord utterance there is a difference of an octave.

In employing the diagram of the whispered scale and a mirror to observe the varying facial compositions, one should use the piano to prove accuracy. Thus a correctly whispered *OH* will be in tune with *G* on the second line. A violin would offer a more accurate test, if fingered in un-equal temperament.

The lower of the two notes beginning with *ER* is the pitch of the vowel as it resounds below the glottis, in the trachea and the bronchi, establishing its prime fundamental. Neck and oral resonance net the same pitch for the sounds, *U, OH, OR, ON, AH, UP.*

The diagram as here presented shows the whispered pitches for men.

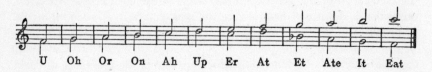

U   Oh   Or   On   Ah   Up   Er   At   Et   Ate   It   Eat

As a further aid to good diction conductors and singers should study the following diagram which is taken from "A Guide to Pronunciation" incorporated in the preliminary considerations of Webster's "Collegiate Dictionary," fourth edition.

	Back		*Mixed*		*Front*	
High	ōō	(food)		High	ē	(Ēve)
	ŏŏ	(foot)			ĭ	(ĭll)
Mid.	ō	(old)	ĕ (evĕr)	Mid.	ā	(āle)
	ä	(ärt)	ŭ (ŭp)		ĕ	(men)
Low	ô	(ôrb)	û (tûrn)	Low	â	(câre)
	ŏ	(nŏt)			ă	(man)

Explanations: "Front" vowels are such as are pronounced with the front of the tongue more or less raised toward the palate, forming a place of con-striction at the front of the mouth. "Back" vowels are such as are pronounced with the back of the tongue similarly more or less raised toward the palate at the back of the mouth. "Mixed" vowels are those in which neither "front" nor "back" articulation predominates. "High," "mid" and "low" refer to the "height" of the tongue, that is, its relative distance from the palate at the place of constriction, the raising and lowering of the tongue being accompanied by raising and lowering of the lower jaw.

4. Important as the correct formation of vowels is for intelligibility and elegance in speech and song, the articulation of consonants must be stressed as of greater importance.

One of the singularities which differentiates English from the Latin languages, is the relationship of the consonants to the vowels. The latter have much freedom, the syllabification of words frequently permitting the vowels exemption from the double stoppage characteristic of the English method of partition.

Thus, *do-mi-na-tio* in Latin, with its freeflowing vowel phonations following quickly upon prefixed consonants at the beginning of each syllable, becomes *dom-i-na-tion* in English with the first vowel stopped by the consonants *D* and *M,* thus restricting the vitality of the vowel. The Latin *de-sul-to-rius* becomes *des-ul-to-ry,* and *be-ne-vo-lens* becomes *be-nev-o-lent.* The site of vowels being frequently between two consonants, the contour of spoken or sung syllables seems to be determined by these. If the Latin method of syllabification were applied to the word cellar, its contour would be ce-llar, but the English method concludes the first syllable and begins the second with *L.*

Experience has proven to many conductors that the accurate articulation of consonants is of primary importance in English diction, and a chorus that is regularly drilled in a definitive management of them is usually noted for its distinctness of utterance. The effort to enunciate clearly two words, one of which ends in a consonant, the other beginning with one, generates an intermediary vowel sound which is distracting; e.g. *from-my* often is heard as *from-er-my.* This interpolation of an extra sound is a fault of over-zeal, and may be corrected, together with other faults, by faithful practice of the exercises prescribed in the Thornfield book.

The scheme of vocal training sponsored in these pages, stressing the use of consonants in all exercises from the earliest stages, prospers the cause of good diction. Units trained according to the principles of the Five Stages and Apposition soon become habituated to acute precision in engaging consonants with vowels. In the matter of singing the pure vowels, however, as well as their many modifications, with the elisions and ligatures, much corrective attention is necessary, always. Fatigue, care-lessness, and distractions thwart the good intentions of chorus singers to excel in diction just as they impede the illustration of many other choral excellences.

Although this chapter is candidly a mere skeleton of the subject, mainly a proposal of the divisions or sub-titles to the student, it is not beyond its scope to suggest some means of improving choral diction which have been helpful in my personal experience.

While the "crazy-quilt" of polyphony offers "such a choice of difficulties that I own myself at a loss how to determine," it is possible, by availing oneself of certain opportunities, to delineate the essential continuity of the text. Such opportunities present themselves at moments of coincidental expression, at entrances of single lines, and upon the appearance in the score of striking musical phrases and the ensuing imitative treatment of these by the other lines.

Frequently, polyphonic music invites all parts to participate in a coincidental rhythm and a simultaneous expression of syllables. At the end of phrases or clauses, there is usually an oasis at which all parts refresh themselves together before recommencing their devious wanderings. These coincidences and oases are golden opportunities which must habitually be seized upon to present a word or words with univocal articulation. The concomitance of parts at such places makes the unison expression strikingly clear, in contrast to the miscellany of the contrapuntal combinations. Therefore the conductor is urged to mark all such auspicious places in the score for special clarity of enunciation.

A choral line, entering or re-entering after a period of rest, draws attention to itself. Therefore the text of this line can be slightly emphasized, due regard being observed for the idiomatic features of the figure. Canons and fugues lend themselves admirably and with enhanced effect to the underlining of entering parts, and in much of the fifteenth, sixteenth, and seventeenth century polyphony, it is possible to make clear the text of the entrant without jeopardizing the parity which must be maintained among all the parts.

In canons and fugues, the stressing of the entrants' words is accomplished according to the principle of *accentuation by diminuendo*,[1] the other parts being made less conspicuous momentarily, rather than by bringing the entrant too noticeably *en dehors*.

A bold melodic pattern, which presently will be reiterated, imitated or inverted in the other parts, merits the same underlining and after the same fashion as entering parts. The melodic figure, which *per se* arrests attention to itself, should, during the progress of its curve, have textual

[1] See Chapter XII, "Control of Dynamics and Tempo."

"right of way" as well. It is easy, by slightly moderating the activity of the associated lines, to set forth the text with gratifying explicitness. By accepting such opportunities, even in the most complicated polyphonic forms, the text can at least declare itself at strategic points, with sufficient clarity to convey a general impression of its meaning.

Exaggeration is another recommendation to soloists and to choral bodies. The phonation and articulation which may be adequate for conversation is probably altogether inadequate for public performances, particularly in large auditoriums. Many of the most renowned actors have prescribed exaggeration as a basic desideratum for effective elocution. Intonations and inflections require augmentation if they are to be audible in the theatre. Sonority is not always indicated; special distinctness and lucidity of syllables are involved, and these qualities can be achieved only by an increase of activity in the muscles which control vocal expression. The development of the public address system and increasing use in spacious halls and theatres may make the need of exaggerated lip and facial movements unnecessary; on the other hand, the constantly improving devices for mechanical amplification of sounds may divert the attention of singers and speakers from the necessity of achieving a cultured diction. The electronic increase of amplitude favors sonority rather than distinctness, and amplified syllables will always be more or less intelligible in the ratio of the qualities of excellence at the point of origin, i.e. in the mouth of the speaker or singer. The vocal mechanism produces the sound, and it will never be within the capacity of mechanical instruments to compensate for inaccuracies in the initial construction of vowels or consonants.

The use of the whispered scale has already been recommended as an aid to the proper phonation of vowels. The shape of the oral apertures in the making of the several sounds may profitably be copied in actual singing. Any deliberate effort, however, to try to adjust and readjust the soft palate are not only futile, but definitely prejudicial to the reflex-action which puts all the component parts of the vocal mechanism into action. Singing is guided solely by mental control, the actual sounds being generated by reflex processes.

With consonants, directly controlled action can and should be cultivated, for pure consonants are not sustained sounds; they are the joints between the explosive, the explosive transitions towards, or the complete stoppage of vowel sounds, even though they be classified as open or closed, voiced or voiceless. If consonants are to accomplish their part in promoting good diction, they must be articulated deftly and disposed of quickly.

A high degree of clarity and differentiation in applying the articular letters to vowels may be attained by careful practice of each consonant prefixed to each vowel. The exercise should begin by the recitation of *ba, bee, by, bo, bu,* etc.; the same sequence should then be sung on a single note in the middle low and high registers.

In order to assure systematic progress, it is well to practice all the consonants of each class—labials, labio-dentals, palatals, and gutturals—before mixing them. In initial exercises in which unrelated consonants follow one another, there is not sufficient opportunity for concentrating upon the action of the tongue, the lips, or the throat, the three agencies which produce the consonants. *Too, Poo, Goo* or *Lee, Mee, Key* is a poor pattern for beginners. *Too, Doo, Loo, Bee Mee Pee, Vay, Fay Vay, Gah Kah Gah,* etc. are obviously better paradigms for those who lack the vigor or speed required for trenchancy and precision. Each class of consonants should first be perfected separately. Then only is it opportune to mix them.

It is profitable, occasionally, for groups of choristers to retire in turn to a distance during diction exercises to observe for themselves the excellences or defects of their colleagues. A special combination of sounds should be set, of which the listening group has not been apprised. The critique of the group is of benefit to the others, at the same time reacting advantageously upon each member of it, since it focuses attention upon faults which are seen to be characteristic and probably general.

Much has been written on the technique of clear enunciation. The bibliography is so extensive and complete that teachers and conductors can offer no plausible excuse for persistently unsatisfactory diction of singers, except in the circumstances of the polyphonic "crazy-quilt," the acoustical conflict between the fundamentals of notes and vowels, and the high speed utterances of a note-for-a-syllable figures.

In the early years of my professional career, I was so intent upon setting forth an ideal of tone-quality, that I quite willingly relegated the needs of diction to a place of unimportance. It seemed necessary to emphasize, at whatsoever expense to other phases of the choral art, that the prevailing choral tone in Europe and America should be amended. Furthermore there was little information available in the writings of the grey-beards of the choral fraternity at the turn of this century, to guide young conductors. The art of choral technique had been "splendidly neglected" and the candid guesses of a young experimenter might uncover a valid *modus operandi* as well as the academic, albeit conjectual, surmises of confirmed traditionalists. That all song is a combination of words and music is patent. That singers and conductors of choral organizations should keep the factors of the two elements in felicitous correlation is equally evident. In general, a fair appositeness can be attained and maintained but in certain circumstances one of the two elements must grant precedence to the other. In these circumstances which outranks the other?

Since the time of Dufay, musicians have been divided, some ceding the high prerogatives to music, and others to text. The rigorists among church musicians have naturally registered with the latter.

Music, as an accessory to the liturgy, must certainly be so regulated as not to interfere with the words of the sacred offices; at the same time, no sounds which are definitely unmusical must be permitted to mar the decorum with which the liturgy must be exemplified. Therefore, such music as, by its structure, impedes or compromises the intelligibility of sacred texts is unsuitable for use in Divine Services.

For concert performance, if there be a conflict between the two elements, the music must be granted first consideration, for if the choral-art is a phase of music, it must necessarily concern itself primarily, consistently, and ultimately—giving no quarter—with the essential character of music which is compounded of quality, pitch, and quantity, and furbished to its brightest by the greatest of these, which is quality.

CHAPTER XIV

The Art of Vocalization

Competence in any craft or art depends ultimately upon assiduous, regular, and systematic application of the principles which are essential to it, and upon a highly developed control of its peculiar technicalities.

Genius lessens the rigors of study and practice for those upon whom it bestows its gifts, but it cannot dispense even the most brilliant talent from the necessity of learning the science and precepts of an art or of acquiring facility in the management of its constitutional factors.

Supereminence in music can be attained only by faithful adherence to an enlightened progressive plan; it can be maintained consistently only by a routine of suitable exercises. A celebrated pianist commenting upon the need of daily practice, admitted that if he had missed one day's practice, he himself was conscious of loss, and if two days', the public would be aware of his neglect.

The practice upon which singing depends for beauty, fluency, and effect, is itself an integral if secondary art, i.e. the art of vocalization.

Soloists, almost universally, follow some plan of daily vocalizing, though frequently the plan is ineffective or injurious.

But the average choral director has no scheme of vocalization for his chorus.

Many, if not the majority of choirs and concert choruses are never directed to vocalize, their leaders being concerned exclusively with the study and practice of repertoire.

There is no doubt that, in this era, the chorus generally presumes to interpret the masterpieces of choral music without preparation in the essentials of choral technique. One seldom discovers a choral conductor who is as intent upon building up the vocal controls, balance, blend, etc., as upon the study of repertoire.

The chorus is the most neglected instrumentality in the whole field of musical expression.

Without a definite plan of vocal exercises, comprehensive enough to correct abuses, develop positive qualities, promote elasticity and assure accuracy of pitch, a choral conductor can never produce a singing unit of superior artistic merit.

Solo-singing relies for effectiveness upon careful exercising of the vocal mechanism, and in no less degree is a group of singers teased by this need. Careful exercise of the voice requires study of the fundamental facts of tone-production as synthesized by physics and physiology. All plans of vocalization which ignore the facts of these sciences are necessarily futile or dangerous. Effective plans are predicated further upon an understanding of the specific abuses or faults to be corrected. This understanding is the reward of frequent diagnosis of vocal conditions by teachers of individuals and conductors of groups.

The "patent-medicine" type of vocalization may help one singer while hurting another. A certain form of exercise which promotes a vocal virtue in some circumstances, may, in others, abet a serious defect. Vocal exercises must be prescribed after examination of symptoms. Teachers and conductors must be diagnosticians; otherwise the doses administered at their rehearsal clinics will be as uncertain in effect as tablespoons of a patent compound given indiscriminately to each of the patients in a hospital ward.

One of the first lessons to be learned by vocal teachers and choral conductors is that specific prescriptions must be furnished for specific conditions.

A general dosage of all one's pupils or choral singers with standard measures of standard catholicons, selected at random from the Pharmacopoeia of singing masters, hints at covert quackery. Aesculapius and Apollo can charge the chronic disorders of many stomachs and larynges against drug stores and vocal studios.

In some standard books of vocalizations, there is of course much valuable material. But the material is there in the same sense that the components of a patent-medicine are noted in the Pharmacopoeia. A high degree of selectivity is indicated as essential.

For instance, upward vocalizations which abound in published sets of exercises obstruct the freedom and volatileness which initial stages of voice-training must prosper. The employment of the low register before the lightness of the upper has modified it is prescribed in some popular volumes. The premature use of certain vowel sounds, although a practice antagonistic to the interests of vocal progress, is a feature of many traditional vocalizations.

It is not my intention to satirize the published vocalizes altogether, or to intimate that, with superior tutelage, none of these has value. My argument is merely, but forcibly, this: published sets of vocal exercises generally provide scale and arpeggio progressions which in some circumstances may meet particular needs, but which in other circumstances are very definitely inadequate or obstructive.

An impression prevails among singers that almost any series of notes, on any vowel sound, in any register, at any tempo, or in any dynamic panel will serve admirably as "setting-up exercises" for the voice.

One hears practically the same vocalizations emanating from the studios, ricochetting and repercussing through the noisy corridors of conservatories in America and Europe. There is a formula that encircles the globe at every latitude where mature or student songsters and songstresses deliver ejaculations preparatory to their canzonets and arias. With slight modifications in some climes, the vocal formula is compounded thus:

FIG. 1

It is the vocal shibboleth of the great international fraternity of chanters, bards, and *cantatrices;* a voucher for mediocrity, a symbol of misdirection.

The claim, often made, that great voices have been developed under the egis which carries this formula or a variation as its heraldic device, cannot be substantiated. The voices were either great before being kidnapped into the fraternity, or became great in spite of the fallacies sponsored.

It has been stated already that the choice and use of vocal exercises constitute a collateral art. Choice must be determined after diagnosis. Symptoms must be examined, chronic habits of voice-production analyzed, and the type of exercise prescribed which is suitable to the condition.

The practice of vocalization has two major purposes:—first, the removal of impediments to the free action of the vocal mechanism; second, the sharpening or refining of qualities which will add lustre and distinction. There are, therefore, both physiological and musical phases to be considered.

Vocalization is the exercising of anatomical parts. It is essentially like all physical exercise, being a process by which muscles, tendons, ligaments, cartilages are made free to function correctly and easily. Physiology, the science of normal bodily functions, posits as its fundamental fact this principle: in proportion to the correctness with which any bodily part operates, are there comfort, ease, and efficacy.

Specialists in therapy are applying this principle more extensively now than formerly, and much helpful as well as interesting information is accruing to their experiments. For instance, some of the most uncomfortable and crippling afflictions, long defying adequate explanation, such as arthritis and muscular rheumatism, are now being attributed to encroachments upon the freedom of the feet. The vanguard of the orthopedic specialists asserts—with much dramatic proof available—that the proper exercise or manipulation of certain muscles of the feet (after diagnosis) establishes such a freedom of movement that the ills associated with or consequent upon unnatural posture, carriage and gait, unequal distribution of weight, or idiosyncrasies in the functioning of internal organs, rapidly disappear, if not altogether, at least in notable measure.

Vocalization, in its physiological aspect, must be guided by an analogous method and proceed in the same manner, if the many defects of speech and song which muscular abuse and constriction have created, are to be eliminated.

First, symptoms must be observed and tabulated. Next, the causes of the symptoms must be sought. Upon discovery of these, a specific technique of vocal exercise must be applied, which will remove these causes.

The needs of pedal ailments are met by *direct* positive exercise, while the laryngeal mechanism must be freed *indirectly* from interferences, chiefly by avoiding certain movements and the exercise of associated muscles which affect the tone-making factors.

The resemblance between modern therapeutic methods and the art of scientific vocalization is only analogous it is true, but nevertheless enlightening. The physiological *raison d'être* of the latter is identical with that of the former, i.e. the freeing of muscles to function properly and therefore without discomfort. Discomfort is an obstruction to facile natural operation, causing physical and mental preoccupation; it is a sign that something is amiss, that some elementary piece of the physiological mechanism has gone awry, that adjustments are necessary.

The major and most common defects of voice production have been discussed throughout this treatise. To a well schooled choral conductor, these defects and their causes should identify themselves upon first hearing. Weight and sluggishness, "swallowing the tone," the shock of the glottis, the husky eliptical tone, whiteness, opaqueness and the hoot, lack of resonance, shrillness, flat or sharp intonation, these and other categorical faults are immediately evident to an expert, readily noted, and the specific condition of singers at once diagnosed.

Some muscular encumbrance or irregular activity is responsible for the particular fault detected. It is the obligation of the *maestro* to assign the type of exercise which will most promptly remove the encumbrance or make the faulty movement normal.

Indiscriminate use of the "formula" is obviously as futile or injurious as the application of a standard manipulation by orthopedic masseurs to any and all pedal conditions. The "formula" or any of its sundry variations increases the obstructing activities which are responsible for the first four faults enumerated above.

The earlier Chapters of this volume treat of the specifics to be applied to all the major faults. The Five Stages prescribe the types of exercise which guarantee correctness, ease and comfort in the production of tones. The principle of "apposition"[1] is applied in further paradigms of exercises which stimulate growth of tonal strength, at the same time conserving physiological freedom.

The employment of consonants has already been urged as an invaluable aid to voice-placing and balancing. It constitutes an indirect way of exercising the larynx properly, for by relieving undue strain from the laryngeal muscles, it assures freedom to the reflex action of these. This point has been adequately discussed in foregoing pages, but the efficacy of prefixed consonants is so striking that the student is again directed to it. Labials, labio-dentals, dentals, and palatals, all serve to develop auxiliary activity in the lips, facial and lingual muscles. This auxiliary activity lessens the pressure and constriction at the cords, thus permitting greater freedom to the thyro-cricord and the thyro-arytenoid muscles.

Much experimenting with the various influences and values of the several consonants is required before a conductor can with assurance select those best suited for particular needs. Thus, the choice of *P* or *B* to promote a forward poising of the tone, would be unfortunate if the singers were prone to be prodigal of breath supply, for these consonants allow a popping or bursting of the vowel to which they are prefixed. *F* or *V,* requiring the placing of the upper teeth on the lower lip, would serve better in this circumstance. On the other hand, *F* or *V* might be undesirable if a tendency to set the jaw rigidly were detected. The use of *M* would then be indicated. Examples might be multiplied, but suf-

---

[1] See Chapter IV "The Positive Development."

ficient suggestion has already been offered to interest the student in personal research and experiment.

The use of *K* and the hard *G* is not recommended, generally, for these explode their associated vowels too near the cords. Sometimes, however, these consonants can be used effectively in cases of chronic sharpness. The fact that they stop the vowel and presently explode it by the back of the tongue, deters the facial muscles from becoming rigid, and the pitch established by the cords is less likely to be modified.

The use of appropriate vocal exercises to prepare singers for the special needs of compositions about to be sung is another phase of the art of vocalization which must be examined by directors. It is clear that if the "Kyrie" from Mozart's "Requiem" is listed either for rehearsal or for performance, long sustained *adagio* exercises in a medium tessitura provide poor preparation for the rapidly moving sequences of that intricate fugue. Similarly, sixteenth notes, *allegro* and *staccato,* if not complemented by *sostenuto* phrases, put the larynx in the wrong mechanical mood for Palestrina's "Lamentations."

The proper choice of exercises, in proximate preparation for performances, as well as in the habitual culture of the voice, is one of the marks of mastership which betokens the accomplished tactician.

The tuning-up exercises which precede public performances should include both prophylactic and therapeutic elements, the former to prevent errors, the latter to correct them. The Stages offer the preventive material. The curative elements must be selected from the recipes prescribed for particular ailments.

Downward vocalization, *pianissimo* and *staccato,* with prefixed consonants, can always be employed, with the knowledge that these agencies will quicken the voices to a degree of buoyancy which will preclude common faults. But the particular weaknesses which a director knows to be characteristic of some of his singers cannot be remedied by a panacea. Thus, the shrillness of reedy-tenors and the heavy darkness of certain basses cannot be tempered by the same vocalization. Specifics must be applied. Throughout these pages, the student will find the *materia medica* applicable to the varying vocal conditions which a conductor must encounter in routine experience.

Each vowel sound promotes certain harmonics, and these harmonics promote certain qualities. *EE* is string-tone, *AH* reed, *OO* flute, etc. According to the various needs, therefore, the various vowels should be assigned in vocalizations.

The first purpose of vocalization has been seen to be the removal of impediments to the free muscular activity of the vocal mechanism.

The second major purpose is the enrichment of timbres and the cultivation of latent qualities.

This phase of the subject involves the study of tone-quality in general and of the differentiating characteristics of the many colors and hues in the tonal spectrum.

It is impossible to lead singers to the attainment of vocal distinction unless the leader himself be a master-judge of timbres.

The temperament of his mind must be imbued with appreciation of the specific differences in tones. His imagination must present ideals and norms so clearly to his tonal perspicacity, that he is never in danger of rating tones by incorrect or uncertain criteria.

Vocal teachers and choral conductors must recognize that their paramount obligation to art and professional sincerity is to become musical contemplatives. They must habitually meditate upon the vocal elements and factors which promote beauty, grace, elegance, charm and intrinsic values. Otherwise they are as the "blind leading the blind." No technique, however vigorously and faithfully applied in the external forum of a rehearsal room, can avail against the confusion or dim-sighted aural vision of myopic muddlers.

Some directors nurture the illusion that any highly approved method will of itself produce splendid results.

Like dramas which are so obvious as to require a minimum of study or discretion from untalented actors, being dubbed "actor-proof," certain rehearsal plans are *presumed* to be "singer-proof."

But *in actu* there are no such schemes available.

Successful application of the soundest principles of choral technique depends ultimately upon the conductor's understanding and appreciation of them.

The gyroscope has been an invaluable aid to mariners, but its use does not exempt officers from bridge duty on the ocean liners.

I have sometimes attended rehearsals presided over by directors who evidently expected the logarithms of the technique which they had superficially perused, to accomplish the factorings, approximations, and integration necessary to an artistic production.

The exercises, which led by a master would have undoubtedly proved effective, were on such occasions altogether futile.

Without a cultivated intuition for identifying and treating tonal symptoms, it is unreasonable and even conceited for individuals to assume the role of conductor or choirmaster.

Personally, I learned in the first years of my professional career, that understanding of tone-quality is the *sine qua non,* the outstanding pre-requisite, the signally important dependence of the choral art.

As the years passed, this conviction became increasingly stronger, confirmed by my own experience and that of others. A voicer of organ pipes, tamped, as it were, this dogma into my subconsciousness. He was engaged in the re-building of my organ, which at its original best was scarcely more than a "box of whistles." He took lodging near the church. On almost every evening for many weeks, I saw him walking slowly along the street, stopping from time to time to muse,—evidently oblivious to his surroundings. I questioned him once about his curious habit. His explanation was that he was thinking about the tones of my organ. Only by much quiet meditation, he intimated, could he set before his mind a tonal picture of the sounds which he was invited to produce from inferior pipes. "You have poor diapasons, shrill flutes, flamboyant reeds—and the worst *quintadena* I have ever heard. How can I transform your organ, if I do not give my mind to it unreservedly?" He worked a near miracle with the old music-box, and left me a dramatic proof that concentration on tone-quality is the first duty of conductors, performers, and all craftsmen who have voluntarily accepted the obligation of creating the consonances designated by an oft harshly treated word, music.

The student who has established this doctrine as the genetic influence of his musicianship will gradually become aware of the more mystical elements of music; he will discover himself increasingly to be more cognizant of its subtle and secret variations, and subconsciously he will eventually become a tonal strategist, selecting, with fine discrimination, the technical processes which are emendatory and efficacious.

With his growth in tonal consciousness, the choral director will find increasing value in the use of multi-part, as it were *orchestral,* vocalizations. Such exercises are not only admirable agencies for the development of qualities and perfect adjustments among the several choral lines, they also furnish fruitful opportunities to the conductor for determining the ratios of timbres best suited to various styles of composition.

Some indication has already been given of the value of exercising choral singers in two or more parts.[1]

Many conductors of modest ensembles are timid about introducing six- and eight-part numbers. They should overcome this timidity, for there is a large repertoire of such numbers, the single parts of which are easily

[1] See Chapter XI, "Blend and Balance."

learned. The reaction on himself and the chorus will be much more gratifying than "singing in the wide open spaces" of the standard *S.A.T.B.* The interstices between the lines in four-part songs tend to isolate the parts, whereas the *beau ideal* of the choral art is to effect appropinquation. The blend and coalescence of harmonies, timbres, fundamentals, and harmonics which accrue from frequent practice in many parts, should persuade directors, after a few experiments, to make such practice a routine feature of rehearsals. When used as purely vocal exercises, the texts of the numbers should be discarded, and appropriate vowels (with prefixed consonants) substituted.

A few measures of the "Hymn of the Cherubim" by Rachmaninof are given below, with some suggestions for using them as orchestral or color vocalizations.

Fig. 2

Arrangement A

Soprano I,	one half, *Foo* (flute)
	one half, *Mee* (string)
(*F* promoting forward focus	
M promoting resonance as well)	
Soprano II,	two thirds, *Fee* (string)
	one third, *Fah* (reed)
Alto I,	one half, *Mah* (reed)
	one half, *Maw* (horn)
Alto II,	one half, *Mah* (reed)
	one half, *Maw* (horn)
Tenor I,	entire group *Mee* (string)
Tenor II,	entire group *Mah* (reed)
Baritone,	entire group *Mee* (string)
Bass	one half *Mah* (reed)
	one half *Mee* (string)

This movement must be sung *pianissimo* in performance but, when employed as an ensemble vocalization, it should be sung at all dynamic levels, and with dynamic variations in the single parts.

The combination of timbres indicated in *arrangement* A presents a vocal orchestration of flutes, strings and light reeds in the treble parts; broader reeds and horns in the alto; cello and bassoon analogies in the tenor, and a combination of broad string and reed effects in the baritone and bass parts.

It is profitable to vary the combinations of timbres, lest the natural resources of all the voices be denied full opportunity for development. Thus the first soprano choir should sometimes be assigned to the second line, the first alto to the second, etc.

Similarly, it is well to set forth the parts as comprising an ensemble of kindred timbres. Thus:—

Arrangement B

All voices on *Mee* or *Fee*
(cultivating a definite blend of string tones throughout the parts)

Arrangement C

All voices on *Mah* or *Fah*
(cultivating the relationships of light and broader reed timbr

Arrangement D

Sopranos I and II,	*Foo*
Altos I and II,	*Maw*
Tenors I,	*Maw*
Tenors II,	*Moh*
Baritones	*Mah*
Basses	*Mah*

(approximating the color scheme of flutes, horns and trombones)

Exercising the voices of the ensemble in arrangements similar to these is a traditional practice in the Paulist Choir hall. New motets are always studied in this manner, for while the intervals, progressions, and rhythmic features are being learned, the vocal aspects of the numbers are revealing themselves, and a blend and balance of parts is accomplished as a by-product of the study of the notes.

The astute director, economizing both effort and time, considers the possible by-products of vocal exercises as well as their primary purposes. It is essential that the primary purposes be served with intention and attention, but secondary ends can be prospered at the same time. Reference was made to this desideratum at the introduction of melodic phrases in the Third Stage.[1]

While emphasizing a principal point, directors must insist upon the exemplification of all the choral virtues, lest stressing one they neglect the others.

Thus, steadiness of *tempo,* or an indicated variation, a nuance of quantity, accurate intonation, continuity of tonal integrity throughout the registers, avoidance of unseemly impacts at the beginning of new phrases, these and the many other facilities which are indispensable to the worthy performance of choral music should be re-enforced and confirmed by every vocalization employed whether in the single lines or in the concerted exercises.

Vocal exercises constructed on the principle of apposition can be made to include factors which produce several results concomitantly. For instance, if it were my primary purpose at a given moment to improve a *crescendo* in an upward progression starting in the middle or low register, I would assign a vocalization designed to accomplish this chief end, but which at the same time would tend to deter the singers from carrying weight upwards and the likely consequence of singing flat.

[1] Chapter III, "The Five Stages."

FIG. 3

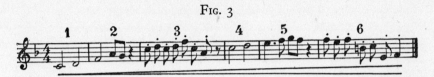

In measures 2 and 5, the notes of the third beat, if conceived high, will tend to keep the pitch true; the *staccato* passage of the third measure aids both pitch and flexibility; the sixth measure is obviously an encouragement to avoid forcing, as the apex of the *crescendo* is approached.

Similarly, if a vocalization be proposed to prepare singers for elastic delivery of difficult intervals, several important related features may be emphasized, as:—

FIG. 4

The first derivative to be sought in such an exercise is steadiness of *tempo,* which on account of the triplets and eighth note octave jumps is in jeopardy; another is homogeneity of tone in the alternating registers. A further by-product is fidelity to the *accentual* pattern which is prejudiced by the introduction of accidentals at awkward points, as in measures 5 and 7; finally, the temptation to vary the quantity of tone will present itself, according to the degree of confidence felt by the singers. Thus a *crescendo* will mark measures 1 and 2 and 5, because the intervals are easy and suggest animation, whereas the groping for the middle *A#* in measure 3, the middle *G* in measure 4, the low *F* natural and *B* in measure 7, will be attested by a lessening of quantity.

These examples seem sufficient to illustrate the opportunities offered by well constructed vocal exercises of furthering several choral interests while mainly intent upon accomplishing a specific point.

The studied art of vocalization is a choral director's richest resource. Careful exercise of the various voices according to their needs and to the relationship of the parts, gradually develops a choral tone which is almost as reflex as the muscular actions by which it is produced. In other words, through intelligent and *regular* vocalization, each singer becomes habituated to the proper use of the voice and to its proper contribution to the integral unit.

The mind controls the muscles of the larynx, habit directs the mind, and vocalization infixes the habit.

Therefore it is not idly repetitious to reiterate here that the successful choral conductor must be a specialist, a master of every phase of vocalism, a sure judge of symptoms, quick to enjoin, prescribe, or impose.

To be a true artist, he must be a scientist, well versed in the lore of physics, physiology, and aesthetics.

An important aspect of the art of vocalization is the use of accompaniment with the exercises. All types of exercises are impaired by indifferent or injudicious accompaniment. Those designed chiefly for blend or balance are usually more effective *a cappella,* while ingenious and carefully studied accompaniment enhances the value of those employed for developing certain vocal virtues.

Indifferent accompaniment to vocalization is an indication that the *maestro* regards as inconsequential the reaction of the singers' subconscious hearing to the mechanical sounds of an instrument. The loveliest falsetto I have heard was developed by the ukelele. Loud strumming of the piano, note for note with the vocalists, is certain to bring a harsh percussive effect to their attention, establishing a standard which unwittingly they tend to copy. Considering the influence which all synchronous sounds have upon the musical sensibilities of singers, it is important to set down as a guiding principle in this connection that *the piano or organ accompaniment to vocal exercises must be so subdued as to be scarcely audible.* A modification of this general precept will duly be permitted, but except in the special circumstances to be noted, it may safely be insisted, that the regular accompanying of vocalizations with loud chords, or single notes, is a most baneful practice, destructive of the inherent values of the exercises, and a deplorably pernicious influence.

Some of the qualities which make accompaniment an efficacious ally of vocal exercises can be deduced from the above considerations. First, *subordinacy,* which means that not only loudness, but all features which might distract the singers unpleasantly must be excluded. Among such features are the use of extravagant harmonies antipathetic to the simplicity of the melodic figure, the constant choice of dominant and subdominant chords whenever the melody permits (these chords being atmospherically new tonic-chords which tend to make the effect of the progressions too angular), furnishing full chords for all the single notes of the exercise, and, in organ accompaniments, the selection of registration which is repugnant to the color scheme of the voices.

Second, *elasticity,* which by its graceful buoyancy suggests freedom, volatileness, and comfortable ease to the vocalists. The very fact of being unobtrusive predisposes the accompaniment to affect the singers advantageously, and if the player make special effort to apply a notably light touch, his participation in the exercises will be a valuable asset.

Other features which increase the worth of accompaniment in vocalizations are:—

(*a*) playing the notes of the exercise (if it be necessary to play them) one or two octaves above the singers.

(*b*) playing only chords at important rhythmical intervals.

(*c*) playing a light, high, unobtrusive discant.

(*d*) the use of rich harmonies (urbane and within the implications of the melody) and especially the dissonance.

(*e*) the use of light open fifths.

(*f*) the occasional restriction of the accompaniment to chords in the tenor-bass area, if sopranos or altos are vocalizing, and to chords in the soprano-alto range if tenors or basses are being exercised.

(*g*) the use of the left hand alone, playing the single notes of the tonic or dominant, according to implications of the rhythmic and melodic patterns.

(*h*) in organ accompaniment, (1) the use of the stops most suited to the development or complement of specific timbres; (2) application of the drone of a double pedal-point, carefully "pointed-up" with string color; (3) the use of the unison-cancels.

(*a*) Groups of inexperienced singers require aid from the piano at rehearsals. Much time is lost in the useless effort of teaching the vocal exercises without instrumental delineation. A new vocalization should be set forth clearly by the pianist in the register which the singers are to employ; it should be played similarly to support the first trials of the singers, and thereafter it should always be played in a higher register. The high tessitura of the theme-accompaniment lifts the melodic line well out into the open where the choristers can take aural *cognizance* of it readily—and at the same time retain their independence of it. When played in the same register, the identity of vocal and instrumental pitch predisposes singers to merge their utterances with the tonal effect of the instrument. This is obviously prejudicial to the suavity of vocal intonations, which qualitatively have little in common with the distinctive sounds of a piano. Furthermore, the light prevalence of the high theme-playing suggests the buoyancy which all singers, and especially novices, must cultivate as a primary quality. I have observed this practice to be most fruitful equally with adults and children. If the exercises are carried to the highest normal registers, it is sometimes advisable to play the vocal themes an octave or two below the singers, to avoid the thin tintinnabulary tinkling of the upper piano, and to suggest the concept of solidarity which prevents upper notes from becoming shrill.

(*b*) After a group has become accustomed to vocalizing together, the regular presentation of a vocal theme is unnecessary. The less support given by the piano, the greater are the self-reliance and confidence of the singers. A skeleton accompaniment of light chords at the proper rhythmical points serves abundantly to establish the harmonic elements which give savor and vitality to the theme. These chords should be played at 8va lightly, occasionally rolled *quasi arpa* and the bass given some prominence.

(*c*) In connection with the skeleton harmonic accompaniment, a delicate discant frequently adds a charm to the vocalization which communicates itself pleasantly to the singers. In using contrapuntal figures, whether in the interior structure of the harmonic procedure or in the offing as counter-melodies, care must be exercised to avoid "overloading" the accompaniment. If an accompanist be facile in the elaboration of discant, the temptation to make of a vocal theme a *cantus firmus* for contrapuntal invention is frequently alluring and in equal degree dangerous. "Overloading" destroys the contour of themes, replacing the simplicity which should prevail with elements, academically correct and interesting perhaps in themselves, but cumbersome and unfavorable to the purposes of vocalization.

The recent efforts (1937) of choirmasters to alleviate the monotony of long hymns by assigning a part of the chorus to elaborate discants, are laudable indications of a desire to improve church music. But the discants have been too heavy, too complex, too alien. The simple straight line, so to speak, of the hymn tunes is frequently hidden under the cross-bar lattices of ingenious but imprisoning counterpoint.

But if the obligato be simple in itself, and definitely subordinate to the theme, an adjective merely in the melodic syntax, it can function as an encouragement to tonal concinnity and refinement. During all vocal practice, the synthesis of all the elements employed must be an influence towards ease of production and beauty of tone.

A single element of the synthesis is sufficient to frustrate the primary purposes of vocalization and to convert a vocal exercise into an agency of deterioration. The use of an out-of-tune piano is such an element. Other elements which thwart artistic results have been considered throughout this volume. Among those whose first fruits are poisonous, in lethal degree, to vocal health, are loud singing to loud accompaniments thumped out in middle registers, premature upward exercises, the frequent use of vowels without prefixed consonants (especially *AH* and *EE*) and the unstudied choice of vocalizations.

When, however, the combination of elements employed in vocal exercises nets a fusion of qualities agreeable to the canons of physics, physiology, and aesthetics, the growth in vocal freedom, elasticity, and richness is immediate and unhindered.

(*d*) Ingratiating harmonies increase the productivity of accompanied vocal exercises. The choice of these harmonies, as has been stressed before, must be limited to the proprieties of the melody, chords which have no simple affinity with the key being excluded. The brevity of most vocal exercises does not permit the introduction of harmonic dialects which are foreign to the environment. They distract attention by their alien accents. But within the idiom of a melody, the resources of appropriate harmony are multiple. Diatonic harmony is generally more stabilizing than chromatic, for it establishes and supports a clear aural picture of a definite key-tonality. Perhaps one of the sources of choral stability which one may conclude to have been a virtue of the Renaissance choirs, was *modality,* i.e. the strict adherence to a definite scale form, which was a primary criterion of rectitude among the polyphonists until the amiable hypocrisy of *Musica Ficta* became general. It is interesting, parenthetically, to note here that in these days when the invention of modernistic details by which to recreate the arts of painting, architecture, poetry and music has become the mark of alertness, some of the most acceptable music publications have been as modal or diatonic as any motet of the early sixteenth century; e.g. the Russian school of composition up to the date of the revolution.

The prepared dissonance is the chief asset available for enriching diatonic harmony. Its importance in the elaboration of the masterpieces of the polyphonic era is recognized by all specialists in this style. One of the most engrossing items for study in the interpretation of polyphonic *a cappella* music is the treatment of the dissonance. The three great settings of the "Crucifixus" by Antonio Lotti (1667-1740) are predicated structurally upon the extension of notes beyond the vertical consonances of which they are a part.

No choir can sing polyphony with ease and grace which has not achieved facility in managing inharmonic extensions.

The most formidable book ever published on any musical topic is Knud Jeppeson's "Palestrina's Style and the Dissonance," [1] in which the specific references to the great master's employment of the device make an amazing total. The charm accruing to the harmonic fabric from a well ordered and ingenious use of inharmonic tones which resolve presently in a diatonic stepwise progression, is unescapable. It promotes a taste for dissonant tone-relations, stimulating in the singers an important curiosity and interest in the *quality* of the tones. Tones of poor quality cannot successfully be combined in such relations, for dissonance readily becomes discord. Tonal mozaics require a choice calcedony of compatible timbres.

Therefore the use of prepared dissonances in accompaniments and in the two or multiple part *a cappalla* exercises has a threefold value; it mitigates the coldness of diatonic harmony; it betters facility in singing inharmonic relations; and it provides to the director an infallible test of the tonal condition of the single lines and their status in the blend and balance of parts. The introduction to the eight-part "Crucifixus" of Lotti should be practiced frequently as a dissonant *a cappella* vocal exercise.

It is superfluous to give examples of dissonant tone relations, but in order to provide instant illustration of the value of suspensions in the accompaniment of vocalizations, two harmonizations of exercise B (p. 87), are offered here for comparison—the first plain, and the second with the embellishment.

FIG. 5

[1] Available through Organ Interests, Inc., 467 Richmond Sta., Staten Island, N.Y.

At Fig. 6 is a harmonization in dissonance of exercise C (p. 65).

FIG. 6

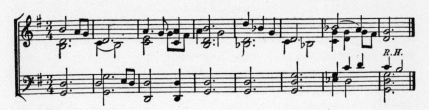

(e) The use of open fifths has already been suggested as a valuable aid to accurate pitch.[1] The simple fifth is a cold, uncompromising officer of the acoustic law and insists upon exposing infractions, giving warnings which persuade vocalists to adhere strictly to the canons of physics. Under the menacing scrutiny of unbribable fifths no chorus can continue long to violate the fundamental statutes of the art. Triads can be bribed by the third of the chord to lend a deaf ear to slight deviations from pitch, for the third is a saccharine element, the sweet beguiler of harmony. But the fifths and dissonances operating in conjunction, as at Figs. 1 and 2 (p. 123), offer an invitation to accurate intonation which singers are hard pressed to decline.

(f) The occasional restriction of the accompaniment to the tenor-bass area during the vocalizing of sopranos and altos and *vice versa,* is recommended as suggesting solidarity to the higher voices and lightness to the lower voices. It is unnecessary to expound this recommendation at length for it is clear that the harmony of chords below the treble clef stimulates

a sense of key tonality to the voices singing above, simultaneously inculcating a realization that the high voices are actually what their designations imply—*alto* higher than the tenor and bass, *soprano* (*sopra*) above the rest of the ensemble.

[1] See Chapter V, Fig. 1 (p. 93).

A grievous and general fault of choral direction grows out of indifference to this point. Today, choruses are, in great majority, top-heavy. There is too much *soprano*. Directors and singers have yet to become aware that in choral as well as in architectural ensembles, the top is consequential only for balancing, shaping, and animating, the foundation and the mid-sections with their consistence of stamina and solidity conveying the real stable notes of the structure.

Sopranos and altos must be brought to comprehend the underlying general principle of choral line relations, i.e. the tone-fundamentals are usually in the low parts, the sopranos and altos frequently only re-enforcing the harmonics, even in homophonic music. All procedures that help to keep the details of the tonal-structure subservient to a general plan as indicated by blue-prints of acoustic factors, should be added to the routine practice of choruses which aim at perfection. Choral soprano tone-quality must be conceived as a fleecy cloud effect.

The intimation of elasticity furnished by light chords in a high treble tessitura is of assistance to tenors and basses in their exercises. The increasingly compact and dark consistence of successively lower tones is mitigated by a mental control which is being influenced by a concept of tenuity and imponderability. The reflex action of the vocal muscles is admonished by buoyant disembodied tones to restrain and temper the more cumbrous elements of low intonations. The principle involved here has been consistently invoked throughout this volume as a dogma of choral technique of which most of the other tenets are merely developments or ramifications. The first article in the creed of a specialist in chorophony is without modification or reservation: lower notes must be qualified by the quality of upper notes; the top must communicate easy volatility to the middle and bottom; the starting point of choral technique is *downward progression*.

(g) The suggestion of furnishing a sort of monochrome, black and white accompaniment occasionally during vocal exercises, is consistent with the recommendation to maintain simplicity, albeit an interesting simplicity, in the harmonic associations. Alternating octave tonics, low and high, in the left hand, without any contributions by the right hand, establish a feeling of key-tonality, at the same time promoting independence and self-reliance. This practice is akin to the use of the pedal-point, having the advantage over the latter of indicating the time pulsations. Occasionally, the dominant can effectively alternate with the tonic, producing a distributed double pedal-point.

(*h*) 1. The pipe-organ can serve as a most effective ally of the choral director, or it can readily frustrate and destroy the good results of patient work in the rehearsal room. Rehearsing regularly with the organ is a practice vigorously to be condemned, for unless the stops of the organ be most judiciously selected, and unless the organist be free from the vicious tendency of his many brethren to "over-play" the singers, the harsh or shrill timbres will injure the good timbres of the voices, and the "over-playing" will conceal many faults, thus defeating a principal purpose of rehearsals.

Occasional practice with the organ, however, is recommended for two reasons. First, if the registration be selected carefully with the aim of setting examplars of good timbres before the choristers, the latter will unconsciously copy the quality of the pipes. Having been impressed with the suggestive values of such practice early in my career, it has become a traditional feature of my rehearsals. A smooth round flute-tone 8′ allied with a light string-tone 8′ is a perfect combination to set before lyric sopranos *stopped diapason* 8′ plus an *orchestral oboe* 8′ serves the vocal needs of counter-tenors admirably. A *melodia* 8′ helps mezzo sopranos to moderate their natural over-brilliance, while *salicional* 8′ gives point to the accompaniment for contralto. If the pipes be well voiced and under the control of expression pedals, they can serve as admirable influences of refined quality, the freedom, evenness, and balance of their tones giving direction persuasively to the imaginations of the vocalists.

The second reason which commends occasional practice with organ accompaniment is the freedom from the accentual effects produced by the piano and upon which a chorus can quickly come to depend. The piano is an authoritative vivifying rhythmical agency, while the *sostenuto* speaking of pipes, the characteristic *legato,* and the even placidity of the great church instrument concur to make the organ less of a leading influence than an associate participant. Conductors frequently fail to advert to the chronic weaknesses which reliance on piano accompaniment can foster in a chorus. Renditions which are commendably accurate and secure in the rehearsal room, are not infrequently followed by humiliating performances when the accompaniment is transferred to the organ. There are certain means of improving the leadership of the organ in accompaniments which are discussed in another volume, but in general the organ cannot be ceded high rank as a beneficial accompanying influence, especially in the rhythmical aspects of singing.

2. Pedal-point and tonic-dominant-tonic in left-hand accompaniment have already been recommended.

Basso-continuo was a feature of accompaniment during the seventeenth century, having been developed by Viadana, Peri and contemporaries (probably its first appearance was earlier) to supply an uninterrupted bass to units which could not assemble a complete chorus. This, in the sense of *Basso-marcato,* is recommended as valuable practice in the accompaniment of vocal exercises, for, like the pedal-point, it establishes a steady basic color which tends to steady and co-ordinate the timbres of the voices. *Ground-bass* provides similar support and suggestion.

Below is an excerpt from my "Rhythmic Trilogy for Easter"[1] which serves admirably as an illustration of the effect of the synthesis of *basso-marcato, ground-bass, tonic and dominant* alternation, and, if the encircled notes are played, of double pedal-point. It is given here in a higher key than the original, as a vocalization for any of the parts except the low basses (singing the soprano line), or for the ensemble in harmony. The contrapuntal figure played by the right hand adds the feature discussed under letter *C* of this Chapter.

FIG. 7

[1] "A Rhythmic Trilogy for Easter" by Father Finn, published, J. Fischer & Bros., 119 W. 40 St., New York City.

Double pedal-point on the organ provides an excellent fundament for vocal exercises, especially if a good blend of Bourdon and string tones is available. The organ point can be played

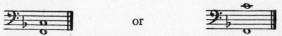

as in the drone effect which permits the two part vocalization *C* on p. 224 to float gracefully about, but securely anchored to the key-tonality. Thus:—

FIG. 8

3. A mechanical gadget on the organ, named "unison-cancel," permits the mixture of *sub* and *super* octaves which in the accompaniment of the

lighter types of vocal exercises is most effective. The unison cancel eliminates the unison pitch of a pipe, and the use of the 4' and 16' couplers
produces a synthesis of octaves which in reality is a fundamental, plus its
fifteenth, the voices singing at the half-way register. Such a combination,
especially when applied to such delicate timbres as those of the *Rohr Flute*
4' or the *Triangle Flute* 4', promotes limpidness and lucidity which prosper
the interests of lyric voices.

The use of the piano and organ in the accompaniment of repertoire
is expounded in another volume. In the foregoing chapter these instruments have been discussed as accessories to vocalizations. It is of importance to the success of vocal exercises that these accessories be well
understood, and their association with the principal undertaking of choral
technique be determined by principles of physics and art. Some purists in
chorophony excluded both instruments in the practice of both exercises
and repertoire, notably the celebrated conductor of Henry Leslie's
Select Choir (late nineteenth century, England) and the late Dr. Haslam
of Toronto, Ontario, who, in moments of most generous magnanimity,
permitted the violin to assist their struggling choristers.

Vocalization is the disciplinary basis of singing. Tyros, submitting to
its regulations and exactions, soon graduate from a fruitful novitiate and
may be fashioned presently into convincing expositors of a Fine Art.
Vocalization is indeed more than a disciplinary force; it has personality;
it is the real factor of choral destiny; it is the animating agency of growth,
assuming in fact the titular responsibilities so naïvely assigned to Dr.
Heyther's *Choragus* and *Coryphaeus*.

If, therefore, a conductor install the true art of vocalization in his
choir-hall, according it the place of honor at all rehearsals, he will have
entrusted his chorus to the only sure medium through which it can pay
fitting tribute to the Muses, and through which *per retro,* he will hear
Euterpe's sweet sounding *jubilos* of approval undulating back from
Olympus.

CHAPTER XV

Baton Technique

For authoritative direction of a choral group at ensemble rehearsals, as well as at performances, a precise baton technique is required. This technique must be distinguished by clarity and simplicity. It must also be comprehensive, adapted to communicate to the singers the special messages, warnings, and hints which a conductor may find necessary to convey. Furthermore, effective conducting includes facility in creating and modifying the moods which particular musical movements indicate. The modern conductor is himself a performer. His instrument is the ensemble, and to elicit a co-ordinated vital performance from all participants, his skill must be that of the virtuoso. He needs to evoke immediate response to his interpretative intentions. He must at all times superimpose his conceptions and discriminations upon the unit, holding it steadily to a high standard of vocalism, forewarning of possible lapses, and indicating by appropriate gestures the particular needs of the moment.

Perhaps the value of the modern conductor's contribution to the artistry of ensemble performance has been exaggerated. Frequently the convulsions of agitated *maestros* on the podium seem meaningless. Sometimes they are a grievous distraction. But considering the elaborate style in which so much modern music is written, the rhythmic and harmonic features, and the ever-changing tone-colors indicated in both orchestral and choral scores, a conductor can discharge a very important function.

Until the nineteenth century neither orchestras nor choruses were directed by baton-conductors from a central platform. There were few hidden elements of importance in the earlier music which required the concentration of an individual leader for proper exposition. The Gregorian Chants had been regulated and steadied by arching up-and-down movements of a precentor's hands—cheironomy. Polyphonic music depended upon a leader only to indicate the time. This leader, one of the singers, using a scroll called "Sol-Fa" was accustomed to indicate the pace so that the involved contrapuntal figures might fit neatly into the integral pattern. Except for the preservation of rhythm and tempo, there was no need for

conducting in the modern fashion, all the factors involved in the interpretation of Gregorian Chant and polyphonic *a cappella* music being
immediately discernible to the singers. The undulatory *crescendo* and
diminuendo of arsis and thesis, and the stress to be accorded to notes in
various neumes, are component features inseparable from the essential
structure of the Chant. The melodic, rhythmic, and dynamic independences of the modal polyphonic school, and the interpretative resources by
which these are established are evident in each choral part, and a choir
that has been taught to sing polyphony correctly, needs but little conducting
in public.

The earlier styles practically conduct themselves. The chief duty of
the modern maestro presiding over performances of polyphonic music,
in addition to indicating the pace, is to maintain the proper quantitative
relations between the parts. At times, also, he must give hints about the
vocalism.

But the conductor of modern music assumes a more complex responsibility. He must present the emotional elements of compositions
with discerning perception. He must direct the dramatic progress of
movements so carefully as to secure gradual growth to climaxes. He
needs to be constantly on the alert to prevent inopportune *animandos*
which will rob the real climaxes of their efficacy,—and to relate the
dynamic variations to the acoustics of the auditorium in which he is conducting.

Richard Wagner insisted that the conductor's principal obligations
were to choose the proper *tempo* (which includes a sensitive gauging of
rubato modifications) and to find in which part the melody lies. Perhaps
the latter is the more difficult of Wagner's demands upon a conductor,
for in modern music the melody is constantly wandering from one part
to another, sometimes manifesting itself clearly and at others concealing
itself from easy view in the subtleties of contrapuntal richness, or instrumentation.

In order at all times to be able to influence an ensemble with a sort
of magnetic flux, it is necessary for a conductor to use gestures and sundry
indications which are easily observed and immediately understood. Time-
beaters with the "Sol-Fa" were adequate for the earlier music, but the
modern conductor has more extensive responsibilities. Polyphonic music
is generally found to be simple in its color scheme. Being impersonal, with
tranquil curve lines in the melodies, little or no imagination was or is
required to present its characteristic qualities, but modern music, both
orchestral and choral, is richly colored, demanding many hues and
nuances of tonal color for the transmission of its refinements. The con-

ductor of modern music, therefore, must have a technique for controlling these hues and nuances.

Audiences, nowadays, quickly perceive if a conductor be merely a modern "Sol-Fa" or if he be indeed a solo-artist, playing upon the ensemble as upon a great instrument, revealing a highly sensitive and aesthetic reaction to the music, through his manipulation of each individual participant.

Some celebrated conductors are difficult to follow, having no definite code of signals; others make the rhythmical patterns perfectly clear, and convey their interpretative intentions with simple and unmistakable gestures.

It seems to be of little import whether a conductor uses a baton or conducts only with his hands. But it is useful and expedient for him to divide the directional gestures appropriately between the right and left hands. In conducting an orchestra, the left hand is not generally so important as in choral direction, since there are fewer signals to be given to the instrumentalists.

Tradition has established the right hand as the custodian of rhythm and tempo.

It is incumbent upon conductors to select simple diagrams of gestures by which to indicate the beats of measures. An indifferent technique in this particular causes much speculation, distress, and irregularity among the performers.

Not infrequently, it is quite impossible to determine by watching the gestures of a conductor, the time-form or the progress of a measure. Obviously the down and the up beats are of paramount importance, indicating the beginning and end of a measure.

A high vertical up beat is of particular aid to players and singers for it not only designates the termination of the measure, but prepares them for the ensuing down beat with its usual stress.

There are various diagrams which can successfully be employed to indicate the divisions of the time-forms, and it is of little consequence which of these are chosen, as long as the first and last beats are identified by vertical strokes, down and up, respectively.

It is not the purpose of this chapter to set forth in detail the diagrams which are suitable for all the rhythmical patterns to be encountered. There are three admirable brochures which provide the forms for this technique.[1]

---

[1] The concluding Chapter, published separately, of "A Treatise on Modern Instrumentation" by Hector Berlioz, "A Handbook on the Technique of Conducting" by Adrian C. Boult and "Technic of the Baton" by Albert Stoessel.

Some young conductors fail to develop elasticity in their gestures, thus giving the impression of heaviness and awkwardness. Practice before a long mirror, through which one can see his actions as the players or singers see them, is of great aid in achieving an easy, graceful, and natural method. Eccentric mannerisms and exaggerated movements of the head, arms, or body are to be avoided as disconcerting affectations.

Accelerandos are easily indicated by the gradual increase in the speed of gestures, but *rallentandos,* especially if they occur after many measures of a rapid *tempo,* should be preceded by an anticipatory signal, such as leaning over the conductor's stand while making a warning gesture with the forefinger of the left hand.

I have found the habit of counting the first few beats of the *rallentando* passages with both hands, steadying and reassuring to performers.

The left hand can normally assume the regulation of dynamic variations. A conductor should indicate the exact degree of *crescendo* or *diminuendo* to be made. The invention of a code of signals for this purpose is not a severe tax on ingenuity. For many years I have designated *pianissimo* by holding the left hand horizontally with the outside of the hand towards the singers, one, two, three, or four fingers lifted vertically calling for *piano, mezzo-forte, forte,* or *fortissimo,* respectively. If the group fail to respond, I sometimes call attention to the dynamic indication by tapping my left hand with the baton. If a *diminuendo* or a *pianissimo* be unsatisfactory, I slip the forefinger of the left hand down the baton from the tip. Such signals are simple and convey at once to the entire organization the intentions and impressions of the conductor.

A general defect among choral singers, which must frequently be remedied during public performances, is their failure to watch the conductor. Players in the orchestra have no difficulty in watching their parts and the conductor as well, but choristers the world over like to focus their attention upon the notes, thus making difficult and often impossible the nuances and modifications which artistic interpretation requires. A simple signal (frequently it must be repeated before noticed) should be given to warn of inattention. My scheme here is to point to myself with my left hand, and turning towards the most inadvertent group, conduct to it for a few measures.

In the matter of communicating the mood of a composition to the performers, the conductor must be willing to give an intimation of his own reactions by facial expression, tenseness of muscles or obvious relaxation. He must exercise a certain hypnotic influence on the singers; they must recognize the mood he is trying to recreate, and be so impressed by his sincerity as to be guided altogether by his mind, as though they were in reality hypnotized.

It is not necessary to take the audience into one's confidence while fulfilling the duties of a conductor, for, as the art of conducting develops, we perceive that the conductor's most convincing and subtle maneuvers can be made almost surreptitiously. Young conductors, through nervousness or inexperience, and excited by the glamor of public performance, are wont often to adopt extravagant tactics which detract from the aesthetic worth of the program and create the atmosphere of "much ado about nothing." I write this with personal appreciation of its truth, for, as a very young conductor, I bubbled and effervesced with irrepressible ferment and agitation which eventually critics persuaded me to moderate. Restraint is one of the first virtues for the tyro to bring with him to the conductor's podium.

The choral conductor, who unlike the orchestra conductor, is under the necessity of coaching the performers in the production of their tone-quality, must add to his code of signals appropriate gestures which will instruct the singers what to emend and what to avoid during a performance. For example, indifferent breathing must be corrected. A slight tapping by the conductor on his chest will reveal to singers that the breath control must be improved. Perhaps descending intervals are delivered slightly flat; obviously then the singers are not thinking these intervals as sufficiently close together, and the conductor must so inform them; my signal for this purpose is the rapid touching of middle finger and thumb. Conversely, if the difficulty be with ascending intervals, the conductor concludes that the singers are not conceiving the intervals high enough, and he must therefore signal them to think the notes as far apart; my gesture to accomplish this is to snap the middle finger rapidly off the tip of the thumb.

If the posture of some singers be careless, a simple indication like pointing a finger towards the floor will restore circumspection. If tension seem to be developing, especially in such progressions as may easily become sharp, the obvious duty of the conductor is to relax the vigor and to lessen the orbit of his gestures. Symptoms of increasing strain in reaching high notes should be checked by suggesting the lowering of chins, perhaps by the conductor touching his chin. Throaty or murky tone-quality should be similarly rebuked by touching the lips.

All these and sundry other conditions which develop in public performances can be readily prescribed for by the conductor on the stand without giving any impression to the audience that a code of esoteric countersigns is being wigwagged to the ensemble. Such gestures as will prove serviceable aids to the singers can be made effectively without more—probably with less—activity of his left hand than the average con-ductor nervously employs to no purpose.

It must be emphasized that no exercise of ingenious conducting tech-nique can substitute for careful rehearsing. Certain gestures will warn of advance symptoms of flattening, for example, but if the singers have not been drilled thoroughly and consistently to sing on pitch, the warn-ing will be futile.

Some conductors feel more at ease directing by memory; others ap-preciate the security afforded by a nearby score. For the majority, it is advisable to have the score on the stand, as one readily becomes distracted by the exigencies of choral needs, and may become confused about repe-titions, etc. But it is a deplorable habit of some conductors to keep their eyes focussed steadily upon the notes, for a magnetic relationship between conductor and singers is thus impossible. Certainly a conductor should have memorized his scores, using them in public only for reference at strategic points. This recommendation is neatly affirmed in the satire of a music-critic who suggested that a certain performance would have been incomparably more satisfactory "if the conductor had had the score in his head instead of his head in the score."

On the other hand, one observes the occasional phenomenon of a con-ductor who clearly indicates a conviction that conducting by memory is in itself a valuable "stunt." Sometimes such conducting begins and ends with ostentation and affectation, either of which inhibits the presen-tation of the aesthetic sincerities of music. Neither pomp nor pretense should be tolerated on the conductor's podium. The outstanding virtue of the *chef d'orchestre* and the *maestro di cappella,* must be unqualified devotion to the privilege of evoking from their ensembles superlative per-formances. The technique by which they accomplish this must, there-fore, be only a means to an end, at all times dignified, unpretentious, and simple.

CHAPTER XVI

Sight Reading

Many of the obligations of a choral conductor must be fulfilled without compensations to artistic sense. Among these onerous duties are the preliminary tasks of the Stages, the inculcating of sensitiveness to accurate pitch, the persistent need of examining symptoms and prescribing remedies, the maintenance of blend and balance, and the altogether pedagogic undertaking of teaching singers to read music.

I have observed the reluctance of many good musicians to face such uncongenial tasks, which, like teaching the "bone-rules" of a language or the multiplication table, become eventually a plaguesome bore. The burden of years, or merely the unceasing need of applying dull principles and precepts has tempted many artists of skill to abandon the high ideals of the noblest form of musical expression. Some, yielding to the temptation from sheer fatigue or its affinity, ennui, have lessened their vigilance to the left, others to the right, but the one insistent obligation of choral direction which conductors, young and old, ambitious and lethargic, insistent and careless, *tout en masse,* evade with alacrity, covering their evasions with convincing if specious alibis, is the task of developing facility, thoroughly, and throughout the chorus, in translating faithfully into sound the hieroglyphics of notation.

In some countries choirmasters and conductors are bound by the high standards of a severe tradition, and must *nolens volens* accomplish the task within a specified time. In the English foundation choirs, skill in sight singing is a *sine qua non* for adult members, and the boys from their admission as probationers are given systematic and thorough instruction.

Two experiences at Westminster Cathedral, London, indicated to me that a degree of skill in sight reading which would be considered prodigious in America is taken for granted as a normal facility in the English Cathedral choirs. On one occasion, a new Mass *a cappella* was given to the choristers to be sung at sight for the Capitular Solemn Mass.

There are six distinct compositions in a complete Mass, two of these being lengthy, the *Gloria* and the *Credo*. The whole Mass was sung with accuracy and grace, due attention being given to its idiomatic features. But a few soprano-boys stumbled over a lead in the "Benedictus"; their uncertainty was slight, not seriously marring the rendition, *but they were severely chastized for blundering*.

The other occasion was the opening of the great International Eucharistic Congress in 1908. A Papal Legate was to be welcomed in England after many generations of absence. It was a major event. The musical programme was selected with great care. The soprano boys had just returned from their holidays and were presumably somewhat "rusty." The distinguished director was so sure of their skill, however, that he altered the programme at the last minute, substituting for a prepared number, a setting which they had never seen before. I shall never forget the perfection with which those small boys and men sang at sight a difficult motet *a cappella* in the presence of the most distinguished assemblage of Catholic dignitaries ever before convened in an English-speaking country. The most skillful choir of professional adults in America would have struggled for hours with the intricacies of the number.

These illustrations are given merely to strengthen the substratum of this chapter which is that children and adults can readily be educated to a high degree of accuracy and facility in singing music at sight. There are few choir-schools in America, and the number of units which require speed and accuracy in reading is negligible. This is probably the explanation of the indifference displayed by conductors generally. But considering the time wasted in teaching the notes of compositions and the uncertainty which must always harass the conductor if his choristers are singing partly by rote and partly by conjecture, it seems unreasonable to shirk the labor of inculcating a knowledge of music's symbols, and readiness in applying the knowledge. Two things have concurred to impress directors with the unpleasant futility of undertaking these tasks, lack of a simple progressive system, and desultory, irregular teaching. The second item can be disposed of immediately, since no argument is needed to convince that regularity, carefulness, and zeal are essential qualities of effective instruction.

The first item, lack of a simple system, indicates that tutors have been floundering about, confused themselves for want of a plan, and confusing their pupils by the medley of unrelated elements which they introduce. No wonder that one who is learning to swim in the quiet waters of the Key of C should be drowned by a sudden submersion into the whirling

eddies of six sharps! Little difficulty is experienced in learning to translate notation to musical instruments. Each symbol calls for a conscious

physical act. These signs  soon con-

vey to the youngest piano-pupils that they are to depress a series of white
keys beginning at a point which they have memorized as Middle C. An
equation is immediately established between the position of a note on
the staff and its position on a keyed or fingered instrument. But the
vocalist cannot "follow copy" so mechanically. The written note indicates
a pitch to the singer which must be comprehended aurally in the mind,
and finally produced by the reflex actions of the larynx. Vocal reading
is therefore more difficult. Many facile performers of instrumental music
at sight are embarrassed when asked to sing a simple progression. It is
not absolutely necessary for students of instruments (except the brass)
to hear the notes in advance of playing them; after some experience, a
note on a certain line or space will at least predispose them to expect a
definite sound. But sight-singing relies altogether upon the "silent-sound"
of advance hearing as its effectual factor. No pitch that is not pre-
viewed in the brain's tone projecting room can be *deliberately* evoked
from the cords. Since singing is physically a reflex action, postulating the
presence of definite impressions in the mind which can be reflected in
the muscular processes of the larynx, the most important feature to be
examined in any system of sight-reading is its method of training pupils
to receive and understand the correct impressions of which the notes are
symbols. If the method of accomplishing this be elaborate, confusing, or
incomplete, it is necessarily unsatisfactory, and the system of which it is
a part should be rejected.

Effective pedagogy is distinguished by three essential characteristics,
simplicity, consecutiveness and thoroughness. Horace's adage "Nulla
vestigia retrorsum" (no steps backward) must guide the teachers of sight
singing. Many follow plans which, promising simplicity, are in practice
complicated, because they fail to proceed gradually, necessitating much
retracing of steps, supplementing and complementing.

If pupils be confronted with the tonal relations which constitute the
key of *E natural,* before having become facile in reading and singing the
written notes of the preceding sharp keys, it is clear that progress will be
made only by retreating, for until the genesis of the use of sharps is thoroughly understood, each of the sharp keys will take on the discomfiting
aspects of the irregular verbs of Latin or Greek. A professor who would

burden his young pupils with the conjugation of the out-of-order verbs before they had mastered the regular forms, would be ruled eccentric by any Board of School Regents. Music in essence is the mathematical development of a few simple principles. This development involves gradual ramifications, and must therefore be presented to pupils progressively, each step forward being taken conservatively and in sequence.

Each written note is of course a twofold indication. It designates both the pitch and the duration of a tone, pitch involving the intervallic relations of consecutive notes, and duration embracing all symbols of time-values including rests.

There are two classes of aspiring singers who need elementary and simple instruction:— inexperienced novices and those who through inadequate teaching have only confused inklings of the subject. For the latter class, the instructor is constrained not only to clear away the confusion but to dispel the lack of confidence which perhaps years of groping have engendered.

Considering the desirability of simplicity, it seems advantageous to begin the lessons in sight-reading with a study of the time-values.

Rhythm is the simplest medium through which the periodic impulses of music are revealed.

Few persons have difficulty in sensing the pulsations of normal rhythmical patterns, and few experience difficulty in learning the symbols by which these patterns are indicated. The process of developing facility in interpreting these symbols is not more involved than the teaching of elementary arithmetic.

Some preceptors prefer to plunge immediately into the more confusing phases of notation, believing that examination of its interval implications should be initiated without delay. Personally, I have secured better and more enduring results by developing a sense of easy security in reading time-values, before introducing the more complex subject of pitch relations. The students are told that there are only two features of notation which need engage their attention. One concerns duration; they set about studying this: very quickly they master it, and lo! one half of their task has been accomplished without difficulty. The students are thus predisposed favorably to investigate the second feature, and if this be set forth simply and progressively, a gratifying skill in accurate singing at sight will gradually ensue.

Although the subject matter to be presented in teaching the reading of time symbols is limited and simple, directors can easily rob it of simplicity by undertaking to convey too many ideas at once.

The first step is to acquaint the pupils with the relative values of the most important notes without reference to time signs, rhythmic patterns, or measures. Only the major notes should be examined and discussed until there is neither doubt nor hesitancy in identifying and understanding them. Thus:—

$$o = \text{whole note}$$

$$\textit{d} = \text{half note}$$

$$\text{Therefore } \textit{d} \quad \textit{d} = o$$

$$\textit{J} = \text{quarter note}$$

$$\text{Therefore } \textit{J} \; \textit{J} = \textit{d}$$

and

$$\textit{J} \; \textit{J} \; \textit{J} \; \textit{J} = o$$

Until this simple formula has been learned thoroughly, eighth notes should not be introduced. When it is opportune to introduce these, the formula should be extended in the same manner:

$$\textit{♪♪} = \textit{d}$$
$$\text{Therefore } \textit{♪♪♪♪} = \textit{d}$$
$$\textit{♪♪♪♪♪♪♪♪} = o$$

Likewise, presently, sixteenth notes should be duly studied. When these have become familiar, the teacher should write sundry exercises on the blackboard asking the pupils to substitute other notes which are equivalent in value.

It is advisable to defer the use of published music for examples of the items under consideration, until all the subject matter of this phase of reading has been presented. The blackboard and specially written forms are safer, for measures chosen from published music, containing perhaps one or more unexplained symbols, will confuse the pupils.

Confusion is as hostile to progress in sight-reading as loudness is to beauty of tone.

Thus:—
Teacher's notes—
Pupils' suggestion—

Dotted notes may now profitably be studied, attention being so concentrated upon them as to inculcate a lasting impression of the functional value of the dot. It is a mistake to examine the character of thirty-second and sixty-fourth notes, the tie, grace notes, triplets and rests, at this juncture. Also, symbols of earlier notation which have still been

retained, as ⊨ ‖o‖ should be postponed to the indeterminate moment

when they will be encountered in a polyphonic or *recitativo* form. Likewise, signs for *staccato* and *fermata* should be omitted from the first pictures presented. However, it should be indicated in the initial lessons, that the speed at which counts are made does not affect the value of notes. I have found some confusion arising later in the minds of children, when without having stressed this point, I introduced *accelerando* or *rallentando*.

When the relative values of the notes are well understood and memorized, there being no uncertainty in identifying the several indications, it is opportune to distribute these symbols in measures according to simple patterns. An easy procedure is to commence with 2/2 time, which, although less often encountered than other forms, permits the pupils to observe a full measure of counts in simple time. Thus:—

FIG. I.

These notes should be sung softly on *MOO* or *MEE, the full value of each being demanded,* lest carelessness in this regard become a chronic defect.

The place of the time-signature should be indicated as important, but curiosity as to the meaning of the G and F clefs should be met by the promise of later explanation. It is well here to comment upon the alternative fashion of combining eighth notes, etc.; thus:—

The symbols for the intervals of silence between notes, i.e., rests, should be studied next, first without reference to measures and later as parts of rhythmical figures. Having followed the procedure suggested for teaching duration-signs, the measures of the exercises at Fig. 1 should be modified to give opportunity for applying the information acquired; thus:—

FIG. 2

A notorious traditional defect of choristers is to sing through rests. Sometimes this defect can be charitably overlooked as a peccadillo, but frequently the heedlessness implied causes the prolonged notes to cross the path of harmonic intentions, producing discord and discommoding musical and textual phraseology.

Therefore the importance of the rests must be stressed and the pupils convinced of their integral part in the structure of phrases.

The time-signatures of the other simple classes of time, duple and triple, should be set forth and studied before compound forms are introduced. 2/4, 2/8, 3/2, 3/4, 3/8 should engage the attention of the pupils in the sequence given. The simple forms of duple time should be emphasized as the natural divisions of whole notes or their fractional parts. Triple time was believed to be the perfect mode during the polyphonic era, but this belief was predicated upon the pious concept "omne trinum perfectum" (everything threefold is perfect) unreasonably associated with the doctrine of the Holy Trinity.

Choristers can quickly become expert time-counters, feeling with accuracy the rhythmic flow of notes, if they are exercised exclusively in the duple forms for a few weeks. The alternation of strong and weak beats characteristic of duple time stresses a reciprocal relation of rhythmic pulsations which they appreciate instinctively. Unconsciously, one finds ease and gratification in all movement which is accomplished by successive alternations. Nature predisposes us to understand laws of motion whose regular mode of functioning is biform. For ascent is balanced with descent; anode and cathode, to and fro, over and under, arsis and thesis, right and left, are respectively reciprocal terms explaining that the normal function of natural forces is by alternation.

In the study of time forms, therefore, it seems desirable to perfect the singers in the duple forms before proceeding to the tripartite angular divisions of triple time.

Just as *downward vocalizations, staccato, pianissimo,* stimulate anew a flagging sense of correct tone-quality, so vigorous practice of duple time divisions improves rhythmic perspicacity and sensitiveness to recurring accents. When lethargy threatens to anaesthetize a chorus, at rehearsal, the first movement of Morley's "My Bonnie Lass," sung as an ensemble vocalization in a sprightly tempo, will clear the atmosphere quickly, galvanizing the metronomic instincts of the choristers into electrified activity.

In this connection conductors are advised, parenthetically, to bear the foregoing considerations in mind, when arranging their music-lists. On many occasions an animated number in duple time has rescued programmes for me which in spite of a feverish baton, had begun to sink into the abyss most feared by the Muses, the sheol of inertia.

In spite of the fact that compound duple time is a modification of simple duple time, it seems expedient to postpone study of this until the simple divisions of triple time have been mastered. Compound forms involve the difference between the strong and less strong accents of a measure, and should not be presented until all single accent measures can be translated at sight into their proper metro-musical values.

It is unnecessary to elaborate the entire plan for inculcating facility in reading the time-symbols. The remaining details should be unfolded with simplicity. The pupils should have ample opportunity to practice each ensuing exercise, until its minutiae are as clear to their comprehension as the letters of the alphabet. Compound time, both duple and triple, must be studied as thoroughly and practically as the simple forms. But such compound forms as 9/8, 12/8, etc. should be examined only when the pupils have become expert in reading the less complex divisions. 5/4 and 7/4 can profitably be postponed to their first appearance in a composition listed for practice, when their resolution into a combination of binary and ternary forms should be elucidated.

Tied notes and the *staccato* dots must now be explained. The *fermata* and simple grace notes having been adequately examined, the singers should now be unembarrassed in reading the time-values of any normal composition which might reasonably be included in their future repertoire. If they be still uncertain or hesitant, the teacher should regretfully retrace steps to the point where the first sign of confusion is indicated. If the pedagogy has been inadequate, or inattentive pupils have been allowed to proceed hurriedly, perhaps this point is not far from the beginning.

The necessity of gradual progress is reiterated here. A master-teacher's book is always a "Gradus ad Parnassum," each step being ascended in unbroken sequence. In the teaching of music-reading, no other manual can take the place of a "gradus" for each item is dependent upon a preceding one, and all upon an unconfused start.

The study of notation as the designator of pitch and intervals is a more complex phase of sight-singing. Through the years there have been scholarly protagonists for widely differing systems of mastering this branch of the subject. Two of these systems are evolved from diametrically opposed premises. One establishes a basic pattern of intervals which is applied uniformly throughout all the keys; all notes must be related to the pattern; in this sense, the system may be called relative. The other proceeds without reference to a pattern, the pitch of each note being ascertained solely by its acoustical proximity to its neighbor; a note is separated from another by an octave, a fifth, a minor third, etc.; in this sense, the latter system may be termed absolute.

Variations and ramifications of these two systems abound. Although large numbers of singers have acquired accuracy and facility through both systems, there are many studious musicians today who feel that neither is simple enough to facilitate the teaching of sight-singing to the majority of students. Personally, of course, I am convinced that one of the two systems can be made a medium for very intelligent understanding of the subject, but I sympathize with the eagerness of many leaders, especially progressive superintendents of school music, to discover a system which will not frighten the teachers as well as the pupils. Sharps and flats, major, minor, augmented and diminished intervals, chromatic and whole-toned progressions, these and other ogres of notation have been causing havoc in rehearsal rooms since the theorist Hucbald of St. Amand, Flanders, inaugurated a new era of music at the dawn of the tenth century. All of the dread spectres which leer at students from the more modern staff did not make their appearance immediately, but beginning with the illustrious monk's introduction of his inchoate notation, the tranquillity of music-masters has been increasingly disturbed. Guido of Arezzo, in the quiet monastery of St. Maur des Fosses, invented a pattern which furnished a norm for the seven scales adequate to the singing compass of eleventh century choirs:

E—*LA*

Gamma—*UT*

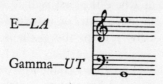

The neumes which up to the eleventh century refreshed the memory of singers (who had really learned their canticles by rote) were often supplemented by the letters of the alphabet to indicate intervals more definitely. A modified form of Hellenic signals was retained, even after Guido had invented the four line staff, for the *notae quadratae* probably were not used until after Guido's death. The proponents of alphabetical reading (acoustical reading or "fixed Do") have therefore an imposing background of history for their system, even though the great Abbot of Santa Croce had already devised the beginnings of solmization (the "movable Do") with the syllables of "Ut Queant Laxis" and the diagram of the "Guidonian Hand."

In the thirteenth century solmization was well established, and guided by the position of the *Do* or *Fa* clef, singers became accustomed to translate the square notes of Gregorian Chant into the actual sounds of the Church's melodies.

It would be outside the purpose of this volume, and probably futile as well, to present the full complement of arguments assembled by sponsors in pleading the cause of their respective systems. The controversy anent the absolute and the relative methods, the "Fixed" and the "Movable" *Do,* has waxed vigorously through the years, and will probably continue to divide theorists into two camps. The "Fixed" *Do* seems rooted in the musical consciousness of the Continent; in England and North America, especially where British views have influenced the shaping of methods, the "Movable" *Do* is commonly used. The absolutists are probably more prejudiced in adhering to their creed than the relativists. The "Fixed" *Do* dogmatists may be, in slight measure, prejudiced because the modern—"Tonic-Sol-Fa" and its variations—emanated from

England, thus being not only transalpine but Anglo-Saxon to boot. The musical conscience was traditionally formed in Italy. It was cisalpine. Even the Netherland musicians were uneasy in their inventions until cisalpine sanction approved them. Tenets of theoretical and tonal rectitude were fashioned or at least endorsed south of the river Po before being accepted into the enchiridion of orthodox procedure. England was too distant from the origins of culture, too far west and north of the fertile lands of the Latins for indigenous blossoms and buds of art to flourish. The flora of music must needs be transplanted to Continental gardens for observation—always—in the time of St. Augustine of Canterbury, in the era of the Tudors, even in the days of John Spencer Curwen, Sir Edward Elgar, and Vaughn Williams. The cisalpine sigillum was accepted almost universally, if often unconsciously, as the official stamp of worth. Even the great musical developments elaborated by the Teutons were ramifications of concepts excogitated or approved in the south.

Thus England's offer of the Tonic-Sol-Fa system of Curwen was unhesitatingly declined by the Continent. Not only did the substitution of letters for staff notation incite the cisalpine bias; the scheme as a whole with its canonical premise of the "Movable" *Do* was antipathetic to their remote and proximate traditions. Nor had the Frenchman, Armand Chevé, been more fortunate, when at Jean Jacques Rousseau's suggestion he begged a Continental hearing for his Sol-Fa method.

Musicians who today follow this "Relative" system cannot reasonably be as inexorable as their "Fixed" colleagues, because when modulations become complex, developing eventually polytonality or atonality, they willingly abandon the "Movable" *Do* as useless and confusing, and humbly borrow grist from the Continental mill. While *Do* is readily discernible, just so long is the "Movable" *Do* system simplifying and efficacious. When the key-note disappears, however, in the haze of modern progressions, the only co-ordinating principle of the system is gone. There is nothing left as a guide except conjecture, which is wont capriciously to speculate in circles.

But for the needs of Gregorian Chant and the classical polyphony, the "Movable" *Do* system is unquestionably the simplest plan of teaching sight-singing. Furthermore, its pattern-scale applied throughout the keys gives a sense of security and ease in all the obvious styles of music. It develops an understanding of notation progressively, and when the singers eventually encounter the more complex idioms in which the keynote becomes lost, they have little trouble in accommodating themselves to the absolute method of acoustical reading. Their general facility can be easily extended to include the technique for meeting emergency needs.

One hears frequently today the hope, wistfully expressed, that some genius will soon invent a method of reading which will eliminate all calculation of keys, the identification of alphabetical symbols and the solmization names (or the numbers) of notes.

A distinguished musician and enlightened pedagogue discussed this point with sanguine expectation at a recent convention (1937) of music teachers. The discussion was not in public forum, being only an intimate but earnest exchange of ideas among a few progressive leaders. Why not convey the impression of the notes to be sung by a sort of musical short-hand? Curves, angles, parallel, horizontal, or vertical lines might be established as a simple code to indicate many combinations of notes, etc. My personal contribution to the symposium was the comment that singers would be hard pressed to find a periapt or amulet which could make such a scheme successful. Such a code would be immeasurably more complex than the most involved system of staff notation. The suggestion, necessarily vague, was in effect a Utopian metamorphosis of the old system of neumes which gave only such impression of sequences as to recall melodies or intervals which were already familiar to singers. Of course, the neumatic system was used to convey unfamiliar melodic concepts as well, but unsuccessfully, since the neumes were not sufficiently definitive to assure univocal performance by a group at first sight. A more informing and instructive medium of pitch-indication was necessary. And so from the days of Hermann the Lame (eleventh century, Reichenau Monastery) to the era of Michael Praetorius (1571–1621) the neumes, various kinds of symbols on staves, mensural and non-mensural notation, and all items relevant to the writing and reading of music occupied the zealous attention of monks, levites, pedants, and composers. Scores of theorists proposed scores of variations in the symbolic language by which music was essaying to make itself comprehensible to the larynx.

Continued examination of the merits of the two surviving methods of reading vocal music has convinced me that the "Movable" *Do* plan provides the easier starting point, clearing away by its own lucidity the multiple riddles of keys, major and minor modes, and solving the enigma of sharps and flats. The other plan seems at the start "obscurum per obscurius," the explaining of the obscure by something more obscure.

The substitution of letters or numbers for staff notation as in the Curwen and Ward systems is not recommended save as a preliminary approach to the subject, for the music which singers generally use is pub-

lished in the standard form of staff symbols, excepting a negligible repertoire sponsored by the Tonic-Sol-Fa Society.

The "Movable" *Do* plan, if set forth simply, thoroughly in each item,
and progressively, will first produce certainty in the delivery of all the
intervals of the diatonic scale of two tetrachords, without reference to
notation. When such certainty has been attained, the plan will proceed
to familiarize the singers with the use of the notes, these comprising a
simple code for indicating the diatonic intervals already understood.

The first undertaking requires more attention than some teachers
suspect. These assume that the scale of *do re mi fa sol la ti do* is as familiar
to pupils as the alphabet and the first formulae of arithmetic. While it is
true that the scale is early learned in the routine of school work, it is also
true that its tonal implications are not impressed upon the full understanding of the pupils. In fact one meets the curious phenomenon occasionally of a choral director who, himself lacking scale consciousness,
is therefore grievously impeded. During a course of lectures on choral
technique, it is my custom at this juncture to test the scale consciousness
of the students. Sometimes the results of the tests are dismaying to a few
who probably had up to the moment considered themselves intelligent
readers of the vocal symbols. I strike a chord and ask the number of its
component parts. A miscellany of modulations follows: in which part or
parts was the harmonic progression accomplished? An accidental appears; in which part? and what is its syllabic name? I identify the key
in which the progressions originate and modulate to another key: in
which part is the mutative note, what is its name, and what key does the
modulation introduce? These simple queries often discover to musicians
that they need a more instant sense of scale intervals and quicker per-
ceptivity of the relations of notes to one another. Certainly they themselves must acquire this tonal sensitiveness before undertaking to teach
others the secrets of sight reading.

Here follows the skeleton of a simple plan for developing with individual singers or choruses, accuracy and a ready proficiency in judging
and singing the intervals intended by composers.

As in the study of time-values, the use of printed copies of music must
be postponed to a later opportune moment. Diagrams upon the blackboard and the baton of the teacher serve to invoke the co-operation of the
"listening-eye" as effectively here as in the acquisition of control of
dynamics.[1]

---

[1] See Chapter XII, "The Control of Dynamics and Tempo."

The scale should be written out clearly, thus:—

DO   RE   MI   FA   SOL   LA   TI   DO

It should be sung several times consecutively without comment. If the students have not yet completed the Five Stages of their vocal training, the scale should be sung only *pianissimo* and twice downwards to once upwards. In the ascending scale each note should be well separated from the preceding one, lest the plan of vocal progress be obstructed.

The scale should then be played upon the piano incorrectly, the students' reactions observed, and suggestions for correcting it invited.

The correction by the students of this first incorrectly played scale is not only a good starting point of their instruction, it is notably skillful pedagogy and an adroit presentation of the rudimentary elements. Therefore the teacher should insist upon the false relations being set right, before proceeding. Sometimes it is necessary to alternate an incorrect scale on the piano with the correct scale of the singers several times before the error or errors are detected and identified. This having been accomplished, it is necessary to describe the correct scale in its tone-relations, concentrating first on the whole tone intervals and presently on the two semi-tones. Many repetitions of *do re re do, do re re mi, mi re re mi, mi fa fa mi,* etc. should be made, before the complete tetrachord is sung. In a short time even very young pupils are conscious of the tetrachord's contour, and the teacher should then proceed to indicate with the baton certain notes of the first tetrachord, thus:— *do re, re mi, mi do, mi fa, fa re,* etc. If these selected notes be sung inaccurately, the complete tetrachord should be sung up and down several times, one half of the class singing, the other half observing. Without much delay the average group, studying in this manner, attains facility in singing the indicated notes. Thereupon, the second tetrachord should be practiced after the same fashion, the identity of the intervals of the two tetrachords being emphasized. When security has been achieved in singing selected notes from *sol la ti do,* it is profitable to alternate between the upper and lower halves of the scale, thus:—

sol la ti   ti la sol
do re mi   mi re do   etc.

The two tetrachords should then be put together and notes indicated to be sung from the complete scale.

It is essential that the teaching here be thorough, patient, and insistent. Many repetitions of the complete scale are necessary to fix in the aural

imagination the sound pictures of notes a few steps apart. The master
who at the outset concentrates on the inculcation of scale-interval consciousness, resisting the temptation to advance too soon, is well advised,
for if a thorough comprehension of the scale relations has been gained
by the students, the most harassing difficulty of sight reading has been
overcome.

Fluent linguists attain mastery of foreign languages by learning to
think in the vocabulary and idioms proper to them. Just so long as they
must translate a thought from their mother tongue into the equivalent expression of an alien speech are they slow, reluctant, and awkward in
gauche attempts to be understood. Until, for example, the concept of a
number of printed pages between covers expresses itself immediately,
without the mediation of an English word, as *livre,* a Britisher or American has not really begun to speak French. Similarly, until one intuitively
senses the relationships between all the notes of the two tetrachords, until,
to illustrate, the musical concept *do re mi sol mi do* fixes an instant pattern
of intervals in the mental ear, independently altogether of high, medium,
or low pitch of the key-note, a singer has not really acquired scale-
consciousness.

Therefore the practical pedagogue, intent upon developing serviceable
skill, is content to pitch his tent near the tetrachords and camp there
stolidly until all the *do re mi's* have capitulated to his perseverance, and
to the pupils' patience.

In the selection of notes to be sung by indication on the blackboard,
after the pupils have become adept at singing small intervals, it is desirable
to perfect them in octave jumps. Two octaves of the scale should be
written out, so that the "listening-eye" may continue to observe the exercise. Thus:—

do re mi fa sol la ti dó ré mí fá sol lá tí dó

establishing the pitch of *do* as *c,* the practice should proceed as follows:

do dó do—repeated several times,

re ré re, etc. concluding with *sol sol sol*

Fifths should next engage attention:

do sol do, re la re, mi ti mi, etc.

Fourths and sixths should follow these, and finally the last wide intervals,
completing the simple table of standard intervals, the major and minor
sevenths.

The next process is to indicate a tune by selecting a melodious sequence
of notes; e.g.

do mi re la sol mi do, dó ti la ti dó

It is opportune now to indicate the time values of these notes, thus:

using only the comfortable range of the singers, more extensive melodies may profitably be fashioned by choosing notes from the two octaves.

Many melodies should be indicated in this manner with various time signatures, the time-values always being written under the syllables as in the preceding exercises. A test of progress is opportune here, and a pupil should be invited to write on the blackboard the names and time values of a simple diatonic melody played upon the piano. If a fair degree of facility in this elementary musical dictation be not evident, it is clear that the ground work must be reviewed for if this had been thoroughly done, the pupils would have only a minimum of difficulty in writing accurately the notes of any diatonic tune. Familiar patriotic and hymn tunes should be proposed to them for translation into the nomenclature of solmization.

Festina lente! Pupils are not sufficiently prepared for the next step forward, which is the introduction of the staff, until they can sing with the syllables of the scale any of the simple songs which they had originally learned by rote, e.g. "My Country 'Tis of Thee."

The course which students most advantageously pursue in acquiring skill in sightreading is analogous to the course which music-script itself followed in the gradual evolution of the current notation. Neumes indicated groups of neighborly notes; these were followed by Hucbald's elementary staff on which intervals were indicated by *T* (whole-tone) *S* (half-tone), then by the colored line staff of Guido and finally by the square and round note systems of Gregorian Chant and Renaissance music respectively.

The period which the pupil spends practicing the syllables selected by the teacher at the blackboard is equivalently the *neume* period. He is concerned with the singing of neighborly sounds. He proceeds next to examine the syllables of the scale written on the staff without notes:

Fig. 3

Do	Re	Mi	Fa	Sol	La	Ti	Do
C	D	E	F	G	A	B	C

Here he is practically in the era of Hucbald and Guido. When square notes take the place of other symbols on the staff of four lines and three spaces, he is in the *notae quadratae* epoch of Gregorian Chant, and on the five line staff he comes up gradually through the diatonic polyphonies to the chromaticism and complex tonalities of our modern music.

If the class is to study the notation of Gregorian Chant, it is opportune to introduce the system here, since it seems easier to accustom the pupils to the locations of Plain-Song notes before addressing the five line system than afterwards. I have met many excellent musicians who felt ill at ease in Gregorian modes and rhythms chiefly because they *worked back* to Gregorian notation from the modern symbols. The rhythm of Gregorian Chant is not circumscribed by time-patterns. The ideal plan of progress is from Gregorian Chant to modern music via discant and polyphony.

In this volume we proceed immediately to the modern notation, referring directors of Gregorian Choirs to appropriate Chapters in Volume II.

The final preliminary point to be established, before beginning to make practical use of Fig. 3, is the identity of the sequence of letters C to C with the scale *do* to *do*. Melodies should be selected from the lettered scale in the manner employed with the solmization tunes. Explanation of the reasons for using the lettered scale may profitably be deferred until the introduction of the first sharp key. Using the baton with Fig. 3 for the diagram, the "listening eye" will quickly become accustomed to recognizing the site of the syllables and their equivalent letters on the staff. Fig. 3 is soon supplanted, the complete scale of Fig. 4 with round notes on lines and spaces taking its place.

FIG. 4

Do Re Mi   Fa Sol La Ti   Do
C   D E   F G A B   C

Presently the identifying syllables and letters should be erased, and the pupils required to sing indicated notes without assistance. But even after the erasure of the prompting syllables and letters from their place under the notes, it is well to keep the sequence in view at a different spot on the blackboard.

A combination of time-values and interval indications should next be undertaken and several exercises like the following be proposed for practice. The function of the G clef should here be explained.

FIG. 5

Published copies of music in the key of C may now safely and profitably be put in the hands of the pupils. Songs without accidentals are preferred, but if such are not available, *disregard the accidentals* promising the class a later explanation of their meaning. Hymns, anthems, glees, patriotic songs—everything available in the key of C should be practiced. The phrases should be "parsed" as carefully as the students of syntax are required to identify the parts of speech in a sentence. The syllables and letters should be read aloud, the time-values of the notes interpreted, and the music sung with solmization, with letters, with preconsonanted vowels, and finally with the words of the song.

All the introductory work had been preparing the pupils for this phase of the study of sight-singing.

They must pause long on this first *mesa* of the journey up to *Parnassus*. They must not venture further until they have become thoroughly acclimated to the staff-terrain of the key of C. Here, iteration and reiteration, duplication and reduplication prepare the students for easy progress to the end. The key of C is the purlieu where aspirants must equip themselves for the last ascent. If they cannot find ease here, they must retrace their steps and make a fresh start.

"Cantilenam Eandem Canis" ("You chant ever the same refrain"), wrote Terence; this is high encomium to the chorus master who confines the study of his choristers, at whatever risk of monotony, to the key of C, until all the possible positions and relations of notes are so familiar to them that a single glance at any page of music in that key immediately discloses a complete tonal picture.

The three primary assets of a skillful sightsinger are fluency in interpreting the time-symbols, scale consciousness, and sure-footedness in the key of C.

Before proceeding further, tenors and basses should become as familiar with the places of the notes on the F clef staff as they are now presumed to be with the places on the treble staff.

The introduction of the sharp keys should now be undertaken.

It seems important to acquaint pupils with the notation of sharp and flat keys according to a definite plan. To permit them to examine the structure of the keys unrelated to their serial acoustic catenation is to sponsor haphazard methods unsuited to a precise art and unworthy of enlightened pedagogy. And yet there are many preceptors who allow their students to drift confusedly from one signature to another, as from four sharps to one flat, from two sharps to five flats, with no understanding of the *raison d'être* of the sharps and flats, or no concept of the simple, orderly, progressive development of musical relations through keys a fifth apart.

The pedagogy used for the key of C must be applied with equal care as the students gradually proceed to multiple sharp or flat scales. Music ramifies through a cycle of fifths. After the octave (a mere doubling of the vibrations of any fundamental), the most important interval is the authoritative fifth, the dominant influence of scale structure. Therefore, the sharp keys should be studied consecutively until the pupils meet the concurrent keys of F sharp and G flat, at which point adequate explanation of the practical reasons for substituting flat keys for increasingly overloaded sharp signatures should be given and the flat keys studied in sequence.

In introducing each scale beginning with G, D, A, etc., it is salutary to play the notes without sharps or flats, calling upon the students to supply these in order to make each scale conform to the original solmization pattern. The student must recognize by his own hearing, the necessity of sharping F to produce a correct scale on G. Careful analysis of each new scale with its added sharp or flat will illustrate and therefore make more tenable in the mind the rules for sharp keys, which while studying the key of D they should memorize, viz:

1. *Sol* of the present key becomes *Do* of the next;
2. Sharp the seventh note;
3. Retain sharps of preceding scales;

and while studying the key of B flat, they should memorize the rules for flat keys:—

1. *Fa* (down a fifth or up a fourth) of the present key becomes *Do* of the next;
2. Flat the fourth note;
3. Retain flats of preceding scales.

Sufficient time must be devoted to the practice of reading the note positions of each key, to assure instant certainty at first sight of any interval in the key. The preceding keys should be regularly reviewed. Ensuing keys should not be introduced until practical infallibility has been acquired in the scale under scrutiny.

Orderly progress through all the keys guarantees a comprehensive, unconfused and practical understanding of the note relations of music and a quick skill in accurate sight-singing.

Some teachers devote much time and energy to imparting information about major and minor scales. The differences between these are irrelevant to the task in hand, i.e. the acquiring of facility in reading notes. Extraneous matter should be postponed until the main end of the undertaking has been accomplished.

Once the complete cycle of scales has been learned, the study of *accidentals* will offer no difficulty, nor will the atonal or polytonal disarranging of solmization patterns embarrass or discommode the singers excessively, for they immediately recognize the alien idioms and discontinue to apply the Guidonian code. Their experience and careful practice in strict intervallic-singing has prepared them to adjust themselves to the irregularities of the modern cacophonies.

A certain amount of guessing and conjectural reckoning must be permitted in the singing of atonal intervals. This license is the justified sneer of art at concoctions which trespass against its well ordered etiquette.

The systematic course outlined in this Chapter follows the successful plan of instruction used in elementary schools in other subjects. It simplifies what seem to be complex and confusing factors, proceeding gradually from primary components to a totality of the important divisions and topics involved.

Students who are thoroughly trained in counting time-values, and well disciplined in visualizing aurally the solmization sounds of diatonic intervals, experience a minimum of difficulty in reading accurately the symbols of musical notation. The inadequacy of the "Movable" *Do* system for the complex, frequently modulating and unconventional demands of atonal music is balanced by the deftness in understanding conventional progressions which it inculcates. This skillfulness predisposes singers to analyze quickly the aberrations from the normal classical style, and to adapt themselves without much confusion to the irregular forms.

Sufficient facility in sight-reading to meet the demands of choral singing, in choirs, oratorio societies or school choruses may be readily achieved if the pedagogy of instructors is carefully planned and patiently continued.

INDEX

287